ASPECTS OF CONTEMPORARY SPORT SOCIOLOGY

Proceedings of

C.I.C. Symposium

on the

Sociology of Sport

University of Wisconsin

November 18-20, 1968

Edited by

GERALD S. KENYON

University of Wisconsin

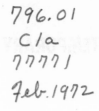

796.01
C/a
77771
Feb.1972

Library of Congress
Catalog Card Number 72-100016

$5.00 PER COPY

The Athletic Institute   SBN 87670-850-5   Chicago

PREFACE

Any attempt to formulate or structure a so-called body of knowledge is fraught with difficulties and is almost certain to fail when placed in the hands of a committee. On the contrary, insofar as knowledge is ever systematically organized, the result is usually accomplished by individuals — such as taxonomists, encyclopedists, library scientists, or even text book writers. Realizing this, the members of the C.I.C. Conference Group on Physical Education, though dedicated to the advancement of knowledge, chose instead, to devote their efforts to encouraging its discovery and dissemination through the sponsorship of a series of symposia in each of the several sub-fields whose members have devoted themselves to the serious study of sport and physical activity. It was felt that such conferences would be most effective in reaching these ends when faculty and graduate students whose interests and research lie in the area encompassed by a particular symposium are brought together to hear about the latest work in the field. The proceedings from such deliberations would in turn be published and made available to all interested persons. The results of the first of such symposia comprise the contents of this report. Although devoted to the Sociology of Sport, no attempt was made to establish a symposium theme, a fact clearly revealed by the Table of Contents. However, as papers were presented and discussed, recurring issues arose which provided considerable, though unplannd for, common ground.

As editor of the proceedings, I would like to bring to the reader's attention the process by which this volume has been prepared. First, each symposium session consisted of the presentation of an original paper, followed by a formal critique and an informal discussion. All of the transactions were both taped and stenotyped, thus permitting the preparation of a complete typescript. Although it is highly presumptuous to tamper with the words and ideas of others, the resulting manuscript was edited, but, hopefully only in the interest of translating oral material to an acceptable written form, while at the same time trying to maintain the spontaneity and informality which characterized much of the discussion.

Despite usual precautions, there no doubt remain some inaccuracies. For example, it is likely that I have at least once attributed statements to one participant which actually were those of another. In addition, it is possible, that as I wielded my sometimes not so sharp red pencil, I may have distorted intended meanings, though never deliberately. To all those so affected, my deep apologies. However, in partial defense I would like to allude to some of my encounters with the limitations of audio communication. As I went through the manuscript, among other tasks, I found myself trying to reconcile differences between what was said and what was heard. To illustrate, after no small amount of pondering, "Meurna Charise's Study" once again became "Muzafer Sherif's Study"; "PJY" became "Piaget," and my favorite, "the man working with you," obviously was meant to be "Mann-Whitney U." Thus, in view of such perplexities and others, and in view of my decision to spare those who prepared papers from the tedium of reading page proofs, *errors may have crept in.* The responsibility, however, rests solely with me.

A number of persons provided considerable support both in the planning of the symposium, and in the preparation of the proceedings. Thus, I would like to express my gratitude to the Chairman and fellow members of our Steering Committee; to Professor Leonard Larson, Professor Karl Stoedefalke, and Wesley White, of the Univeristy of Wisconsin; and to Dr. Frank Jones, President of the Athletic Institute, and Cy Yttri, Director of Publications at the Institute. I owe my greatest debt to Messrs. Loy, Lüschen, Page, Schafer, Stone, Sutton-Smith, and Webb, all of whom gave fully of themselves both in their advance preparation and through their active and most enthusiastic participation in the symposium itself.

G.S.K.
Hayward, California
August, 1969

ACKNOWLEDGEMENT

The Steering Committee is indebted to the Committee on Institutional Cooperation, and in particular to its Director, Dr. Stanley F. Salwak, and to the Deans, Directors, and Chairmen of Departments or Colleges of CIC Institutions, for their generous financial support.

THE CIC

The Committee on Institutional Cooperation is made up of one member from each of the Big Ten Universities and the University of Chicago. Its objective is to foster cooperation among the member institutions through the sharing of human and material resources for educational and research purposes.

THE CIC CONFERENCE GROUP
ON PHYSICAL EDUCATION

King J. McCristal, *University of Illinois, Chairman*

John Alexander, *University of Minnesota*

Louis E. Alley, *University of Iowa*

Gerald S. Kenyon, *University of Wisconsin, Symposium Chairman*

Leon E. Smith, *University of Iowa*

Earl F. Ziegler, *University of Illinois*

FOREWORD

For some time the challenge has been raised, "what is the discipline of Physical Education?" Attempts to answer this highly complex question have been made by individuals, associations and college faculties. Administrators, students and faculty members from other academic disciplines will be even more critical as the demands for higher education increase in our highly complex, sophisticated society.

The Body of Knowledge Project by the Big 10 is a pioneering effort. There has been much detailed planning behind this first of a series of symposia. The leadership exerted by King McCristal (Illinois), Lou Alley (Iowa), the late Arthur Daniels (Indiana) and others has been instrumental in developing the overall plan for the Project. As the various symposia are developed and reported, this thoughtful planning will pay real dividends.

The Big 10 directors should be congratulated for embarking upon this vital project. It very well could raise more answers than it solves. No doubt that the symposia will be challenged by many physical educators throughout the nation. But—when has controversy been all bad?

The Athletic Institute has been very pleased to be a part of this project. On behalf of the Institute it is a privilege to extend congratulations to those who conceived the project as well as those who participated in this, the first symposia. And to Gerry Kenyon, who devoted time and effort far beyond the call of duty, a heartfelt "Well Done!"

FRANK B. JONES

President, The Athletic Institute

CONTENTS

OPENING SESSION: November 18, 1968

Presiding

Gerald S. Kenyon, University of Wisconsin

Welcome

From The University of Wisconsin

Leonard A. Larson, Director
Department of Physical Education

From The Steering Committee

King J. McCristal, Dean
College of Physical Education
University of Illinois

Address

"Some Recent Developments in the Sociology of Sport"

Günther Lüschen
University of Illinois
General Secretary, International
Committee on Sport Sociology

Günther Lüschen

1. Some Recent Developments in the Sociology of Sport

Ladies and gentlemen, it is a great honor to me on behalf of the International Committee for the Sociology of Sport to extend greetings and best wishes to those attending this conference. The Committee, which has been in the center of the more recent developments in the field of sociology of sport, is affiliated with both the International Council of Sport and Physical Education and the International Sociological Association, functioning as a sub- and research committee to both of these bodies. In existence since 1964, it now has representatives from 27 countries among its membership.

The goals of the International Committee have been the promotion of the Sociology of Sport in its broadest sense. For instance, international seminars devoted to selected subjects of the field have been held in 1966 at the University of Cologne in Germany, and just recently (October, 1968) at the University of Vienna. The next conference is scheduled for Moscow in 1970.

Besides the more formal occasions of seminars, this committee also conducts informal workshops, the first having been held at the University of Illinois in 1967 where we discussed cross-cultural aspects of sport, and began preparation for an international research project. Plans were advanced at a second workshop held in 1968 at the University of Leicester in England. In September, 1969, a conference on sociological theory and sport is scheduled for Switzerland.

The Committee realizes, of course, that an international group, with all the attending complications at that level, cannot do all the work. It is only possible to give certain stimuli, and we are well aware that the main groundwork has indeed to be done by national research associations and by individual universities. And so it has always been the policy of this committee to rely on the cooperation of such institutions. What we have recently observed is that in almost all parts of the world, even during the past three years, there has sprung up all types of professional groups as well.

1

We are of course most pleased with this development. At this time we have a rather strong group emerging in East Germany, and Rumania. We have a particularly strong group in the Soviet Union; so strong that the biggest problem of the conference in 1970 will be to keep the number of local participants to 100. Last year, for instance, a conference was held in Leningrad which was attended by 150 sociologists in the field of the sociology of sport.

The situation is perhaps even more encouraging in a country like Japan, which already has had a vast amount of research in the field. If you would look for the major developments in sociology in general you would quickly be able to trace those developments to the work that the Japanese have done.

Of course, this committee highly welcomes a conference as it occurs here, but we are particularly pleased that this is not the only conference scheduled this year. We have had already, under the chairmanship of Professor Page, a round table conference earlier this year at the American Sociological Association's annual meeting at Boston; and one that is coming up later this year as a General Symposium at the annual meeting of the American Association for the Advancement of Science. Thus, this symposium will likely be another milestone in the development of the sociology of sport, and we are therefore very thankful, as I speak for the Committee for Sociology of Sport, that the CIC and the University of Wisconsin have made these great efforts to sponsor the conference. We are, of course, particularly grateful to Professor Kenyon's work in organizing this symposium.

Now, let me just briefly comment on the present stage of the sociology of sport. I see the sociology of sport as a special discipline in the broad realm of sociology, and I think that it is possible to justify that for at least two reasons. One is that the magnitude of sport in society can hardly be overlooked any more, and if you consider just the different types of involvement in sport, from, for example, the rather passive role as a spectator or follower of sports news in the newspapers, up to the top athlete, then you will know that there are not very many people in modern society that can escape sport. The second reason justifying a sub-discipline within sociology that is concerned with sport, is that this field, as I see it, has particular potentialities to demonstrate in its realm basic sociological theory, and even to the point of developing sociological theory.

That I stress so strongly the discipline of sociology at this point and, at the same time, don't give much attention to physical education, is not out of ignorance. It is more a matter of procedure. I think that only after we have discussed and investigated this field in the framework of sociological theory, then we can come up with meaningful results that will be applicable to physical education theory, and also be applicable to sports practice. By this, I don't mean to rule out certain research findings which might be applied already to sport practice, but at a rather low theoretical level.

The present state in the field of sociology of sport may be characterized by the fact that, by my rough estimate, if you do not define the field of sociology of sport too rigidly, you may count as of today something like 3,000 related publications internationally; a recently published selected bibliography[1] lists something like 1,000 titles with the emphasis on those works appearing since 1965, with the remainder included to characterize the earlier development of the field. If we look at the topics that have been tackled in these publications, most prominent are programmatic discussions. These have been quite numerous recently coming from scientists in sociology and in physical education, and point to topics that should be discussed or point to the magnitude of the problem, or the benefits that could come out of proceeding with this discipline. Such articles have appeared in many parts of the world in professional journals, whether they be for physical education or for sociology. If, however, you then look at the different subject areas you will find that the topic of sport in society, on the one hand — the structuring of sport through its affiliation with paricularly types of societies or to particular cultures — stands out quite prominently in publications. On the other hand, attention has also been given to the role that sport plays, i.e., the function that sport fulfills for societies at large.

One problem that since the beginning of the century has caused quite a bit of interest, and one that I would like to include in the field of sociology of sport as well, is the study of games and culture. However, it is just recently, and I would say in particular through the efforts of Professor Roberts of Cornell and Professor Sutton-Smith from Columbia, that the former orientation towards the problem of cultural diffusion has now been in a way reversed to the making of inferences from the study of games to the structure of culture and society itself.

A subject about which I think the contributions have been quite numerous, and I would also say quite valuable, is the field of sport as it relates to social class. Another area, one on which I will comment this afternoon, also seems to have come up with a number of studies, namely, the field of small groups and small group research as it relates to sport. Still another area that could be mentioned, is that of sport and leisure. I would say here that in the vast literature in sociology of leisure, the number of studies that have been contributed from the field of sociology of sport stand out quite prominently, and as such, I consider them to be among the very few studies that can be taken seriously as good solid sociology. I may mention here in particular the studies that have been produced by Professor Heinila in Finland and by Professor Dumazedier in Paris.

On the other hand, it's quite amazing that a number of problem areas in the field of sociology of sport have not gained very much attention. I would mention among others, that the sociological analysis of sport as it appears in schools and institutions of higher learning is almost empty of research. Here we have to do something, particularly in view of the direct implications for physical education. Furthermore, problems of sport and

---

[1] Lüschen, Günther, "The Sociology of Sport," *Current Sociology*. Vol. XV, 1967, No. 3.

delinquency, within the broad realm of sport and social problems, have not received very much attention, although as you know it has often been claimed that sport fulfills a very important function in prevention of delinquency or in the resocialization of the delinquent.

There are some other problems that you could name that represent shortcomings in the field of sociology of sport. Up to now, publications have been mainly on the descriptive level. While I must say that there is nothing wrong with having good description of an area of sociology, very often researchers in the field are not very careful. For instance, sociological concepts are used rather loosely, which brings me to comment that the consciousness of methodological procedures in the field of sociology of sport does not stand out very prominently in the field.

The quality and structure of theory in various parts of the world should be of some concern for the field in the future. However, I would say that for a number of years this picture has been definitely changing, and I think that there is a rising awareness of the different methodological positions from which to go on. I have seen and noticed this in particular at the conference in Vienna, although I was personally, as far as the content of the conference was concerned, not very satisfied. On the other hand, the ongoing discussions led to a very fruitful evaluation of the different positions concerning the theoretical aspects in the field of sociology of sport, and thus it was quite interesting to notice the different concepts and theories, that might be used. Where, on the one hand, the western sociology group would like to develop theories in the field for its own sake primarily, and only in the long run expect a certain applicability for social practice; on the other hand, East European scientists in the field would claim that you could develop, or should develop, sociological theories on sport only in the realm of a given system — for them, obviously Marxism and Leninism — and that the theories should have immediately had implicit implications anticipating social change. You can imagine that this stirred up quite a bit of argument which led to the very basis of sociological theory and analysis.

As I see it, in observing the program, I expect that this conference will again, and perhaps more than before, make the methodological position from which we will begin and have to begin in the analysis of sport, quite explicit. So with these thoughts I again extend my greetings as a member of the International Committee. I am not only hopeful but I am convinced that this conference will be making a very strong contribution to the field itself. Thank you.

Gregory P. Stone

2. Some Meanings of American Sport: An Extended View

What this paper represents is an extension of an earlier preliminary paper that I gave at Ohio State University a little more than a decade ago. At that time I had collected just under 200 interviews. The final sample consists of 566 interviews and for all intents and purposes that study is done.

First, a word about meaning — when I talk about meaning I use it in the sense of George Herbert Mead as the responses that are mobilized by a particular event. Consequently, the first matter of meaning has to do precisely with what kind of response people make when they are confronted with the symbol *sport*. It is this with which I am concerned and thus will get into it substantially.

To explore this problem I developed what probably is best called a proposive quota sample. I was interested not so much in making estimates of what's out there in the world or in the parameters of the problem if you like, as I was exploring social relationships that are mobilized by sport and sport activities. Consequently, I developed a box with three, six, twelve, with twenty-four cells. I was concerned in the first place with adults, married adults, with men and women, with older people and younger people, with urban and suburban residents and finally, with upper, middle, and lower socio-economic strata. Within each cell I selected relatively the same number of respondents, because I was concerned with getting at age, sex, residential and socio-economic differences. In selecting the urban sample I employed census tracts, and using about seventeen different socio-economic variables, which I won't enumerate, picked out the top three tracts and told my students to go into those tracts, make a kind of reconnaissance and select only the best residences in their view within those tracts, for their sample. Then I took three tracts in the dead center of the distribution, again asking students to reconnoiter the tract areas in the city and try to reach some agreement among themselves on the model residents in those tracts. Next I took the three lowest ranking tracts and told the students to pick out the worst residences. So, I was trying to get socio-economic extremes, plus the dead center of the middle mass.

With suburbs it was more difficult because at that time, in terms of the tract data available, the suburban tracts were quite large and quite heterogeneous. So, I had to go pretty much on local reputation of the suburbs and thus we picked two of the high status suburbs, Edina and some parts of Minnetonka, two reputedly middle-class suburbs, and two working class suburbs, and then followed the same procedures in gathering interviews. One interesting point, I think, is that it was very difficult to find young, upper urban people who were married. The young upper-class seems to have abandoned the central city.

Now to begin with, all I did was ask these people what activities they thought of when they heard the word "sport." The number of activities that they reported are provided in Table 1.[1] Over 2,600 activities were mentioned, so that each person on the average mentioned between four and five activities. There is a status relationship or socio-economic relationship between the number of activities that were reported or mentioned by these people. In general, the higher the status the greater the number of activities mentioned. This, I think, should be taken with a grain of salt because it may indicate merely a difference in verbalization among the strata and I may be reporting that rather than the fact that sport has a greater saliency for upper status people than for lower status people. But the consistency between the middle and the lower socio-economic strata suggests that this may only be partially true, since there is no great difference between the middle strata and the lower strata. By the way, as is indicated in the footnote of the table, there are only 6 people of the 562 who answered the question who could not come up with any activities relating to sport, so certainly this underscores Dr. Lüschen's observations to the effect that sport has a profound saliency in our entire society.

Some of the activities mentioned are quite interesting. Included as sport were such activities as relaxing, dancing, television, movies, woodworking and sex. Perhaps the inclusion of sex as sport is kind of apt testimony to the inappropriateness of the Freudian perspective for the interpretation of contemporary American sport David Riesman wrote about some time ago in a collection of very good essays on Freud. Freud viewed work as an inescapable and tragic necessity; and sex, too, was for Freud, a realm of

---

[1]For all tables only significant associations are presented. If age is not presented, there is no significant association. I might say that because sport is still pretty much a male world, there are always significant sex differences, and thus I have only reported the ones that seem particularly interesting.

TABLE 1

SOCIO-ECONOMIC DIFFERENCES IN THE RANGE OF ACTIVITIES
INTERPRETED AS SPORT BY METROPOLITAN RESIDENTS

Number of Activities Interpreted As Sport	Socio-Economic Strata			Totals* (Per Cent)
	Upper (Per Cent)	Middle (Per Cent)	Lower (Per Cent)	
0-2‡	9.0	18.1	13.1	13.3
3	15.3	13.2	25.7	18.1
4	16.9	19.8	17.8	18.1
5	18.5	20.3	21.5	20.1
or more	40.2	28.6	22.0	30.2
Totals*	99.9 (n = 189)	100.0 (n = 182)	100.1 (n = 191)	99.8 (n = 562)

Chi square = 26.41　　　.05 > p > .001

*Four respondents, three in the upper stratum and one in the middle stratum, did not respond to the question.

‡Six respondents, two in the middle stratum and four in the lower stratum, mentioned no activities.

necessity. He saw it not as presenting man with a problem to be solved nor with a game to be played nor coupled with love as a road to human closeness and intimacy, but rather as a teleological prime mover charged with the task of socializing and civilizing man and thus preserving the species. Sex could fulfill this task because of its ability to bribe with an elemental release. Work was then the means by which the species maintains itself while performing its endless procreative mission. Although, of course, in Freud's time sex was purchasable in the sporting houses of the day, the purchasers were probably not called athletes as some of them are called these days.

In spite of the mention of these rather unusual activities associated with the term sport, Table 2 indicates that the responses were, by and large, conventional. Spectator sports received the most frequent mention — football, baseball, and basketball; and that the mentioning of participant sports is somewhat less. In short it seems that in the public mind, sport is still primarily a spectator or a spectatorial affair, a spectable, if you like.

Again these are just words that people mentioned when they were presented with the symbol "sport" and I suppose that what is measured here is a kind of saliency of these different activities, but because the question is open-ended, again I would like to have you view these data with a kind of grain of salt. But saliency indicates what is salient. In other words I think we can say from these data that these particular sports are salient, are in the minds of people when we hear this term, but it doesn't indicate what is not salient. In other words, the fact that only 11 per cent of the people mentioned skiing does not indicate that skiing is not salient. The fact that 73 per cent mentioned football indicates that football is salient. Or that 10

TABLE 2

THE DIFFERENTIAL SALIENCY OF VARIOUS SPORTS
FOR METROPOLITAN RESIDENTS

Activities	Selected Social Characteristics*				Per Cent of Respondents Mentioning at least one Sport (N=556)
	Age	Sex	Residence	Socio-Economic Strata	
Football	——	——	——	——	72.7
Baseball	O-Y	M-F	——	L-M-U	66.9
Basketball	——	——	——	——	42.6
Hockey	——	M-F	——	——	21.0
Boxing	——	M-F	——	L-M-U	16.4
Wrestling	O-Y	——	——	L-U-M	10.2
Golf	——	——	——	U-M-L	35.2
Tennis	——	F-M	——	U-M-L	21.6
Bowling	——	——	——	L-M-U	19.4
Swimming	Y-O	F-M	——	U-M-L	30.6
Skiing	——	F-M	——	U-M-L	11.3
Fishing	——	M-F	——	——	29.0
Hunting	——	M-F	——	——	18.7

*Only significant associations as determined by the Chi-square Test are presented in the body of the table. The level of significance has been set at .05. Categories of informants making most mentions of any specified activity are listed first, those making fewest mentions are listed last, reading from left to right. In the age category those less than forty years of age are designated "Y," those forty years of age or more are designated "O." In the sex category, men are designated "M" and women, "F." In the residence category "U" designates respondents living in the Minneapolis city limits; "S," those living in the suburbs. In the socio-economic category, those in the highest category are designated "U," those in the middle, "M," and those in the lowest, "L."

per cent of the people mentioned wrestling does not indicate that wrestling is not salient as a sport in their minds. So some sports not mentioned or receiving very, very infrequent mentions may be much more salient than this table suggests. There may also be a seasonal kind of censure operating here. The fact that the interviews are taken in the fall may also affect these results. There certainly, I'm sure, is a status bias operating. I'm quite sure that people are loathe to confess to a higher status interviewer, a college student, that, in fact, wrestling is their bag.[2] So there are biases operating to distort those figures.

The two primary differentiating variables seems to be sex and status and some age differences which you would expect, particularly in the case of swimming. So that the sport audience, if you like, is "chopped up." As a sociologist might conceive it, it is differentiated. It is differentiated along the primary axes of sex and status.

The thing that I found also very interesting is the absence of any residential differences in these saliencies. I seriously had expected to see suburban-urban differences in conceptions of sport. Of course, there has been a vast literature on the leisure time of suburbia, but I uncovered no differences at all in terms of the saliency of these sports. This may indicate that, as another sociologist, Berger, has indicated, that of the sociological literature on suburbia is as biased as some of my own data are here, namely, dealing primarily with middle status suburban areas, not concerned with working class suburbs as I'm concerned with here or with high status suburbs.

I then asked people "what is your favorite sport?" Now, here we get into less difficulty in terms of saliencies and you can see that in terms of favorites, the people are about evenly divided between the selection of a spectator sport and a participant sport. The one point I think I'd like to make in terms of Table 3, is that we tend to think of spectatorship as being somehow low status or lower class in character.[3] So that we tend to look at spectatorship as being lower class. Now you will see a slight tendency — I don't think it's enough really to warrant a great deal of emphasis — for participation as a favorite sport to be somewhat greater in the lower strata than in the middle strata, which I think is rather interesting. There was one study

---

[2]They are somewhat ashamed of being caught up in that marvelously curious spectacle which manages to outdraw professional basketball in Minneapolis. It will easily outdraw it. I'd say it gets about twice or three times the attendance of professional basketball, and that's only in the city and, of course, the wrestlers are working a circuit four or five nights a week. People probably don't know either that wrestling is probably the most lucrative professional sport. By and large, on the average, a third rate wrestler can count on about $18,000 a year.

[3]I think sociologists themselves are pretty snobbish about sport. I think this is one reason that there has been so little done by sociologists in this country in sport. If you look at the two main journals, *The American Sociological Review* and *The American Journal of Sociology*, you will find that you can count the number of articles dealing with sport on one hand and on the fingers of one hand. I forget what the number actually is; I think it's only about four or five in the two journals. I have a friend who has been doing research on camping, for example. He sent his article first to the *American Sociological Review*, and received a letter back from the editor suggesting that he really should submit this article to Outdoor Life because it didn't belong in sociology. On the other hand, the editor seldom suggests that we submit articles on industrial sociology to Chamber of Commerce publications. However, through some mediation the paper was eventually published in the *American Journal of Sociology*.

done some time ago by Clarke on Leisure and Levels of Occupational Prestige in the *American Sociological Review,* in June of 1956, (Vol. 21, pp. 301-307) where he did find in terms of leisure time activities a kind of

TABLE 3

SOCIO-ECONOMIC DIFFERENCES IN THE DESIGNATION OF SPECTATOR OR PARTICIPANT SPORTS AS FAVORITES BY METROPOLITAN RESIDENTS

Favorite Sport	Socio-Economic Strata			Totals (Per Cent)
	Upper (Per Cent)	Middle (Per Cent)	Lower (Per Cent)	
Spectator	35.6	57.1	54.7	48.8
Participant	64.4	42.9	45.3	51.2
Totals	100.0 (N = 188)	100.0 (N = 175)	100.0 (N = 172)	100.0 (N = 535)

Chi square $= 20.25$ $.05 > p > .001$

U curve with more participation, more active forms of leisure occurring at the extremes of status rather than in the middle, and these data somewhat follow this. He was concerned with leisure activities; I'm concerned with sport, which is different, but there is a tendency to follow the U type of distribution which Clarke uncovered.

In Table 4 you will find the concrete activities designated as "favorites" and you will notice that there were some 26 respondents who did not designate a favorite sport. Again you get the primary differentiation here of sex and status and although there are some differences in the relationships reported in Table 4 as compared with Table 2, I think that the relative presence of similarity in those two tables indicates something, some kind of argument for the validity of the data in the second table.

I'm not primarily interested, of course, in what sports have saliency in the population, because what a sociologist is concerned with is the activities that are mobilized by sport itself and one very important activity is, of course, conversation. I mentioned earlier, for example, if a man in our society does not have at least some conversational knowledge of sport he's viewed as suspect, and I know of at least one psychiatrist, who I men-

TABLE 4

SOCIAL DIFFERENCES IN SPORTS DESIGNATED AS FAVORITES
BY METROPOLITAN RESIDENTS

Favorite Sports	Selected Social Characteristics*				Per Cent of Respondents Selecting a Favorite Sport (N = 540)
	Age	Sex	Residence	Socio-Economic Strata	
Football	——	——	U-S	M-U-L	24.4
Baseball	——	M-F	——	L-M-U	15.4
Basketball	——	——	——	M-L-U	6.8
Boxing	——	M-F	——	L-M-U	3.3
Golf	——	——	——	U-M-L	11.3
Tennis	——	——	——	U-M-L	3.7
Bowling	——	F-M	——	L-M-U	6.3
Swimming	Y-O	F-M	U-S	M-U-L	7.6
Hunting	——	M-F	——	——	3.7
Fishing	——	M-F	——	——	9.6
Others too diverse to analyze	——	——	——	——	7.8

*Only significant associations as determined by the Chi-square Test are presented in the body of the table. The level of significance has been set at .05. Categories of informants making most mentions of any specified activity are listed first, those making fewest mentions are listed last, reading from left to right. In the age category those less than forty years of age are designated "Y," those forty years of age or more are designated "O." In the sex category, men are designated "M" and women, "F." In the residence category, "U" designates respondents living in the Minneapolis city limits; "S" those living in the suburbs. In the socio-economic category, those in the highest category are designated "U," those in the middle, "M," and those in the lowest, "L."

tioned in the earlier article, who used knowledge of sports as a diagnostic device for recruits into the Army during World War II. If the recruit didn't know, for example, who had won the last World Series then perhaps it's better to give him a rather careful test in terms of his maleness or homosexuality.

As to what is important in terms of conversation, it is that in the presumed anonymity of the city a conversational knowledge of sports gives strangers access to one another, so that if they meet in the bar or in other public places or on a plane or a train or a bus, one can immediately start up a conversation with a total stranger and gain access and penetrate the barriers or the insulations of anonymity that presumably we find in the city. So, Table 5 shows that in the first place it is a man's world; that the conversation about sports is quite frequent for men. About two-thirds of

them say that they talk about sports frequently or very frequently, compared
to somewhat more than a third of the women. Women, by the way, resent
this, although I don't have time to go into it, but some of them are avid
sports fans and they have a difficult time in finding anybody to talk about

TABLE 5

SEX DIFFERENCES IN FREQUENCY OF SPORT CONVERSATIONS CARRIED ON BY METROPOLITAN RESIDENTS

Frequency of Sport Conversation	Sex		Totals* (Per Cent)
	Male (Per Cent)	Female (Per Cent)	
Rarely, Almost Never, or Never‡	10.6	28.5	19.8
Occasionally	25.9	32.0	29.0
Frequently	31.8	24.4	27.9
Very Frequently	31.8	15.1	23.2
Totals*	100.1 (n = 274)	100.0 (n = 291)	99.9 (n = 565)

Chi square = 44.45   .05 > p > .001

*One female respondent did not reply to the question.

‡Three males and seven females never discussed sports.

sport because the men refuse to discuss it with them. Imputing female
interest in sports is probably somewhat on the order of an invasion of their
world, and women then become indignant, and frequently you will find
letters to the editors in the paper with women complaining that they are
avid Twins fans, for example, but nobody will talk to them about sport.
So, the fact that it is a man's world acts to seal off the sexual world, and
particularly in the middle and lower strata, to set men and women a little
bit further apart than perhaps they should be.

Table 6 shows the socio-economic differences and frequency of conversations. The most interesting datum is the polarization in the lower strata
between a third or almost a third who rarely or never talk about sports, and
about a fourth of those who talk very frequently about sports. You will
notice that in terms of frequent conversations the differences among the
strata are so slight as to be negligible. I think what this means is that
many lower strata people are left outside the world of sport. Based upon

TABLE 6

SOCIO-ECONOMIC DIFFERENCES IN FREQUENCY OF SPORT
CONVERSATIONS CARRIED ON BY METROPOLITAN RESIDENTS

Frequency of Sport Conversation	Socio-Economic Strata			Totals* (Per Cent)
	Upper (Per Cent)	Middle (Per Cent)	Lower (Per Cent)	
Rarely, Almost Never, or Never‡	10.4	17.5	31.6	19.8
Occasionally	33.3	32.8	21.1	29.0
Frequently	32.3	27.3	24.2	27.9
Very Frequently	24.0	22.4	23.2	23.2
Totals*	100.0 (n = 192)	100.0 (n = 183)	100.1 (n = 190)	99.9 (n = 565)

Chi square = 30.96   .05 > p > .001

*One lower stratum respondent did not reply to the question.

‡Two middle and eight lower stratum respondents never discussed sports.

other data, I have found that there is a general alienation of the lower stratum when using such measures as integration with the neighborhood, and a sense of belonging to the larger city. There is a general alienation and perhaps this lack of involvement as measured by frequency of sport conversation on the part of the lower stratum indicates a larger alienation than being simply alienation from the sport world. But, once people in the lower stratum do get involved as are other people and the differences more or less disappear so that the association in Table 6 is primarily due to the relatively large number of lower strata people who simply are not involved in the sports world through their conversations.

Next, I asked in what situations did they discuss sport and here again we see the same shortcoming of open ended questions because the people answered this question spontaneously without being probed. Again, as shown in Table 7, you find it's a man's world, that most women talk about sports in relatively few situations. Most men identify a relatively large number of situations, three or more, so that sport, then, is not only more salient to men and involves them more, but also carries over into a larger number of the situations of their daily life. Table 8 shows largely the same status differences in terms of the situations as is found in the frequency of the conversation.

TABLE 7

SEX DIFFERENCES IN SITUATIONAL RANGE OF SPORT CONVERSATIONS CARRIED ON BY METROPOLITAN RESIDENTS

Number of Situations Mentioned	Sex		Totals* (Per Cent)
	Male (Per Cent)	Female (Per Cent)	
0-1‡	18.5	32.1	25.5
2	30.7	29.3	30.0
3	30.4	23.4	27.0
4 or more	20.4	15.2	17.7
Totals*	100.0 (n = 270)	100.0 (n = 290)	100.2 (n = 560)

Chi square = 14.75   .05 > p > .01

*Five respondents, three males and two females did not respond to the question. One male respondent gave a "Don't know" reply.

‡Fifteen respondents, four males and eleven females, did not converse about sports in any specific social situation.

TABLE 8

SOCIO-ECONOMIC DIFFERENCES IN SITUATIONAL RANGE OF SPORT CONVERSATIONS CARRIED ON BY METROPOLITAN RESIDENTS

Number of Situations Mentioned	Socio-Economic Strata			Totals* (Per Cent)
	Upper (Per Cent)	Middle (Per Cent)	Lower (Per Cent)	
0-1‡	15.8	26.2	34.8	25.5
2	30.0	31.7	28.3	30.0
3	32.6	26.8	20.9	27.0
4 or more	21.6	15.3	16.0	17.7
Totals*	100.0 (n = 190)	100.0 (n = 183)	100.0 (n = 187)	100.2 (n = 560)

Chi square = 21.85   .05 > p > .01

*Five respondents, one upper and four lower stratum, did not respond to the question. One upper stratum respondent gave a "Don't know" reply.

‡Fifteen respondents, one upper stratum, four middle, and ten lower stratum, did not converse about sports in any specified social situation.

Turning to what situations are used for discussion in the mobilization of involvement in sports, there are several comments I can make about the data in Table 9. In the first place, there is the problem of the open-ended question. Some people would say neighbors and some say friends, and I was very literal in my code. Of course, I know not all neighbors are

TABLE 9

SOCIAL DIFFERENCES IN SITUATIONAL CONTEXTS OF SPORT CONVERSATION CARRIED ON BY METROPOLITAN RESIDENTS

Situational Contexts	Selected Social Characteristics*				Per Cent of Respondents Mentioning at least One Situational Context (n=945)
	Age	Sex	Residence	Socio-Economic Strata	
Family of Procreation	O-Y	F-M	S-U	U-M-L	63.4
Other Family	——	——	——	M-L-U	14.5
Neighbors	——	——	——	L-M-U	8.8
Friends	——	F-M	——	U-M-L	38.6
Parties and Other Social Gatherings	——	——	——	U-M-L	17.2
Work	——	M-F	——	L-M-U	40.3
Clubs and Voluntary Associations without Sports Facilities	——	——	——	——	6.4
Public Places (Bars, Taverns, Stores)	——	M-F	——	L-M-U	7.5
Sport Scene	——	——	——	U-M-L	22.2

*Only significant associations as determined by the Chi-square Test are presented in the body of the table. The level of significance has been set at .05. Categories of informants making most mentions of any specific activity are listed first, those making fewest mentions are listed last, reading from left to right. In the age category those less than forty years of age are designated "Y," those forty years of age or more are designated "O." In the sex category, men are designated "M" and women, "F." In the residence category, "U" designates respondents living in the Minneapolis city limits; "S," those living in the suburbs. In the socio-economic category, those in the highest category are designated "U," those in the middle, "M," and those in the lowest, "L."

friends. Anybody knows that who has a neighbor. But some neighbors are friends and thus there is some overlap between these categories. Nevertheless, there are some interesting differences here. In terms of the family of procreation, that is, the immediate family, I did get a residential difference which may testify somewhat to the sociological contention that familism is enhanced in the suburban environment as opposed to the environment of the central city. The interesting difference, I think, between the status differentiation of neighbors and friends may reflect the fact that in the lower strata there is a greater reliance upon neighboring as a source of friendship than is the case in the upper strata. I have some other materials on that. I would then point out that the prime situations then for the discussion of sports in the lower strata aside from neighbors, are at work. This is a very important activity at the work scene and in public places such as bars, taverns and the like. For the upper stratum it is in the family, with friends, on parties and on the sports scene itself. One of the consequences of this is that sport involvement may operate to increase family cohesion in the upper stratum. Although differences are not reported here, this may well be because membership in associations dealing with sport or peripheral to sport, like country clubs and so forth, are often family memberships in those strata; that sport may further set apart men and women in the lower strata; and in the middle strata simply from the data I have the same impression I had a number of years ago, that the middle class wife has possibly taken a course in family sociology where she has learned that it's important to have a companion in marriage, while the husband, who is a sports fan or sports follower anyway, then goes to the breakfast table, picks up the morning paper and begins reading the sports page. This is very threatening to the middle class wife who has had this course in family sociology because it's hardly companionable. I have the notion that she may be grasping at sport among several other straws as a way to build some companionship into the marriage, that it's a kind of frantic quest for companionship on her part as opposed to the upper class wife. In the lower stratum the sexual worlds are quite different and extend into leisure and work activities. For example, it would be unlikely, I think, in the middle strata of our society to follow a pattern that I've observed where the working class husband will take his wife to a dance hall and order her some beer, etc. and then leave her there to dance and go out with her friend's husband to some other bar to drink beer with a man and perhaps talk about sports with him. So that the insulation of the sexes is extensive in the lower stratum and perhaps sport functions to further insulate the sexes in that stratum. I, of course, have a number of other materials. The analysis is quite extensive but this is about all the time that I have to report today. Thank you.

REACTION TO STONE PAPER — Charles H. Page

I should explain first a major delinquency of Gregory Stone concerning his very interesting paper about which I will have some things to say in a moment. The delinquency, of course, is that so far as I was concerned there was no paper and I am as new to this material as all of you are except that I did have the advantage about two minutes before we began this morning of being passed the nine tables you've heard discussed.

Let me say first that I think the most interesting things about Mr. Stone's presentation are his asides all along, his comments about some of the possible implications of his data, and to three, four, or five of those comments I'd like to speak briefly in the next few minutes. I should also say in a preliminary way that there is no need for me (even if I had the expertise, which I do not have) to comment on his data as data or the possible limitations of those data or his methods because he's done that for us as he's gone along. He has exercised an extraordinary judiciousness, I think, in this respect. Some of you may wish to talk about those limitations, but I'll avoid that. And finally, by way of an introductory comment, I'd like to correct a canard that he has committed, namely, his reference to that sacred journal, perhaps the dullest of all printed publications in the United States, the *American Sociological Review,* which I happened to edit for one term, and indeed preceded the editor to whom Stone referred, who in my judgment was the best editor that the ASR has ever had. At least one editor of that journal, namely myself, tried to find good material in the sociology of sport, solicited articles without success in this area — which is out of keeping or was out of keeping with the editorial policies of that magazine. He's right that very little has been published in the two leading sociology journals in the United States, the ASR and the AJS. I think the figure is six rather than four or five if one includes a piece by a then obscure sociologist that was published before World War II. I think that's the total number plus about three book reviews. I was interested recently to count up the number of books on sports that have actually been reviewed in the *American Sociological Review.* Well, I can say that I've reviewed the great majority of them — three. There have been I think, four such reviews published during the last quarter of a century or thereabouts.

Turning to the paper itself, I'm simply going to make some running comments on the basis of notes I have made during the presentation itself. First of all, early on in Gregory's presentation he emphasized, when he began to talk about the tables, that in general they show that the higher the social status of the respondents or the people interviewed, the more they had to say about sports, the more activities they identified, and so on. I would be pretty strongly convinced until the opposite was proven that he's absolutely right when he suggests that this is pretty much a reflection of more highly developed verbal skills and perhaps a larger range of exposure of people of higher status. They simply read more, for example; they talk more in general, they are more verbal in general. I certainly wouldn't suggest a greater "saliency" (to use his term) in any affective or emotional or psychologically significant sense. At least I would throw that out as something we might discuss.

At two or three different points in the paper there is a discussion of spectatorship and participation. That is something we are all interested in, of course, particularly, I suppose, people in physical education. One of the things I've been interested in discovering from reading papers, mostly unpublished, at Columbia University — I think that Stone mentioned the fairly recent work of Clarke on leisure — is that there is some positive correlation between the growth of spectatorship and participation, so far as sport is concerned in the United States during the 30 years or so, whether the spectatorship is in the arenas of our large cities or, as is the case more frequently, looking at the boob box. While there seems to be a positive correlation between spectatorship and participation in sport, I'm not suggesting that there is any causal relationship between the two. There may or may not be, but it is something that's well worth finding out. (This is even more the case, I would judge, from reading a recent volume on leisure in France by Dumazedier, in Western European countries or at least in France itself. There the amount of participation in sport is even more closely associated with spectatorship.)

My next point also has something to do with spectatorship with respect to lower status people. I think Gregory is correct when he suggests that many sociologists, at least, who do talk about or speculate about — that is what most of them do in fact — about the world of sport, have a biased image with regard to the activity, participation, knowledge, and so on, of lower status people.

STONE: Even the lower status families.

PAGE: Yes, I think this is possibly true. And in this connection, turning to his concluding remarks, I might say that I have occupied from time to time, and for fairly prolonged periods, a strategic listening post, so far as lower status people are concerned — in the saloons, bars, and taverns, talking with and playing the role of an espionage agent in lower status groups. I've been struck over and over again in these fairly informal exercises about the tremendous amounts of expertise with respect to this or that sport or sometimes sport in general, including some of the sports one would not normally or conventionally associate with lower status people. I have heard people discussing the new black polo team that developed on Long Island 10 to 12 years ago, and the skills of that fellow from Texas — Smith — back in the late 1930's who had a ten-goal polo rating. One might ask, why are these people interested in polo? Well, some of them are. I've also heard some very interesting discussions in recent years of tennis matches — a sport which, as you know, historically was associated with private clubs and upper status groups in our society. So, I think there is much to learn, if we are interested in class differences with respect to not only sport activity, but to sport expertise, sport knowledge, the psychological role and the psychological functions that sport play for people of different strata. I believe that this is the kind of factual, if you like, or at least suggestive information, the kinds of "data," that we need to play with.

I was interested in Gregory's comment about one of the functions of sport. This is both its psychological and social function in helping to break down the impersonality, the anonymity, of what is conventionally called our increasingly cold world, our increasingly urbanized world. I certainly would fully agree that this is one of its functions, an important function. It shares it along with some other elements of our popular culture, so-called, and it certainly shares it — again I'm thinking primarily of that strategic post I referred to a moment ago — with the even more ubiquitous and in some respects, but certainly not in all, interesting of sex — which Gregory talked about in passing in a very interesting and I think highly suggestive way.

Which takes me to women. Well, starting out in the 1920's, when I belonged to a barnstorming swimming and water polo playing group (which had as its chief attraction a man named Weismueller), we traveled around the country with about six women. We thought of them as women. They ranged in age between 12 and 15 or 16, but they were women, not only as athletes but as sexually attractive objects. I'm not so sure that Gregory this morning (I'm certain that he doesn't do this normally) didn't engage a little in something that might be called sexnocentrism. I think that more and more — I'll put this point very cautiously — women are involved psychologically as well as actively in the sport world, and I'd be curious to know how many middle-class wives you portrayed a few minutes ago actually get annoyed in any serious sense when their husbands turn, at the breakfast table, to the sporting page; indeed, I'd like to know how many middle class wives quarrel with their husbands about getting that page. Women not only participate in sport, they are interested in sport. The reason they are interested in sport is because sport is an important part of the world, as we all know. It's a culturally very important part and therefore is a psychologically important part — and I don't think that the shutting off of women from the sport world to the extent suggested by the data, to be sure, is something I'd buy without some more convincing evidence. (I'm sorry that I'm addressing at the moment — only one, two, three, or four, so far as I can tell, women in the audience.)

I have another point, which takes me back to a point I raised earlier, in connection with Table 6 and Mr. Stone's discussion to the data when he was speaking about class or status differences with respect to "conversation." He noted, I think quite correctly, that generally speaking or comparatively speaking, I should say, that lower class people (I use the word "lower" here deliberately) tend to be "left out of the world of sport." I am sure this is correct, that this deprivation is related to what Stone referred to as their general alienation from many if not all aspects of conventional "middle class" life, presumably the modal type of life in American society.

As one now reads the increasing number of studies on the so-called "culture of poverty" (as you know, we've rediscovered the fact of poverty with a distinctive culture in the United States in the last dozen years) one is struck by the reportedly large amount of "alienation." I'm not sure that's the correct word (alienation is a term for several concepts), but there is a real separation of the very poor from almost all of the more or less conventional facets of life including sport, which is such an important part of life today.

I was interested in the reference to the psychiatrist that Gregory had made in his earlier (and now famous) article on sport — the psychiatrist who used knowledge of or participation in sport as an index of masculinity and their absence as a possible indication of homosexuality. When I first read the paper I was surprised, and when I heard this idea repeated I was also surprised. I think that most of the psychiatrists I know would turn the idea around and suggest that a great preoccupation with sport may be a possible indicator of not heterosexuality but homosexuality. Indeed, as we all know, this is one of the ways that men often "prove" their masculinity when they suspect otherwise. This is the hypothesis I would entertain, and I think the psychiatrist in question may have known little about the masculinity-proovers among athletes.

Let me conclude by saying that as usual Gregory Stone has proven himself to be the intellectual virtuoso in this all too little worked field in this country. The rest of us who are marginal members of the sociology of sport world are greatly indebted to him.

DISCUSSION

SEYMOUR KLEINMAN: I thought it might be interesting and helpful perhaps if we clearly distinguished in our studies the categories which are involved, which sometimes tend to become muddled in a way. Thus, I would like to ask whether there is a category of the sport of spectating in which we act as spectators, as opposed to the category of the sport of engagement, active engagement in sport. I'm not really clear in your presentation of the data whether there was this kind of flow of one into another when you asked people what they regarded as sport. Were they considering themselves as spectators or as participants or as both? Or where does one leave off and the other begin in the eyes of your question or the responses to it?

STONE: In terms of the saliency thing I didn't make these distinctions. I just listed the most frequently mentioned activities in terms of favorite sport. I asked, first of all, what was their favorite sport. If they had mentioned a spectator sport, then I asked them what was their favorite participant sport, and vice versa, so I got both you see. But first of all I meant the favorite sport. So it's, I think, quite reliable.

KLEINMAN: I have a further comment to make on what I might want to call the sport of spectating itself. The sport of spectating it appears to me might involve a lot more than just observing sports. I think within our contemporary kind of existence, we become a kind of society oriented toward observing things. We just watch things and we get caught up in a watching or observing kind of business. It almost doesn't make any difference what you watch, you are just engaged in a kind of sport of observation. Whether it happens to be observation of a sport, a variety show, a dance, or drama, the act of observation becomes an end in itself, regardless of what you're watching. This is the kind of activity in which we are engaged over and above what we generally consider to be within the framework of sport itself.

PAGE: I'd like to briefly respond to one statement you made about that subject. I fully agree, myself, that spectatorship or what you nicely referred to as the sport of spectatorship or something like that, today involves much more than watching. It involves (to use fancy terms in true sociological fashion as Gregory would say) a great deal of cognitive activity on the part of spectators. It involves knowledge, an increasing knowledge. It involves expertise. Probably, however, the audience studies that are being made at Columbia and elsewhere today show that audiences break down into various types of spectators. I suppose I have a misleading image of the women who watch Gregory Stone's professional wrestlers because I have seen a few of them. I can't stand that interesting exercise myself, but I've seen some matches and I have a stereotypical view of kindly old ladies with knitting needles screaming "Kill the so-and-so" and so on at these matches. So this might be one type that doesn't involve any great knowledge or expertise. On the other hand, people who watch a great deal starting at about the age of 9 or 10 on their television sets at home not only develop knowledge, but in order to see the things they increasingly want to see on the field or in the arena they develop more and more knowledge. Their internal psychology becomes adjusted to this sort of thing. You have all had the experience of 10 year olds, for example, or 11 year olds, who psychologically and in terms of knowledge are better prepared to watch, say, a basketball game or a football game on television than many adults who don't have the child's knowledge. I wish that we had some — I don't care whether we call it sociology, it's the field that's important, not the disciplines — good studies of spectatorship, as such. Some are underway at the present time.

STONE: It isn't only a cognitive participation, but a vicarious and empathic participation. It's not unusual to come away from a football game or from a boxing match with your shoulders aching. But I didn't mean to imply that spectatorship was merely a passive kind of thing just because I used the word. I think, however, that most of the snobs writing about sports do make this implication. I suggest that sport functions in a very positive way in terms of urban identification. I'd like to comment also on the work I've done in wrestling, which is fascinating. Women certainly participate very actively. One of my wrestler friends still has scars on his back which he received when a little lady came in not with knitting needles, but with a bagful of broken glass in her handbag and threw it at him as he was going down the aisle. Probably the major occupational hazard for the wrestler, second to heart attack, is precisely the spectators. A list of injuries suffered by wrestlers at the hands of spectators is much greater in number than the injuries they suffered at the hands of other wrestlers.

On this business of women in sport, although Page may not agree with the data, the only exception that I can think of in terms of spectatorship, or in terms of the act of participation of women, is in wrestling. The most frequent incidence of spectators in wrestling are older lower status women, when you combine these three factors. Now I can explain to some extent the age and the status relationships particularly in terms of wrestling being a con game with the older people and lower status people more or less accepting appearances as they are, and not probing behind the mask. But, I can't explain women being interested in this, although I have tried. Since wrestling is kind of a great passion play or morality play, I thought perhaps it was because women are the custodians of morality in society and they consequently get much more involved in the struggle between good and evil that is depicted in the wrestling arenas. I actually had data to test this out, but it didn't work, so I still don't know what's bringing these ladies into this very active observation of the wrestling pageant in the arenas. I seriously think that it's still pretty much a man's world. Now it's changing. One of the obvious research projects that I asked for years ago which nobody has taken up — nobody ever acts on my suggestions — would be to do a content analysis of advertisements in outdoor magazines, over a considerable period of time and notice when women began to appear in the ads in these magazines. I think it would be fascinating to pin it down historically and see what historical processes are operating. Obviously women are increasingly coming into some sports, but I think it's still by and large a male world. The people who complain about the New Year's football binge — which now lasts almost a week, and God knows how long it's going to last now that we have this expansion of conferences and we can play off games until Easter — are the housewives. Maybe they will come in and watch a particular game, but they cannot be part of this binge. I can think of no other word for it than binge. And they wonder how the husband can sit there, and I wonder how I can sit there sometimes day after day and on into the evening, watching these various pageants. I think that's probably the best term for it. I do think it's a differential thing, but we need more data on it. We need more data rather than thought.

PAGE: I don't want this to be a discourse between the two of us. I'm keen to answer him, but I will restrain.

NANCY BALDWIN: I don't want to belabor the participation of women, but I would like to ask you, do you not think that many times the verbalized or expressed interest in sports by women is so much governed by what she perceives the man to expect her to be?

STONE: That's right. That's why I'm talking about the middle-class housewife.

PAGE: I'm so glad you asked that question.

BALDWIN: Do you not think as men perceive woman to become more and more a participating or at least a knowledgeable individual in these areas, that she would feel more free in becoming involved or interested?

PAGE: Offhand, I'd have two answers. Clearly, and in keeping with basic differences in character structure between the sexes, one of the strong bents of many, many women is to be attractive to men, whereas one of the basic bents among men is to prove themselves, as we all know, whether it's in sports or business or anything else, to demonstrate our capacity to do things. So this, I think, is a sort of constant in the picture and I think your point is well taken. I might say this in connection with your question and also a comment that Gregory made — and I say this lightheartedly, but with some degree of seriousness — that increasingly I think that women are less and less the custodians of morality in our society and more and more such types as college and high school coaches are the custodians of morality.

STONE: Things are coming to a terrible pass.

PAGE: And I think there is a great deal of evidence of this.

GÜNTHER LÜSCHEN: May I comment on the social class problem. Although I believe as you do, Professor Page, that just to elicit a response is more likely from the upper class, I think there is by and large enough evidence that there is some, although not linear, correlation between social class and participation in sport. I said this is not completely linear since what we have observed for instance in Germany is that particular groups in the lower class, which I would call more the progressive group — those who are employed as industrialized labor — participate quite strongly in sport where, as Mr. Stone mentioned, the very lower class almost does not participate at all. In a paper given at the International Sociological Association meetings, we proposed the hypothesis that this signalizes a redefinition of the social class system. I don't know how much there is in it, but what we saw was, for instance, that the traditionally lower middle-class people were not participating in sport but that they were, in their leisure time, participating in activities that were traditionally lower lower-class activities, so there seemed to be some switch, and we in our hypothesis felt that this would signalize a redefinition of the class system. As far as the relationship between passive and active participation is concerned, I agree that this is a very bad distinction in general. It's also that in general there is —

STONE: Not a term by the way that was used, I don't think. I don't think this distinction was made either in my paper or —

PAGE: Mr. Kleinman made the conceptual distinction. He didn't use that terminology.

LÜSCHEN: The situation is that you have here a somewhat positive correlation between both, so that those who participate also view sports. But if you compare, for instance, this along the social class dimension, then you will find that there is a certain inverse relationship between active participation and call it passive or spectatorship, which is much higher in the lower class, which I would think in a way signalizes high interest. On the other hand, considering a certain deprivation that the lower class faces, as suggested by James Coleman in his high school studies, interestingly enough, if there was not enough sports participation supplied for the adolescents then they would turn to viewing sports on TV. The TV viewing was much higher among those that weren't able to participate that much.

One point that may also be studied in the future is the change of social class affiliation with the same or different sport disciplines. I think there is some evidence that you have something like what a rather old German sociologist by the name of Naumann has once called *Sinkendes Kulturgut* — thinking is cultural material, which somewhere it starts in the upper class and then moves down all the way and you have the same hypothesis inverted. It would be interesting to see for instance, whether the upper class gives up certain sports, or whether sport that they have formerly engaged in moved down to a lower class. Also, what new types of sport do the upper classes now create, or whether they do it at all.

PAGE: Just one comment: I hope that we will have an opportunity later in the conference to pursue this theme. There is good historical evidence that the development of specific sports to a point of popularity, general cultural popularity, can be a development that has either upper class origins, lower class origins or middle class origins. My own study of sport illustrates these different class origins.

STONE: May I make some observations here. I think that in the first place it's very difficult to talk about sport in an all-inclusive manner. So I think that some of the things that Dr. Lüschen says will be true for some sports and not for other sports, and this is the implication of your comment. There are also very important variables that are left out of this discussion. One is age, which is certainly quite important in terms of explaining sport participation, and then, of course, the whole process of urbanization. In terms of these two we have little decent material. Probably the best material that I know of in terms of data was gathered by the Outdoor Recreation Resources Review Commission, but this refers only to outdoor sports. In terms of urbanization, at least as far as outdoor sport is concerned, I have gathered some data which indicate that as suburbia becomes urbanized, as our suburbs become more and more similar to cities, participation in outdoor recreation tends to decline in proportion.

WALTER GREGG: I wonder if you could go back and clarify your ideas about participation as related to heterosexuality and homosexuality. I'm not sure right now whether I should reexamine my boy or not!

PAGE: Well, I would be very glad to speak with you privately about this or alternatively to discuss this matter. I gather that we are approaching closing hour, aren't we?

GREGG: Well, I wasn't clear what you said in contrast to what Mr. Stone had said.

PAGE: I'm sorry I goofed up the illustration. Gregory referred in passing to a psychiatrist, in this case in the Army, who was apparently using knowledge of sport as a possible indicator of masculinity. I suggested that the opposite hypothesis might be more in keeping with at least traditional Freudian views, that intensive knowledge of and capacity in sport, or at least certain sports, might be just the opposite. That's all I was suggesting.

HARRY WEBB: I'd like to address a question to Dr. Stone. I'm wondering, did you take into consideration race in your particular sample?

STONE: I specifically did not include Negroes in the sample. It would have simply complicated the cells. You see this would have added two more and I would have then had 48 cells in terms of sampling. I might say that we do have some data which I haven't really had a chance to look at yet, gathered in St. Paul a couple of years ago in the Negro area, with a few questions pertaining to sport and particularly favorite players and sports heroes and this sort of thing. So that if I ever get around to it, the data are available and if anybody would like to look at it I could probably make it available to them.

CYRIL WHITE: May I address this question to Dr. Stone. You mentioned the concept of the culture of poverty in relationship to sports. I'm particularly interested in the unusual happenings at sport contests, particularly the hostile outbursts. From the investigations I have been involved in over the past two or three years now, I feel that one of the structural strains is a cultural one. In fact it's a sub-cultural one. And in these investigations which have gone into the hostile outbursts taking place not only in the United States but in Britain and South America, it is very clear that the two competing elements which act as predisposing factors toward hostile outbursts, that one of them is certainly sub-cultural strain. We see this if we look at one that I am particularly interested in which took place at a high school football game in Washington, D. C. in 1962. I read very extensively about Washington, D. C. and the background of one particular team and it's very obvious that the cultural poverty here is a very worthwhile concept in identifying the value systems. It's very different from the value system of the other team. Now when those teams come in conflict in violent exercise like American football for example, the results can be on certain occasions not only explosive but a catastrophe. In some cases over 500 people can be seriously injured, in other cases over 300 people can be killed. And this is not something that is just happening now and again. We are now seeing this happen about twice a year in sport, so your mention of the cultural poverty is something I'm particularly interested in, and I think very apropos to this when we talk about social class. Thus, I would like to ask Dr. Stone what type of lower class respondents was he dealing with? Was it people who could be identified as impoverished people?

STONE: You remember I mentioned that I picked the areas, three tracts that were furthest down the scale and within those tracts I told the students to go to the lousiest places of residence that they could to pick the sample. The sample was then reclassified in terms of perhaps more sophisticated techniques. That was just the way of getting these people, but I would say probably half of the 190 people classified as lower here are really lower.

WHITE: Then you would say that they would be in the culture of poverty rather than just being impoverished, being poor?

STONE: I don't know what the culture of poverty is, but they are very poor. Whether they are in the culture of poverty, it's difficult. The culture of poverty can be Puerto Rican and a number of other things.

PAGE: I was very interested in your comments and I would like to respond to one of them. You were discussing the possible relationship between distinctive sub-cultures and violence or potentiality for violence. I'm sure this is a relationship that we should know a great deal more about (however, I'm sure that you know more about this than I do because you are obviously studying it and interested in it). When one examines comparative studies, a look at the Latin American developments, for example, at football games and soccer games where you sometimes, as we all know, have really violent outbursts resulting in all sorts of things, it is very questionable to me whether a distinctive sub-culture is involved in that kind of episode as contrasted, say with the incident in Washington, D. C. you were referring to. I just don't know.

WHITE: I could answer you here and now: yes, it is. It is even more so than Washington, D. C. This has been clearly identified. Dr. Stone, I would like to suggest that it would be useful if some type of partitioning system be used to see which of the cells in your tables contributes most to your overall Chi squares. As it stands now it's difficult to see what the difference is between upper, lower or middle classes, or whether it's part of your rating system.

STONE: In general I cannot tell you. As I recall from the file of data that I have, the directions were fairly unilinear, but I'll have to look and see.

VERDELLE PARKER: I would like an elaboration on the part of the panel on the subject of cohesion and insulation as you mention it as they fit these two stratas, the lower and the upper. This would be of real interest to me and it might be for the group.

STONE: That would take some time. What I was concerned about in that step, and I really wish I had some tables that are interesting on this, was whether people under objective conditions of low integration would develop a subjective identification with a larger community by virtue of relatively active spectatorship measured by their designating themselves as sport fans. In other words, a fan, certainly a self-designated fan, would be a more active spectator than one who said, "No, I'm not a fan." In general, I found out that spectatorship or active spectatorship as designated by being a fan, or fanatic if you like, did not have this effect, unless it was combined with active participation in sport. Once active spectatorship was combined with active participation, then the sense of subjective identification was developed, at all levels irrespective of status. But, again there was much less active spectatorship and active participation in the lower levels. But, when those who were active combined their spectatorship with participation, this did have a cohesive influence. I hope I didn't make that too complicated.

Walter E. Schafer

3. Some Social Sources and Consequences of Interscholastic Athletics: The Case of Participation and Delinquency*

Interscholastic athletes share with other competitive sports the distinction of being among the least studied of all social phenomena. Like collegiate, professional and sand-lot athletics, high school sports are marked by rich and abundant folk-wisdom about the reasons for their existence and strength, their internal dynamics, and their consequences for the society, the community, the school, and participant. Systematic sociological investigations of these issues, however, are only now beginning.

This paper is one of a series intended to help fill this void in our knowledge by identifying significant research questions, drawing on more general theory to suggest hypotheses, and reporting research on one limited problem, the relationship of participation in interscholastic sports with delinquency. As a means for setting this specific problem in a wider context, I will begin with a more general discussion of the sociology of interscholastic athletics.

ATHLETES IN THE AMERICAN HIGH SCHOOL

Almost everywhere one looks in this country, interscholastic athletics occupy a central place in the life of the high school. In fact, James Coleman has suggested that athletics may really be a more important part of the school experience for many teenagers than academic achievement, which is intended to be the principal goal and interest of the student.[1] So dominant and apparent is the attention and energy given to sports that ". . . an impressionable stranger . . . might well suppose that more attention is paid by teenagers, both as athletes and spectators, than to scholastic matters."[2] Coleman's argument must indeed be taken seriously when we consider what the stranger is likely to see during a typical day in a typical high school.

*This research was supported in part by a curriculum development grant from the Office of Juvenile Delinquency and Youth Development, Welfare Administration, United States Department of Health, Education, and Welfare in cooperation with the President's Committee on Juvenile Delinquency and Youth Crime; by the Center for Research on Social Organization of the University of Michigan; and by the Office of Scholarly and Scientific Research of the Graduate School of the University of Oregon. Professor Rosemary Sarri of the University of Michigan generously helped in the collection of the data on delinquency.

A visitor entering a school would likely be confronted, first of all, with a trophy case. His examination of the trophies would reveal a curious fact: the gold and silver cups, with rare exception, symbolize victory in athletic contests, not scholastic ones. The figures adorning these trophies represent men passing footballs, shooting basketballs, holding out batons; they are not replicas of "The Thinker." The concrete symbols of victory are old footballs, basketballs, and baseballs, not works of art or first editions of books won as literary prizes. Altogether, the trophy case would suggest to the innocent visitor that he was entering an athletic club, not an educational institution.

Walking farther, this visitor would encounter teenagers bursting from classrooms. Listening to their conversations, he would hear both casual and serious discussions of the Friday football game, confirming his initial impression. Attending a school assembly that morning, he would probably find a large segment of the program devoted to a practice of school cheers for the athletic game and the announcement of a pep rally before the game. At lunch hour, he would be likely to find more boys shooting baskets in the gymnasium than reading in the library. Browsing through a school yearbook, he would be impressed, in his innocence, with the number of pages devoted to athletics.

Altogether, this visitor would find, wherever he turned, a great deal of attention devoted to athletics.[3]

Despite rather serious methodological deficiencies, Coleman's research strongly suggests that athletics do occupy a central place in the informal sub-culture of teenagers. For example, more boys reported they would rather be remembered as an athletic star than a brilliant student, athletic success was found to be a primary criterion for popularity and leadership, and top athletes were heavily represented in the leading crowd and in leadership positions.[4]

Coleman's analysis was not the first to be carried out by a sociologist. Some three decades earlier, Willard Waller presented a brief but penetrating and suggestive analysis of high school sports in his book, *The Sociology of Teaching.*[5] He, too, remarked on the central role of athletics among youth.

Of all activities athletics is the chief and the most satisfactory. It is the most flourishing and the most revered culture pattern. It has been elaborated in more detail than any other culture pattern. Competitive athletics has many forms. At the head of the list stands football, still regarded as the most diagnostic test of the athletic prowess of any school.[6]

Not only are athletics at the heart of the collective life of the school and its informal subculture, but, to a lesser extent, of the larger community as well. This, too, was noted more than thirty years ago by the Lynds in their study of Middletown.

An even more widespread agency of group cohesion is the high school basketball team. In 1890, with no school athletics, such a thing as an annual state high school basketball tournament was undreamed of. . . . Baseball received much newspaper space, but support for the team had to be urged. Today more civic loyalty centers around basketball than around any other one thing. No distinctions divide the crowds which pack the school gymnasium for home games and which in every kind of machine crowd the roads for out-of-town games.[7]

While we know little of the conditions under which this pattern varies, it is probably safe to assert that interscholastic athletics are a major focus of attention and energy and a major source of cohesion in most American schools and communities.

SOCIAL SOURCES OF INTERSCHOLASTIC ATHLETICS

Why are interscholastic sports so important? Part of the reason is that school authorities (boards of education, superintendents and principals) have decided this is the way it should be. This may seem too simple an explanation, and indeed it is not the total answer. Yet it is clear that without present resources in money, staff time, and facilities, which are allocated by decision-makers, athletics would not flourish as they do. But we are still left with the question, why have school authorities decided athletics warrant such a central role? No research has been conducted on this question, but several reasons can be suggested.

First, a strong athletic program is thought to provide a number of educational benefits. A typical statement of such alleged benefits comes from a 1954 pronouncement by the prestigious Educational Policies Commission.

> Participation in sound athletic programs, we believe, contributes to health and happiness, physical skill and emotional maturity, social competence and moral values.
>
> We believe that cooperation and competition are both important components of American life. Athletic participation can help teach the values of cooperation as well as the spirit of competition.
>
> Playing hard and playing to win can help to build character. So also do learning to "take it" in the rough and tumble of vigorous play, experiencing defeat without whimpering and victory without gloating, and disciplining one's self to comply with the rules of the games and of good sportsmanship.
>
> Athletics may also exemplify the value of the democratic process and of fair play. Through team play the student athlete often learns how to work with others for the achievement of group goals. Athletic competition can be a wholesome equalizer. Individuals on the playing field are judged for what they are and for what they can do, not on the basis of social, ethnic, or economic group to which their families belong.[8]

The expectation of such outcomes does not by itself explain school officials' decisions that athletics should provide a major source of entertainment for the rest of the school and community, since these alleged benefits pertain only to athletes themselves and could be expected in athletic programs conducted on a much smaller scale.

A second reason is that school officials see athletics as an effective means for channeling interest and loyalty of the student body and the community into the school. As Coleman has put it,

> . . . the importance of athletic contests in both high schools and colleges lies in part in the way the contests solve a definite problem for the institution — the problem of generating enthusiasm for and identification with the school and of drawing the energies of the adolescents into the school.[9]

A third and related reason is the social control value seen in interscholastic sports. Part of this perceived function lies in the harnessing of the energies and impulses of athletes themselves. Waller perceptively noted that:

> Part of the technique, indeed, of schools and teachers who handle difficult cases consists in getting those persons interested in some form of athletics. This constitutes a wholesome interest, opens the way to a normal growth of personality, and inhibits abnormal interests and undesirable channels of growth.[10]

As Matza points out, the social control of athletes takes place largely because they are ". . . enjoined to be 'in training'; they are to refrain from smoking, drinking, staying out late, and other forms of dissipation which violate the expectations of adult authority."[11] Whether or not athletes in fact conform more often (a question to be investigated later in this paper) is immaterial. The important point is that school authorities see it this way.

Not only will the time and energy of athletes presumably be channeled into controlled non-delinquent activities, but, to a lesser extent, the same is thought to be true for the rest of the students as well, if the athletic program is healthy and well supported. Waller cogently depicted in the following way the social control function of sports — and the support given athletics by school authorities. for this reason.

> By furnishing all the members of the school population with an enemy outside the group, and by giving them an opportunity to observe and participate in the struggle against that enemy, athletics may prevent a conflict group tension from arising between students and teachers. The organization of the student body for the support of athletics, though it is certainly not without its ultimate disadvantages, may bring with it certain benefits for those who are interested in the immediate problems of administration. It is a powerful machine which is organized to whip all students into line for the support of athletic teams, and adroit school administrators learn to use it for the dissemination of other attitudes favorable to the faculty and the faculty policy.[12]

Matza has pointed out that competitive sports are really a "routinization of violence."[13] Physical force and strength are encouraged, yet controlled. But he also notes that the control of violence is not always complete, as when players engage in rough or dirty play, when spectators join the battle on the field or court, or when the violent conflict is extended to the streets after the contest. The recent upsurge of post-game fights and destruction in many of our large cities makes one wonder whether school authorities will soon change their minds about the general social control value of sports and try to reduce the program to a modest scale. Indeed, potentially explosive championship games have already been eliminated in some cities.

There is another, more subtle way athletics is thought to serve a social control function. Many school authorities believe, as Waller puts it, that ". . . athletes may simplify the problem of police work in school . . ." by embodying the kinds of behavior judged to be moral and upright.[14] A high school principal recently illustrated this point very well when he told the student body attending an awards assembly, "I want you to see that none of these letter-winners are wearing long hair or sloppy clothes." An even more direct use of athletes for social control of other students was also illustrated by the same principal who gave the letter winners' club permission to "persuade" a group of alienated intellectuals, during school hours, that they really should attend pep rally assemblies, which they had refused to do in violation of school rules. He refused to take action against the athletes despite the fact that they roughed up the intellectuals enough so the incident was reported in the newspaper in the community involved.

Interscholastic athletics, then, have come to assume their central place in most schools partly because school authorities see value in a healthy and well-supported program for educational ends, student and community involvement in school affairs, and social control.

But this can only be a partial explanation. One must still ask, why do students and adults give their interest and energy to athletics to the exent they do? In short, why do they get so involved in competitive contests between schools? One reason is that normative influences pull them in that direction. Put differently, it is the *thing* to support your school's football, basketball, and, where I live, track team.

A second reason is that fandom, to use Gregory Stone's term, provides a sense of belonging, of identification with a collectivity larger than the family or friendship group. To the best of my knowledge, no research has been conducted on the significance of the "affiliation motive" for fandom, but it is probably considerable, not only because of the opportunity for involvement with the collectivity of spectators itself before, during, and after the contest, but because of the chance for direct involvement with various subgroups as well, such as friendship groups, the band, the cheerleading squad, or the concession club.

Third, adults and students alike become so strongly identified with the school team because the team represents an extension of their own sense of self or, if you will, of their egos. Stated differently, by identifying with the team, the fan is afforded the chance to affirm his own worth and quality. But he does it at some risk. If his team wins, he feels good about himself. Through a kind of extension of self, he too is a winner. But, if his team loses, especially if it loses consistently, he too is a loser in his own eyes. Perhaps it is in this way that we can better understand why fans become so intensely concerned that their team win, and why attendance and interest fall off so markedly when a team consistently loses.

In summary, I have argued that the central role of athletics can partly be accounted for by decisions by school authorities, and partly by intense, voluntary involvement by fans. Of less importance, perhaps, but not to be overlooked is the pressure from college athletic departments on high schools to develop or maintain high quality programs — and high quality recruits for collegiate sports.

CONSEQUENCES OF ATHLETIC PARTICIPATION AND FANDOM

The preceding section focused on the social and social psychological causes of the present strength and centrality of interscholastic sports. Another, equally important, question is, what are the consequences of involvement in athletics, either in the form of participation or spectatorship? A large number of possible consequences might be identified, but in the interest of time, I will suggest only a few.[15]

First, fans and especially participants might be expected to identify more strongly with other facets of the school's program, following the reasoning outlined above. On the other hand, involvement in non-athletic curricular or extra-curricular affairs might have the same result, that is, serve as a functional equivalent, for non-athletes and non-fans.

Second, fans and especially athletes might be expected to display more than usual achievement values and behavior, the fans through identification with the athletes, and the athletes through internalization of the subcultural influences in athletics on high aspiration, hard work, postponement of gratification, and achievement. Matza has pointed out that athletic participation represents one of the only opportunities for the modern teenager ". . . to make real the conception of aspiration."[16] The playing out of the success ethic might be expected to be especially vital in the development or reinforcement of achievement values for the athlete, especially if he is successful.

Third, athletics often serve as a channel for upward mobility, especially for boys from lower class and ethnic backgrounds. Elsewhere, we have pointed out that there are several ways in which this might occur.[17] Athletics might contribute to educational attainment which in turn increases occupational success chances. Recent research by Rehberg and myself suggests that participation in high school athletics in fact increases the chances of attending college. Similar findings have been reported from Project Talent data. Further, participation in athletics might develop those personal qualities which make for occupational success. Moreover, athletes sometimes benefit from "sponsorship" in hiring and promotion. That is, they are hired or promoted purely because of their reputations or public images.

Fourth, student fans and especially athletes might be expected to be less deviant in their behavior in and out of school, partly for the reasons already discussed in connection with social control. A more elaborate theoretical discussion on the deviancy of athletes is presented in the following section.

Fifth, Coleman contends that the present emphasis on sports results in a "flow of energy" away from academic achievement toward participation in support of school teams.[18] Despite his conclusions, his data do not indicate this to be the case.[19] In fact, recent research by my colleagues and I suggest a minimal, but if anything, positive effect of participation on grades. At the very least, more research is needed.

Sixth, athletes whose sense of identity and self-worth is entirely linked to athletic achievement often experience an identity crisis when the athletic career has ended, and it becomes necessary to move on to something else. How often athletes have difficulty getting new meaning from activities other than sports is not known, but countless examples can be cited of men who have never successfully made the transition, and, as a result, linger on as marginal men in the world of athletics, have family or personal problems, or fail to adjust to a new work role. Research is clearly needed on this general question, as well as on the type of athletes, in terms of personality, background, and nature of the athletic career, who are most vulnerable to such identity crises.

Seventh, it is often suggested that athletes, partly as a result of influence from their coaches, tend to be more intolerant of "non-conventional" interests, life styles, and political views than most students.[20] This is illustrated by increasingly frequent incidents of conflict at both the high school and college levels in which athletes have physically or verbally attacked hippies or radicals. Certainly, this question needs to be investigated.

Finally, what are the consequences of failing in sports? Little is known — and little mention is made — about the boy who invests a great amount of physical and emotional energy in sports, then fails to play or make the team. We might speculate that there would be important negative consequences for his self-esteem, his status among his peers, his view of the world, his tendency toward rebellion, and his future aspirations.

These, then, are some speculations on possible consequences of involvement in sports, through either spectatorship or participation. In the following section, we narrow our focus on one possible consequence, delinquent behavior.

ATHLETIC PARTICIPATION AS A DETERRENT TO DELINQUENCY: THEORETICAL FRAMEWORK

Earlier we pointed out that interscholastic athletics are supported by school administrators partly out of the belief that participation in sports is an effective deterrent to delinquency. Yet the validity of this belief remains untested.[21] Fortunately, six general theories of delinquency provide a basis for formulating a hypothesis on this relationship.

Albert Cohen has remarked that adequate theories of deviancy must account for conforming behavior as well.[22] Therefore, we will draw on these theories to predict that other things being equal, participation in inter-scholastic athletics will have a deterring influence on delinquency. Stated in testable terms, athletes will have a lower delinquency rate than non-athletes, other things being equal.

Delinquency as a Result of Differential Association. Sutherland, and many other sociologists since him, posited that delinquency was the result of exposure to deviant influences.[23] From this theory it follows that a lower class youth in a neighborhood with a high crime rate will be more likely to become delinquent than a lower class youth in a neighborhood with a low crime rate. Further, a boy who attends a school with a high proportion of delinquents carries a greater risk of delinquency than one who attends a school with few delinquents. It also follows that, within a particular school, the chances of becoming delinquent vary directly with the amount of exposure to deviant subgroups and inversely with exposure to conforming influences.

As we noted earlier, coaches set strict standards of behavior, not only on the field but off as well. Thus, there are rules prohibiting smoking, drinking, maintaining late hours, wearing beards or long hair — and delinquent behavior in the community. Violation of such rules often results in expulsion from the team. Most athletes internalize these standards, as well as other less formal but just as conventional standards, and, moreover, exert pressures on other athletes to conform to them as well. Since the influence from coaches is likely to be high, as is the amount of intra-athletic friendships and influence, any particular athlete is thus not only less likely than a comparable non-athlete to be exposed to deviant influences, but he is more likely to be exposed to strong conforming influences. Such influences are further reinforced in the wider school and community, where basic training rules are fairly well known and the athlete's behavior is under constant public scrutiny, especially in smaller communities.

In short, athletes should be delinquent less often than non-delinquents on the basis of the theoretical reasoning of differential association.

Delinquency as a Result of Weak Social Controls. Reiss, Gold, Cohen, and others have concluded that delinquency is sometimes the result of weak external social controls. That is, other things being equal, boys who are exposed to strong social controls from parents or other authorities are less likely to deviate.[24] It may be that the training rules regulating off field behavior of athletes deter some youth from engaging in delinquent behavior. If so, we would expect athletes to be less delinquent than non-athletes.

Delinquency as a Result of Rebellion. Albert Cohen, Arthur Stinchcombe, Kenneth Polk, myself and others have contended that delinquency is mainly a result of rebellion against the school.[25] For Cohen, many youth become delinquent because of a motivation to strike back at the school, where they are measured against universalistic achievement criteria which they cannot reach. For Stinchcombe and for Polk, rebellion flows from the perception that the school will be unable to pay off on their occupational aspirations. For Polk and myself, rebellion sometimes arises out of failure, perceived lack of payoff, or resentment against punitive sanctions. Running through each position is that, for some youth, school is frustrating, an outcome of which is overt rebellion in the form of illegal behavior.

For the athlete, especially the successful one, school is less likely to be a source of frustration than for the comparable non-athlete. Rather, school is a source of success-experience and a positive public and private evaluation of self. If school in fact has this meaning, then it follows that athletes will rebel and become delinquent less often than comparable non-athletes.

Delinquency as a Result of Boredom. Several theorists contend that delinquency often arises out of sheer boredom.[26] Slashing tires, stealing, beating on drunks, and smoking pot are simply ways of getting one's kicks. Clearly, athletes are less likely to be bored and thereby be susceptible to delinquency than comparable non-athletes, since sports take up so much after-school and week-end times. Even when not directly occupied in practice or competition, the athlete's psychic energies and loyalties are still directed in a conforming direction.

Delinquency as a Result of Need to Assert Masculinity. Cohen, Ferdinand, Parsons and others all contend that delinquency sometimes results from the motivation to assert masculinity to themselves and their peers through daring, adventuresome, or illegal acts.[27] It is argued that this is especially true of boys from middle class homes, for whom conformity is linked to mother. As Ferdinand points out, however, interscholastic athletics, as an institutionalized display of force, skill, strength, and competitiveness, represents a visible non-delinquent means for public and private demonstration of masculine prowess and competence. Insofar as delinquency arises from the need to establish one's manhood, then, athletes can be expected to be law-abiding more often than comparable non-athletes.

Delinquency as a Result of Labelling. The labelling or interactional view of deviant behavior, as discussed by Lemert, Becker, Erickson, and others, holds that deviancy is not something inherent in an act, but is created by the definitions of those who enforce social standards of behavior.[28] Thus, Becker states,

> Social groups create deviance by making the rules whose infraction constitutes deviance, and by applying those rules to particular people and labelling them as outsiders. From this point of view, deviance is not a quality of the act the person commits but rather a consequence of the application by others of rules and sanctions to an "offender." The deviant is one to whom that label has successfully been applied; deviant behavior is behavior that people so label.[29]

Whether or not an act is defined as deviant depends not only on the nature of the act itself but on a number of factors extrinsic to the act: who is enforcing the norm; the situation and its social context; and the status, reputation, and friendship patterns of the actor himself. Thus, for example, a white middle class youngster may well not be referred to the juvenile authorities for a minor theft. For him, the act is defined as a mere adolescent prank. On the other hand, a lower class Negro youth is much more likely to be apprehended and referred to the court for the same act.

Similarly, athletes, especially those who are successful and live in small communities, are more likely to be "protected" from apprehension and referral to the court by the public image they enjoy as being clean-cut, all-American boys, even when they commit delinquent acts. They may well be just as delinquent in fact, but turn up less often in delinquency statistics.

The interactional view of deviancy also leads one to predict that athletes are less likely to develop the image of bad boys, cut-ups, or hoods early in their school careers. As a result, they are less likely to get caught in the negative, self-fulfilling cycle of action, labelling, repressive or alienating sanctions by teachers, increasingly negative self images, identification with other troublemakers, rejection of school standards, further deviancy, further labelling, etc., ultimately resulting in overt rebellion in the community. Rather, because of their conforming public and private identities, athletes are more likely to become involved in a positive self-fulfilling prophecy with respect to their conduct.[30]

In short, each theoretical position leads to the same hypothesis: Participation in interscholastic athletics can be expected to exert a deterring or negative influence on delinquent behavior. In testable terms, athletes should be delinquent less often than comparable non-athletes.

DATA AND METHODS

During the summer of 1964, complete high school records were examined for all 585 boys who began as tenth graders three years earlier in two midwestern senior high schools. At the time the records were examined, most of the class had already graduated from high school. One of the three year high schools had a total enrollment of 2,565 in the fall of 1963 and was located in a predominantly middle class, university community of about 70,000. The other school had a total enrollment of 1,272 and was located in a nearby, predominantly working class, industrial community of about 20,000. For purposes of this study, boys from the two schools are treated as a single sample.

Of the 585 boys in the total sample, 164 (28 per cent) were classified as athletes. These boys completed at least one full season in any interscholastic sport (varsity or junior varsity) during the three years of high school. Any given boy could participate in three seasons each year; for example, football in the fall, basketball in the winter, and track in the spring. Thirty per cent of the athletes completed one season during the three years, 34 per cent completed two or three seasons, 21 per cent four or five seasons, and 15 per cent six to nine seasons.

Delinquency, the dependent variable, was measured by examination of the juvenile court records of the county in which the two schools are located. Since all those included in the sample were over the legal age of juveniles when the delinquency data were collected (1967) the records used were all in the court's inactive file. Since we are interested in the possible effect of participation in high school sports on delinquency, only those boys who had a court record after the beginning of high school were classified as delinquent.

It must be recognized, of course, that court records underestimate actual delinquent behavior, especially for middle class boys and perhaps for athletes, as we suggested earlier. Therefore, this measurement must be viewed as only a gross indicator.

Even if we find a relationship in the predicted direction, we will not have proven the hypothesis, of course, since boys who go into sports might not be very apt to become delinquent anyway. In short, the findings might simply be due to selection. As a means for eliminating some selection influences, we will control for academic achievement during the final semester of junior high school and father's occupation. Academic achievement was measured by obtaining the grade point average of all major courses during each semester ranging from 4.00 (all A's) to 0.00 (all F's). For this paper, G.P.A.'s were dichotomized into equal categories. Father's occupation was measured using census categories and dichotomizing into white collar and blue collar. By controlling on 9B GPA and father's occupation, we can also determine whether the original relationship varies among different types of boys.

In addition, athletes were divided into major-minor sports and high-low participation, in order to determine whether the deterring effect of participation on delinquency varies according to the type of sport and the amount of participation. Football and basketball were labelled major sports, based on their popularity, and all other sports were labelled minor. Boys who completed three or more seasons, either in different years or the same year, were placed in the high participation category, while low participants were those who completed one or two seasons.

RESULTS

The results in Table 1 indicate a negative association between athletic participation and delinquency, as predicted. Seven per cent of the athletes had a court record, compared to 17 per cent of the non-athletes. This finding suggests that participation in interscholastic sports might well have a deterring influence on delinquency. However, it is entirely possible that athletics simply do not attract the type of boys who have been or are likely to become delinquent. This is, of course, a distinct possibility, which we cannot entirely rule out with available data. However, we can partially

TABLE 1

	Delinquent	Non-Delinquent	Total	N
Athletes	7%	93%	100%	(164)
Non-Athletes	17%	83%	100%	(421)

test this alternative hypothesis by, first, seeing whether two factors, academic achievement and father's occupation, which have shown relationships to delinquency in past research, are related to the independent variables in this study; and, second, if so, whether controlling for them will lessen or eliminate the relationship reported in Table 1.

In Table 2, we see that previous academic achievement is rather strongly related to athletic participation. That is, 40 per cent of the boys who had

TABLE 2

	Athlete	Non-Athlete	Total	N
Hi 9B GPA	40%	60%	100%	(284)
Lo 9B GPA	18%	82%	100%	(284)

achieved in the top half of their class in the second semester of the ninth grade completed at least one season of high school sports, compared to 18 per cent of the boys who had achieved in the lower half of their class. Table 3 indicates that previous academic achievement also relates to delinquency,

TABLE 3

	Delinquent	Non-Delinquent	Total	N
Hi 9B GPA	7%	93%	100%	(284)
Lo 9B GPA	14%	86%	100%	(284)

although somewhat less strongly. Whereas 14 per cent of the low achievers developed a court record, this was true of 7 per cent of the high achievers. Since previous GPA relates to both the independent and dependent variables, then, we will control for it and then re-examine the original relationship.

Table 4 reveals that white collar boys participate more often than blue collar boys (33 per cent versus 22 per cent) while Table 5 shows that white

TABLE 4

	Athlete	Non-Athlete	Total	N
White Collar	33%	67%	100%	(298)
Blue Collar	22%	78%	100%	(239)

collar boys are less often delinquent (7 per cent versus 17 per cent). The chance of a confounding influence of father's occupation also arises, then, and suggests that this factor, too, should be controlled.

TABLE 5

	Delinquent	Non-Delinquent	Total	N
White Collar	7%	93%	100%	(298)
Blue Collar	17%	83%	100%	(239)

Table 6 contains the delinquency rates for athletes and non-athletes within each of the categories of father's occupation and 9B GPA. Examination of the findings reveals that for white collar, high GPA boys the relation-

TABLE 6

	Delinquent	Non-Delinquent	Total	N
White Collar				
High 9B GPA				
Athlete	4%	96%	100%	(74)
Non-athlete	8%	92%	100%	(113)
Low 9B GPA				
Athlete	11%	89%	100%	(27)
Non-athlete	5%	95%	100%	(94)
Blue Collar				
High 9B GPA				
Athlete	8%	92%	100%	(36)
Non-athlete	11%	89%	100%	(57)
Low 9B GPA				
Athlete	10%	90%	100%	(20)
Non-athlete	23%	77%	100%	(126)

ship declines to a four percentage point difference, while for white collar, low GPA boys it is slightly reversed. In both cases, then, the relationship virtually disappears.

Among blue collar, high GPA boys, the relationship is in the predicted direction, although I would hardly regard a three percentage point difference as a relationship at all. Interestingly enough, however, the relationship among blue collar, low GPA boys is rather marked: whereas 10 per cent of the athletes had a court record, this was true of 23 per cent of the non-athletes.

In short, controlling for father's occupation and previous GPA virtually eliminates the relationship, except among low achieving boys from blue collar homes, for whom athletic participation appears to make a substantial difference in the chances of becoming delinquent. If one is such an athlete, the chances of becoming a delinquent are reduced by more than half. It must be pointed out, however, that the difference in size of the N's for athletes and non-athletes in this category is rather large, making it necessary to draw conclusions with caution.

Is there a difference in delinquency rates among participants in major and minor sports? Table 7 shows that the delinquency rates for the two types

TABLE 7

	Delinquent	Non-Delinquent	Total	N
Major sport athletes	7%	93%	100%	(83)
Minor sport athletes	7%	93%	100%	(74)

of athletes are identical at seven per cent. Table 8 reveals that there is also a virtually identical rate for boys who completed three or more and one or two seasons (6 per cent vs. 8 per cent).

TABLE 8

	Delinquent	Non-Delinquent	Total	N
Participants for three or more seasons	6%	94%	100%	(79)
Participants for one or more seasons	8%	92%	100%	(60)

CONCLUSION

We have seen that, as predicted, athletes are less often delinquent than non-athletes and that the overall relationship is almost entirely the product of a sizable association among blue collar, low achievers. Of course, it is still possible that athletics attracts conforming types of boys in the first place. Stated differently, the negative relationship between athletic participation and delinquency may not be the result of the deterring influence of athletics at all, but rather to selection of conformers into the athletic program. This alternative interpretation must be taken seriously, since we have not controlled out all the selection factors, and since deviant boys are likely to have been formally or informally screened out of sports by coaches during junior high school or even before.

Nevertheless, the deterrence hypothesis warrants further investigation, since the data we have presented are consistent with it. If there in fact is a preventive effect of participation in interscholastic sports on delinquency, what are the processes by which it occurs? Is it because of greater exposure to non-delinquent influences? Stronger social controls? Less internal and external pressure toward rebellion? Less boredom? Less need to assert masculinity through deviant behavior? Or less chance of being labelled and detected? Unfortunately, the data available for this study do not allow us to put these interpretations to a test, although each must be viewed as plausible.

Hopefully, this paper will stimulate further thinking and research on the reasons for the present central role of interscholastic athletics in the life of the American high school and about some of the consequences of active participation in athletics. It is especially hoped that this preliminary study will direct attention to the need to study the role of athletic participation in deterring delinquency.

REFERENCES

1. James S. Coleman, *The Adolescent Society*. New York: Free Press of Glencoe, Inc., 1961; James S. Coleman, "Athletics in High School," in his *Adolescents and the Schools*. New York: Basic Books, Inc., 1965, pp. 35-51.
2. Coleman, "Athletics in High School," *ibid.*, p. 35.
3. *ibid.*, pp. 35-36.
4. Coleman, *The Adolescent Society, op. cit.*, Chapters II-V.
5. Willard Waller, *The Sociology of Teaching*. New York: John Wiley and Sons, Inc., 1932, 1965, pp. 112-117.
6. *ibid.*, pp. 112-113.
7. Robert S. Lynd and Helen M. Lynd, *Middletown*. New York: Harcourt, Brace and World, Inc., 1929, 1936, p. 435.
8. Educational Policies Commission, *School Athletics: Problems and Policies,* Washington, D. C., 1954, p. 1.
9. Coleman, "Athletics in High School," *op. cit.*, p. 49.
10. Waller, *op. cit.*, p. 114.
11. David Matza, "Position and Behavior Patterns of Youth," in R.E.L. Faris (editor), *Handbook of Modern Sociology*. Chicago: Rand McNally, Inc., 1964, p. 206.
12. Waller, *op. cit.*, p. 116.
13. Matza, *op. cit.*, p. 205.
14. Waller, *op. cit.*, p. 116.
15. For related discussions, see Walter E. Schafer and J. Michael Armer, "Athletes Are Not

Inferior Students," *Trans-action*, November, 1968, pp. 21-26, 61-62; Richard A. Rehberg and Walter E. Schafer, "Participation in Interscholastic Athletics and College Expectations," *The American Journal of Sociology*, LXIII (May, 1968) pp. 732-740; Walter E. Schafer and J. Michael Armer, "On Scholarship and Interscholastic Athletics," in Gregory F. Stone, *Sport, Play and Leisure* (forthcoming); Walter E. Schafer, "Athletic Success and Social Mobility," paper presented at annual meetings of the American Association of Health, Physical Education and Recreation, April, 1968, St. Louis, Mo.; Walter E. Schafer and Nico Stehr, "Participation in Competitive Athletics and Social Mobility: Some Intervening Social Processes," paper presented at the bi-annual meetings of the International Committee on Sociology of Sport, Vienna, October, 1968.

16. Matza, *op. cit.*, p. 207.

17. Schafer, *op. cit.;* Schafer and Stehr, *op. cit.*

18. Coleman, *The Adolescent Society, op. cit.*, and "Athletics in High School," *op. cit.*

19. For a methodological critique of Coleman, see Schafer and Armer, "On Scholarship and Interscholastic Athletics," *op. cit.*

20. For an interesting journalistic discussion of this point, see "Grades and Styles," *Eugene Register-Guard*, November 30, 1968.

21. For unsupported discussions suggesting that athletic participation is likely to prevent delinquency, see James B. Nolan, "Athletics and Juvenile Delinquency," *Journal of Educational Sociology*, Vol. 28 (1954-1955), pp. 263-265; Joseph H. Fichter, *Parochial School: A Sociological Study*. Garden City, New York: Anchor Books, 1961, p. 214. For discussion of the position that athletic participation is not likely to prevent delinquency, see Paul W. Tappan, *Juvenile Delinquency*, New York: McGraw-Hill, 1949, p. 150; and Edwin H. Sutherland and Donald R. Cressey, *Principles of Criminology*, Seventh Edition, Chicago: Lipincott, 1966, p. 169.

22. Albert K. Cohen, "The Study of Social Disorganization and Deviant Behavior," in Robert Merton, Leonard Broom, and Leonard S. Cottrell, Jr., (editors), *Sociology Today*. New York: Basic Books, 1959, p. 463.

23. Albert K. Cohen, Alfred R. Lindesmith and Karl Schuessler, (editors), *The Sutherland Papers*. Bloomington, Indiana University Press, 1956. Part I; Sutherland and Cressey, *op. cit.*, Chapter 4; Donald R. Cressey, *Delinquency, Crime and Differential Association*. The Hague: Martinus Nijhoff, 1964.

24. Martin Gold, Status Forces in Delinquent Boys. Ann Arbor: The University of Michigan Research Center, 1963; Albert K. Cohen, *Delinquent Boys, op. cit.;* Albert J. Reiss, Jr., "Delinquency as a Result of Personal and Social Controls," *American Sociological Review*, 1951, pp. 196-207.

25. Albert K. Cohen, *Delinquent Boys*. New York: Free Press of Glencoe, Inc., 1961; Arthur S. Stinchecombe, *Rebellion in High School*. Chicago: Quadrangle Books, 1964; Kenneth Polk, "Delinquency and Community Action in Non-Metropolitan Areas" in *Task Force Report: Juvenile Delinquency and Youth Crime*. Washington, D. C.: President's Commission on Law Enforcement and Administration of Justice (U. S. Government Printing Office), 1967, pp. 343-352; Walter E. Schafer and Kenneth Polk, "Delinquency and the Schools," in *Task Force Report, ibid.*, pp. 222-277; Walter E. Schafer, "Rural and Small Town Delinquency: New Understanding and Approaches," address to the National Outlook Conference on Rural Youth, October, 1967, Washington, D. C. (mimeographed).

26. See, for example, David Bordua, *Sociological Theories and Their Implications for Juvenile Delinquency*. Washington, D. C., U. S. Government Printing Office, 1960.

27. Cohen, *Delinquent Boys*, op. cit., pp. 157-169; Talcott Parsons, "Certain Primary Sources and Patterns of Aggression in the Social Structure of the Western World," (May, 1947), pp. 167-181; Theodore N. Ferdinand, *Typologies of Delinquency*. New York: Random House, 1966, Chapter 4.

28. For illustrative statements of the perspective, see Howard S. Becker, *Outsiders: Studies in the Sociology of Deviance*. New York: Free Press, 1963; Kai Erikson, "Notes on the Sociology of Deviance," in Howard S. Becker (editor), *The Other Side: Perspectives on Deviance*. New York: Free Press, 1964; Edwin Leinert, *Human Deviance, Social Problems, and Social Control*. Englewood Cliffs, New Jersey: Prentice-Hall, 1967. Discussions with Gregory Stone were helpful in developing this point.

29. Becker, *Outsiders, ibid.*, p. 9.

30. Variations among the following tables in total N are due to missing data for some individuals on particular variables.

REACTION TO SCHAFER PAPER — Brian Sutton-Smith

I think we ought to congratulate Dr. Schafer, first for introducing some refreshing data into an area where we have had for a hundred years a lot of assertion and speculation and very little data. I think it's very difficult, or more difficult than it used to be, to associate the reduction of delinquency with the virtues of sports and athletics. At the turn of the century it was much easier because they were theoretically linked by the recapitulation theory which said that in effect, we were all born with a variety of atavisms, primitive impulses of various unfortunate sorts which we could only get rid of if we played them through; and a delinquent was, of course, one who hadn't had a chance to play them through. So the association between sports and the reduction of delinquency was much clearer than I think we can hazard it is today. I liked, too, all the suggestions in Dr. Schafer's paper concerning the possible characterological effects of sports, whether referring to the social control aspects or the personal self control aspects. I have a naive belief that there is something in this although the thesis has been more of a mythology with us than ever being established as a fact. I think any of us who have worked with children or athletes have noticed changes in their behavior over a time on a purely case study basis. I do have the feeling that the experience was a self-organizing one for them, but we are still waiting for someone to really demonstrate and prove it in an empirically sound way. In recent years we have had the unfortunate effects of Freudian psychology suggesting to us that the athletes were mainly reducing their tensions on the field. We have got a little bit away from an orientation towards what sports do as a form of self-organization. I think we are on the verge of moving back somewhat; the pendulum is swinging. I like to think that the work that Roberts and I did on games as models of power, and the notion that various games induce knowledge of personal strategies for example, really is within the original characterological concept. Goffman in his last book called *Interaction Ritual** makes the point that in the game the person can test his character cheaply. He suggests we cannot really take chances on testing our character in ordinary life. If you would test your character with your wife, for example, you would probably have a divorce; but in a game, you can test your gallantry, your courage, your coolness, your confidence, etc., without any great consequences. And his line of argument is that society really requires you to keep your character up. If your character is not kept up, then you are not really ready for emergency situations. The games are, as Roberts and I would say, buffered models where you can test your character. When I worked with Fritz Redl, who was an ego psychologist of a post-Freudian persuasion, character control was our main focus. That was in the first part of the 1950's. We mainly focussed on the way in which, with disordered boys, disturbed boys, we could use games to induce self control in their behavior. And while unfortunately that line of research didn't go past the period I spent with Redl,

---

*Erving Goffman, *Interaction Ritual*. New York: Doubleday-Anchor, 1967.

I think we have a fair bit of evidence suggesting that some games were superior to other games with some types of clinical syndromes in leading to a greater organization for a period anyway, a period of time in which the child was less disturbed than when he was out of the game.

Now let me return to the paper. I think it's very difficult, as I said, to make an association between delinquency and character. Delinquency itself has become much more differentiated as the years have gone by. It was a much simpler concept at the turn of the century when this association was made with great force. I don't know whether you know it — I'm sure you *do* know it — actually you are specialists in the field — I'm usually talking to psychologists and they don't — but you may remember the playground movement made a great deal out of this. This was one of the main foci of the playground movement's ideology, that putting up playgrounds having recreation programs would reduce delinquency. Today delinquency is differentiated into a variety of categories. Dr. Schafer cautiously suggests that most of his data may be due to pre-selection and I'm afraid I would be more inclined to choose that alternative than the other one. I'm thinking of the Glueck studies, and the pre-delinquent syndrome, and the fact that delinquent children already in the early grades of school tend not to go into any formal organizations. They tend to have selected themselves out of any sort of formal club organizational activity promoted by the school so that the so-called pre-delinquent syndrome which is leading the boy towards whatever type of delinquency he ultimately gets involved in, in a sense predisposes him to be a non-athlete. Secondly, I think of some of the work that has been done on the different types of delinquency in the different social classes and different racial groups. White middle status delinquency tends to be a more deviant form. Let's say, it's deviant with respect to norms, at least to the extent of involvement in narcotics and car theft, stealing, assault, and so on, whereas if you take Negro delinquency you more characteristically get a type of expression which is normative for their particular group. It involves much greater activity and much greater aggression. It's almost as if the delinquent gang group in the Black culture stood to the rest of the culture as the athlete stands to the rest of the culture in the white culture. So the question one has to ask about a study which compares "delinquency" with athletics is, which delinquency? And using his sort of an approach an interpretation which one might put on these figures here is that the blue collar and the white collar cultures through which athleticism and delinquency are being expressed are quite different entities. If we look at the literature I agree that it certainly suggests that in high school the boy athlete in general tends to be the all-around personality. The high school is the last stage, anyway, in the middle class American culture for the Renaissance phenomenon. The boy who is good at one thing tends to be good at all things and athletics tends to be associated with prowess in scholarship and social life and so on. But also in some of the longitudinal studies of children we've had from Fels Research Institute, Yellow Springs,

Ohio, one additional characteristic is that the athlete — and this is positively related to what I just said — tends to be more of a "red blooded American boy." He has more precociously developed sexual appetites and activities than the non-athlete. Now this boy and his sports are in a sense an expression of much greater vigor. And in a sense while the data hardly support it — in fact you cannot make anything out of the figures on the left hand side upper portion of Table 6 because the differences are so small; it is possible that with these white collar boys there are not going to be so many records of their delinquencies. More often their fathers are going to be lawyers, or judges, and have influence over the local police force and they are less likely to be found on the court blotter as a result of this. So the differences might feasibly be larger particularly for that lower grade point average white collar boy. These are the red blooded stupid boys or alternatively the red blooded boys who didn't have time for doing anything much at school. Their athleticism expresses but doesn't control their vigor. I would like to have a study of this sort carried out with a sense of what's going on within the particular culture group.

Now on the other hand if you particularly look at urban groups where you have blue collar boys characteristically the boy who is in athletics is an upward aspiring boy. He's upwardly mobile and the athletics is a part of that upward mobility. The boy who goes into athletics is a boy less typical than others in his particular group. Over in the lower right hand corner of Table 6 there are twenty in the athletic group and a hundred and twenty-six in the non-athletic group. The athlete is less typical and he's striving apparently for acceptance in the upper status group. His athleticism is an expression of that and so in joining athletic groups he's also at the same time assimilating the greater middle class control, the middle class control system. Here the athletics are indeed a form of character control.

At any rate, this is the way I would react to these two sources of data. I think the paper is an excellent one because it opens up questions of this sort by giving us a few facts.

DISCUSSION

GUY REIFF: We fiddled around some with problems similar to this in terms of academic success of athletes and non-athletes and so forth, and I'd like to point out, though not offering a solution, that the grade point average has been a very difficult thing to try to use as any criterion, any absolute criterion. In the first place the difference between a high and low grade point is not an independent advantage. The kids who are out for athletics will tend to get higher grades many times if they are on the verge because of the very fact that they are out for athletics. I can think of some of the kids in some of the major cities, for example, who are out for athletics and who are barely scraping through school but the guy who is an all-state basketball or football player I can't see anybody giving him a D or an E on the course and making it out to the parking lot alive. Again, I think the criterion of grade point is very difficult to equate. Some people are taking the college prep course, other people are not; and the lower grade point kid may be striving or he may not, he may have a part-time job, and so forth. There are so many other variables that come into this thing, as you know. The solution to this particular type of analysis may be to take a group of youngsters and follow through. Perhaps a better method would be to construct some type of a very small probability sample of three or four different schools that may have been purposely selected and run through on the case study method rather than the broadest logical approach. I would be interested in comments. I'm looking for some answers myself.

SCHAFER: I hope you weren't studying the same sample I was. You might have been. But let me react to what you said. Let me react to the last point first. It might be suggested that one might use objective tests of some kind to get a measure of grades that is independent of the situation. My reaction is twofold. On the one hand, I agree that if you want to measure achievement objectively then grades are not an effective way of doing that, because it's not only the performance you are measuring, it's the evaluation of the performance, and there are all kinds of things that enter into the interaction between the student and the teacher resulting in the grade. On the other hand, however, I would suggest that grades have an importance beyond what is reflected in an objective test; that is, a student's grade point average is a representation of his identity, his place in the system, and it influences his future career. And so I think there are merits to using grade point average as an assessment of academic performance, taking into account the fact that we are not measuring objective performance but a combination of objective performance and assessment of that performance. It's also true that there are problems of comparability between schools in the meaning of grades. I mean the grade distributions in the two schools were not exactly the same. However, we classified students according to the rank within the school which really standardized that problem. I might say also in this particular study we took account of curriculum differences in the meaning of grades by matching athletes and non-athletes on curriculum. That was one of the four factors that they were matched on. This is the academic achievement study which appeared in *Trans-Action,* and which involved the same sample. We matched them on curriculum, father's occupation, IQ, and academic achievement during his last semester of junior high school. In other words there were 152 pairs who were matched on these four factors and we suggest that they are rather equivalent, then, on selection factors and that the curriculum problem which you mention is partly taken into account.

Your first point as I recall, was that eligibility standards might themselves account for higher achievement among athletes. And I would agree that that is one possible interpretation for such a relationship especially among marginal students, that is, those who are in danger of becoming ineligible. I think as an interpretation it has less plausibility for students, who are above, say, a 2.5 grade point average and who are not in danger of becoming ineligible. If there is a positive effect, which we haven't proven, then I would suggest that for students other than marginal ones, there are probably other interpretations. For example, the one that has come into all of your minds is probably the possibility of more lenient grading for the athlete. He is seen as something special. He perhaps in a subtle, unconscious way, is thought to be more deserving of better grades and it may be that athletes then don't perform higher objectively but are assessed higher at the same level of actual performance. But there are still other interpretations if there is a positive effect on grades. It may be, for example, that other things being equal an athlete comes into contact with achievement norms more often than a comparable non-athlete, that is, norms would pull in the direction of achievement. It may also be that athletes make more efficient use of their time, as coaches would like to argue. It's also possible that there is a purely psychological effect or mediating effect, namely that participation in sports results in high prestige and status which in turn results in an elevation of self-concept within the individual, which in turn results in higher aspirations in other activities including academic performance. There are several others which we might suggest as well, so coming back to the question of eligibility I would not use that argument to discount the findings but rather to interpret the findings.

CHARLES PAGE: I'd like to raise two points that bear upon both your excellent paper and Mr. Sutton-Smith's comments. They are of a rather general nature. They have troubled me for a long time. One, with respect to any possible relationship between sport and delinquency or participation in athletics and delinquency; I wonder if anyone has ever been interested in what I would call the delinquency of athletics. Certainly it's been the experience of a good many of us sitting in this room that we have been taught by coaches and those of us who have been coaches have probably been guilty of teaching these lessons occasionally. We have been taught a lot of delinquency, a lot of dirty play, and in a good many respects I don't think this was a phenomenon merely of the 1920's. I think it still goes on, at least in some sports at even the high school level, but I suppose more significantly at the college level. I would guess that I would just raise this as a question.

The other point is that so far in this afternoon's discussion I haven't heard any reference, explicitly at least, to the appeal, it seems to me still a very powerful appeal, of athletics in secondary schools, as a cultural activity, that is, the *end value* of sport. I've heard a good deal of comment about sport as a possible mobility channel or aid in mobility or aid in achievement and matters of this sort. But don't quite a few kids get into athletics because they enjoy it, that is for the same reason that they smoke pot, not because it's illegal; or for the same reason in the 1920's that they drank quite actively in this country, or for the same reason that kids engage in erotic exercises, not because of the instrumental value of these exercises but because of their terminal value, because sport *is* something for an awful lot of us, a lot of people. That answers itself and it seems to me that this is a very important element that should be cranked into almost any consideration of sport, whether it's with relationship to delinquency or anything else.

SUTTON-SMITH: I'll respond to that if you like. I think one of the reasons is that in scholarship we are used to functional interpretations of adaptation. Now you are suggesting a notion of adaptation which is sort of non-Darwinian in the sense that sports are useful without being useful in some specific way; that as ends in themselves, they do something valuable for the human organism. I accept this without any problem at all but it's a very uncustomary way of thinking. The history of our social science scholarship is an attempt to prove that something is meaningful because it works in some way. And by "works" we mean makes money, gives good sex, reduces delinquency, or whatever, and it's very difficult to think this other way. I put sports with art and other cultural activities and the way I look at it is, that these things are very delicate parts of human behavior easily put to one side and, therefore, during the history of capitalism and industrialism easily treated as trivial. In fact, they are not trivial but they are delicate. We can always do the other things first; we can fight and we can eat, and so on and so forth, but these are the things that even in very early childhood are the unique manifestations of the organism's own response to its environment, cognitive, expressive, affective and so on. And on the sports level they're the culturally unique things about a particular culture. Sports, along with other forms, of course, are the unique expressions of group life, you might say, but you know we are not used to thinking that way. That's what makes it difficult.

SCHAFER: Could I add to that? I would just point out that the question I was raising early on in the paper was the question of why athletics are such an important factor in the total sub-culture of the school. I think the suggestion that athletes join because of the consumatory value is not an adequate answer for that question. I think one would have to rephrase it by saying that fans become so involved and, therefore, athletics become so important because *fandom* is consumatory. You know, it's fun — I like to go to football games and other people do too, because of the inherent joys of watching the contest. I think that's a good point.

DAN LANDERS: In reference to your point that we don't go about it that way because we are not used to it, perhaps we ought to start getting used to it or start investigating avenues and approaches by which we can get at it, because what a great deal of our studies and our theories do is to provide intellectual after-thoughts. They come after the fact and then we try to get explanations for the reasons people behave the way they do. We come up with as many explanations as there are theories or as many explanations as there are interpreters of data or interpreters of behavior; and perhaps we may hit upon a good theory or we may hit upon good reasons but in the final analysis we don't really. Our approach in this fashion perhaps demands second thoughts, and perhaps we ought to utilize some internal instrumentalizing in some way, so that we don't look at the thing from the outside in, when in effect the behavior is coming from the inside out.

SUTTON-SMITH: I guess my reaction to one part of what you said is that I think we are always going to be stuck with these sorts of problems when you deal with multi-dimensional phenomena like sports. There are many, many meanings in them and, therefore, conceptual systems to account for them are going to have varying value and varying payoff. But I think with sport you have both fun and payoff, and you are in there for both reasons. I think perhaps if you get to some other cultural activity, if you get out towards art and music, maybe the ratio is higher on the expressible fun value — I don't want to use the word "fun" — but it's higher on the expressible value and less on the pragmatic value, but sports probably are closer to the latter. They are, as we know, a fringe phenomena. Many people are in there for the practical payoff. Many high school athletes drop out when it no longer makes any sense to their future careers, but sport is right on the borderline where both of these clusters of variable are quite critical.

SCHAFER: The problem is that in any research effort it's difficult to separate them. I mean, do you ask someone "Why do you attend a contest?," "Why do you participate?" and have a set of categories "Because I enjoy it," "Because I can identify with my friends," or "identify with a larger collectivity." All of these things are happening which we may be totally unaware of, or which the spectator or participant may be totally unaware of and unable to respond to, so it just makes it that much more difficult to separate.

GÜNTHER LÜSCHEN: I want to throw one very bad name in the discussion. I think on the basis of Parson's theory you may well be able to explain why there can be cause for this. I would think he would treat the whole thing as a matter at the personality level whereas if you think of fun as being on the level of the social system, then in engaging in fun for sports' sake you will always be rewarded and so there would be, as I would reason, an immediate payoff. However, what I want to comment on here again is on the problem of value which I think that may supplement your point that sport in a way internalizes. In true sports you value certain orientations. However, sport does not necessarily always provide you with the means to gain those values in ordinary life. It may even be that sports provide you with the wrong means, as for instance in cheating in sports, and I may just remind you of the very fancy role of the hustler — you may know the article by Polsky — who is indeed keeping the interest of his audience by pretending a lower skill than he actually has. You will also know of other cases. So, I would say, that sports have the potentialities to lead into delinquency. Also, if I remember correctly there is a study by Thrasher dealing with gangs, where he comments on so-called athletic clubs as focal points for delinquent gangs. Somehow I think the best material so far available on the whole question of delinquency is still the investigation by Ethel Shanas done in the '40's, where she studied recreation and delinquency and found, and indeed confirmed from Dr. Schafer's suspicions, that people who are delinquent were usually not going to recreation programs. However, if delinquent people go into recreation programs then just where do they go? They go to sports and not to other delinquent programs.

SUTTON-SMITH: One of my responses to that would be, that sports train in character delinquency and delinquency is very necessary in our society. Deception and cunning and so on. I always remember the case we had of the poker players whose fathers gave them so much money — this was at Cornell and Roberts and I have reported this before — some of them were getting $500 a month to play poker from their very wealthy business fathers who knew very well where they would learn the necessary skills, so this is a double-edged thing, this delinquency in sports. I suspect that the coaches who encouraged a little chicanery and otherwise in their teams were also turning out players who could use that very nicely in battle and business.

SCHAFER: I wonder if I could just add two comments. You know Gunther, a way to test the problem of selectivity very simply would be to match athletes and non-athletes on their pre-high school delinquency careers. Among a matched sample, what happens when one goes into athletics and another one does not. So one could test for selectivity which I am unable to do here.

Let me make a second point if I can, and this goes back to a point you made Greg, about delinquency and character. I would like to offer a distinction. I would argue that I'm not addressing myself here to the relationship between participation in athletics and character. Character or characterological qualities, as you put it, denotes internal subjective characteristics of people, that is, personality traits, and I think that's another question. I'm not interested in what happens to the personality or the internal dynamics. I'm interested in the investigation of behavior and I would suggest that the former is really a separate question.

GREGORY STONE: While we are on this business — I think your point is a very good one that society needs a witness — I am reminded of Kai Erickson's work on the "Wayward Puritan" which is beautiful. What's he's assuming, whether it is correct, is that we need a certain proportion of deviants to provide what he calls a "system-maintaining boundary for the society," which I like. I like his play on words, we can always find one. There have been several studies which have been done that show that all of us at any particular time could have wound up in prison for one or another reason. The thing is that delinquent acts must be situated. If we carry out some forms of delinquency in our bedrooms at home, where we are fairly well sheltered, we are not apt to wind up in prison. Now this being the case I think there is a theory missing, Walter, in your paper. That is the labelling of this business which has recently come up despite Goldner's concern, and

Becker's material on the outsiders, and so on. The fact is, if Erickson is correct and if you are correct, in that any society needs delinquents, then, the question is, "who's going to get labeled?" Isn't it the case, then, that athletes may well be in a sense protected from this labelling process. I don't know about the high schools but in a large midwestern university at which I'm not teaching at the present time, I remember that there were at least nine of the first string football players at one point who were up on various charges ranging from drunken driving, to car theft, rape, and criminal assault. I was at the trial of one of these athletes where the athletic direc-tor of that institution, presently still the athletic director, testified as a character witness in this person's case. I happened to know what the case was and the fellow was let off. What I'm trying to suggest here is almost the same thing as I was arguing about before. One of the consequences of the academic standards in the Big 10 has been to increase pressures, at least in some high schools which are sources of recruitment of Big 10 athletes, to raise grades for the athletes competing for those high schools. Similarly there is delinquency and certainly there is a protective sense that shelters the athlete. I certainly know this is true in college and professional foot-ball. It's two years ago when a current professional football player was up for exhibitionism, which of course is not a very harmful act at all. But, all that happened, was that he was traded. He was one of the outstanding pass receivers of the NFL, but he was traded quite a distance away from his team's home city. Also, I know that when pro athletes are publicized in the paper for criminal acts, there is almost a pained reception of this informa-tion by the sports columnists. This happens particularly in the case of boxers once they go over the hump. I think your identity crisis is very well taken, that they get caught in criminal acts; so I would just raise the same question that I raised to you earlier about the pressure for keeping athletes eligible in high school by being a bit less exacting in terms of grades. Now, I know you cannot answer with your data. I think your study is really excellent in terms "tickle of the mat" samples. I think it's beautiful. But, I mean, don't you need to make a kind of revisitation of some of these schools to find out if you can, what kind of pressures are operating in these situations? I think it would be very useful.

SCHAFER: Yes. Those are excellent points, Greg, and you know they are points that are ignored by using entirely quantitative methods in a study of this kind. I liked your suggestion for a fifth theory, I should have thought of it, obviously. It would lead to the prediction that perhaps rates of actual deviant behavior would be no different, but rates of labeled behavior would be likely to be different.

STONE: But you see Becker's point isn't the fact of deviant behavior, because we all engage in it.

SCHAFER: Yes, that's right. It's the status change that's important. I'm also interested from another theoretical point of view in using the labelling theory to understand deviancy inside the public school. What are the social processes whereby the labelling occurs? Who gets labeled? What are the characteristics of the individual, of the situation, of the person who is doing the labelling? I now have a fellow doing a dissertation on this problem using some data from New York State. Again we would predict that an athlete is likely, given the same behavior, to be protected because of different perceptions of him. It may not be deliberate.

STONE: Oh yes, I'm not saying this is conscious protection, although I know in some cases it is.

SCHAFER: Yes. In some cases there may be an effort to protect a kid from being expelled if he's done a particular act. But on the other hand, what I've called, in another context, a halo effect may influence the perception of teachers and other school authorities of the athlete, quite subconsciously.

LANDERS: Dr. Schafer, I was curious to know what were the nature of the causes of delinquency in your study? Was it things like drunken driving, or theft? Do you recall what some of these were?

SCHAFER: I had someone else do this and I am embarrassed to say that it was just recently done and I haven't looked in enough detail at the delinquency categories to be able to respond to that.

LANDERS: I was wondering if a lot of it might be due to getting traffic tickets or drunken driving, or things to do with a car, things that a lot of non-athletes may go into. Whereas athletes are devoting a lot of their time to sports after school.

SCHAFER: Yes, that's a good point. Just the probabilities of becoming delinquent are greater if you are out doing things in which you can become delinquent.

SEYMOUR KLEINMAN: Just one other point. It seems to me that there has been some recent evidence in terms of expectations on the part of teachers from pupils when they come to regard them in a certain light. Those who are of higher intelligence or are told they are of higher intelligence, perform better in the eyes of the teacher. It appears to me that the expectations for an athlete would be viewed in a particular light by the teachers in the schools, which has a great deal to do with labelling and also this question of grade point average. There are a lot of subtle things going on between in the pupil-teacher relationship in terms of expectations especially when the teacher sees the student as an athlete or non-athlete or as a potential delinquent. And if you expect the kid to be a delinquent, you're going to see a delinquent kid.

SCHAFER: Yes. Rosenthal and Jacobson point out that there are subtle ways, subtle qualitative differences and interactions when expectations are high, that will in fact elicit high expectations. I'd like to suggest, however, that the opposite may be true; that is, expectations among some teachers may be negative of athletes. We don't know what the positive and negative attitudes are toward athletics and it might be that for every teacher who has a positive perception of athletes there is another teacher or maybe two, who have a negative perception. We just don't know, and it's an interesting question.

DENISE PALMER: This is really just to confuse the issue, but I wondered what consideration you have given to women in the same respects, with the growth now of acceptance of women as athletes. Are they in it for self-esteem, immediate satisfaction, or expressions of femininity, or what?

SCHAFER: Well, I have to admit that as a typical sociologist, I haven't thought much about that question. We don't study girls. It's really true and it's true in the sociology of adolescence, there are very few studies of girls, and so all I could do is speculate off the top of my head. Maybe you would like to speculate.

PALMER: Well, I think pre-selection is quite clear. From my own background the girl who is interested in sports is selected to go to a certain school because there she will get what she wants.

SCHAFER: It's interesting to think about the place of ladies' athletics. Is that how we describe it? How do you term it — girls' athletics?

PALMER: Women, girls or women.

SCHAFER: Well, it's interesting to speculate about the place of girls' athletics in the subculture in the public school. I mean, is it really frowned on in contradiction to boys' athletics? Are girls who are athletes out of it, or are they looked up to in the same way that boys are? I suspect they are not, although I just had a conversation with Margaret Johnson Bales who was on the ladies' winning 400 metre relay team in Mexico City. She is a high school student in Eugene. Although the whole thing is compounded by the fact that she is married and is a Negro, she says that in school people don't care whether she runs or doesn't run. It's quite an ordinary occurrence. She is neither frowned on nor particularly rewarded socially as boys are. Perhaps that will change, however. What is the situation in the midwest in that respect, do you think?

PALMER: Well, I'm at a very new college and the survey work that I did with the incoming students, the only real excitement on the part of girls is to go into track and field. I'm sure this is a result of the news media. Also, they want integrated sport.

STONE: If you want a typical case, at Washington University I think about four years ago there was a girl, much to the embarrassment of the coaching staff, who made the tennis team and she couldn't play.

PAGE: There have been other cases too, at least two that I know of, where women have made tennis teams and have played.

KING McCRISTAL: At the University of Illinois there are ever so many instances in which girls' and women's sports are picking up. This year for the first time they are getting a chunk of the Women's Department budget. There are about 340 girls that are engaging in extra-mural sports, that is, they take trips and have a regular circuit, with competition in about five or six sports.

Günther Lüschen

4. Small Group Research and the Group in Sport

The topic I wish to discuss today has been chosen for a number of reasons. First, I think the area should be included in the sociology of sport, and second, I think there's a certain neglect of it in the field of physical education. You could, of course, expect that psychologists in the field of physical education to work with aspects of small groups, but they are mainly concerned with motor learning and motor performance.

The field of study, which by R. F. Bales has been labeled Small Group Research, originated at the end of the last century in a study on sport. Triplett (1898), in observing the performance of cyclists, noticed the differences in the level of records of individually racing cyclists, of those cycling with a pacer and those with a pacer competing against others. A number of theories to explain the superior performance of the paced competitors over the non-competing paced cyclists and even more over the non-paced cyclists, caused him to design an experiment with fishing reels, in which he was able to control the different factors, from suction to automatic stimulation, that had supposedly an effect on cycling performance. He found bodily presence of a competitor to be one of the stimulating factors to release energy not ordinarily available. A number of questions remained unanswered, yet his study is still a classic example of experimental design in social psychology.

After Triplett, a number of schools may be listed as originators of the small group approach. Mayo and his co-workers (cf. Roethlisberger and Dickson, 1939) explored productivity in industry and more or less accidentally discovered the standards of production of the small work group a determining factor in productivity. K. Lewin promoted experimental psychology, studied the influence of groups on the individual, and among others inaugurated the influence of leadership styles on group morale and the performance of group functions. (White and Lippitt, 1960). In World War II combat groups and their structure were the target of sociologists and social psychologists (cf. Stouffer, 1950). And finally, the promotion of two specific techniques for the study of groups, sociometry and sociodrama, by J. L. Moreno (1953) should be mentioned.

Small group research has, since the beginning of this century, established itself rather solidly. At annual meetings in sociology and psychology one will definitely run into reports dealing with this approach. Even in administration, psychotherapy and education, research techniques and results of small group research are well accepted. The number of relevant studies has cumulated in the last decade. Already in 1954 Strodtbeck and Hare listed almost 1500 titles. Topics investigated range from the effect of audiences on performance, and the situational determination of leadership, to sympathy structures in school classes and the equilibrium of discussion groups. There is almost no question in social psychology, group sociology and their related fields that could not be studied in the realm of the small group. What integrates the field is method of research and a *physical* object of study, a number of people from 2 to 2 dozen, who are called a small group — although they may not be a group at all.

The objective in theory and research is for a number of scientists the *group as a system* (Bales, 1950; Mills, 1967). For others the group has only relevance as a place of study where the *individual's response* to social factors, often in an experimental setup, or the *individual personality as a basis* for social structure, are studied. As Homans in partial retreat from his earlier efforts put it, "The group is not what we study, but where we study it" (1959). This "it" for him contained every aspect of social interaction of individuals which should give insight' not only into micro- but into macrostructures as well. In his later publications, he denounced part of his earlier systems-approach and in an address to the American Sociological Association, "Bringing Man Back In," argued for building sociological theories on psychological propositions only and thus making the individual personality the basis of study (1954). Yet one can not deny that Homans still deals with individuals in a group context, more explicitly with interaction. The problem is here more one of quality of theory or denial of explanatory power of system variables. The points of interest are still questions of power, status or exchange mechanisms in social settings. The ultimate goal is definitely the development of theoretical insights from limited structural units into complex macrostructures, this being quite evident in Blau's work *Exchange and Power in Social Life,* (1964). Yet the small group seems to appear only accidentally. As far as Blau is concerned quite intentionally so, since he wants to focus on dynamics, on what he calls the structure of social associations. In the approach of many psychologists in this field the small group or even interaction as a focus have even less interest. Under study is the individual's behavior in a social situation, but social structure itself is of no particular interest and provides only certain single variables. Many of the laboratory studies are of this type. This has of course led to valuable results for individual behavior. Also the rigor of research designs and the superior formal validity over many sociological studies are quite impressive. Yet for interaction or small group theory these studies have not given much insight. As a psychologist one perhaps couldn't care less. As a sociologist I do care.

The magnitude in the number of studies has also produced quite conflicting results. Not that the tests implied were wrong or the designs were poor. What appears to be one major problem is the negligence of sociocultural factors involved in many of these research setups. Most prominently, there is first the neglect of cultural factors, which indeed exert the strongest control over social behavior. There is second, the neglect of groups as parts of larger systems and organizations. There is third, a problem which has not sufficiently been recognized: the difference between what Stone called interpersonal and structural relations (1966). The neglect of these properties may be partly due to a psychologist's wish to study interactions between controlled factors only. Very often the problem will be due to the structural poverty of the lab situation. In putting 2-5 persons (most "groups" of this type do not go beyond that number) into a lab in order to test, e.g., anxiety, one has not created a group at all. Only gradually will this collection of persons develop a group structure — and often against the actual planning of the experimenter. The neglect of the distinction between interpersonal and structural relations is also a problem in the more recent work of Homans (1961). His concept of distributive justice, e.g., depends not only on investment by individuals but on a distinct normative structure and other qualities of a social system. The critique of Parsons (1964) that Homans did neglect the levels of organization in dealing with interactions is essentially the same as that of Stone. After the psychological approach has dominated the field in the last decade, and after Homans has gone to a pure psychological reductionism in explaining interaction and interaction systems, one may now well reverse the title of his address to the ASA and ask for efforts in "Bringing the Group Back In." Precisely at this point I see the potentialities of the study of sport groups for the small group approach. In the following I will thus deal with groups and interaction systems only and consider the behavior of individuals only insofar as they are performing social roles.

Sport has not only the potentialities to bring the group back in — and for developing theoretical propositions concerning the magnitude of social aggregates, sport will also lead us again out of the laboratory. Not only does sport provide the clearly defined structure of groups and roles, and the ultimate definition of values like achievement in group culture, the clear outcome of winning and losing provide for controlled variable. It is also in this realm quite easy to create experimental conditions with a minimum side effect. Newcomers on a team, backward referees, reinforcement of achievement, and odd rules are all very natural conditions in sport, but could well be used for experimental controls. Moreover, the very structure of sport will be a barrier to dealing with isolated groups only, since the determination of their structure through systems at large and the continuous interaction with other groups in sport's contest can hardly be overlooked.

What we face in sport is on the one hand the spontaneously formed casual play group of children or adults. They engage in play primarily determined by interpersonal relations, out of which a form of game may emerge, yet only for the length of the gathering. The play will show a certain order, yet the frequent interruptions of such games through arguing over rules and the meaning of the game situation (cf. Piaget, 1965) reveal the structural instability of these relations and thus a low degree of system organization. Indeed the social system is always threatening to break down. What integrates this type of play group is mainly interpersonal exchange, and possibly rewards are intrinsic.

On the other hand, the team of top competitors, like a national squad, is defined in its behavior primarily by the social system. The interpersonal structure is of little importance. What we find here is a highly differentiated code of rules determining the activity that this group engages in. There are not only formula rules of a specific sport but other norms as well, which in general will restrict the action of the individual considerably. The extension of all types of social control on this level is strong and determined by system and subsystem structures. What we face here is almost a complete loss of individual freedom in role performance. Interpersonal relations are of low importance. Rewards are extrinsic in this situation.

The argument over interpersonal versus structural (system) relationships is quite easily to be resolved referring to the spontaneous play group and the highly competitive team. Both levels are of importance. The magnitude of structural differentiation, e.g., determined by the amount of extrinsic rewards, will decide where on a continuum between play and top athletics a sport group will be located.

A question which for the clarification of our topic sport group should be answered is: What is the structure of the sport group and what are its functional problems? In Chart I, following Parsons, a sport group is outlined as a social system, which as any other social system has four levels of structure: values, norms, the normative structure of subcollectivities, and the structure of roles. The chart states under each of the structural levels specific examples that could be identified in a sport team. Of course in very small groups like that of tennis partners in a doubles match there may be no subcollectivities. It should also be mentioned that a social system in sport may well be identified as a contest of two sport groups.

In regard to the functional problems that such a system of a sport group has to meet the value and general norm levels are roughly focused on the "internal" problems of the system, having to do with maintenance of basic patterns and with the interrelations between "units" of the system (subcollectivities and roles), while the levels of subcollectivities and norms have to do primarily with "external" problems of goal attainment and adaptation. The "internal" problem of relations between units covers all aspects of solidarity, including not only positive incentives for participation but also the terms of competition and the forestalling, channeling or settling of conflict.

CHART I.

THE SPORT GROUP AS A SOCIAL SYSTEM*

Structural Levels	*Functional Problems*
Values (achievement, fair play)	Pattern maintenance
Norms (defining amateur, foul; rules of a game; defining "good" team member)	Integration
Subcollectivities (offense or defense; "braintrusts" of a team; cliques, friendships)	Goal attainment
Roles (unique clusters of recognized formal or informal rights and obligations of individual members; specific quarterback, peacemaker, scapegoat on a team)	Adaptation

*In regard to the section on Parsonian theory I owe much to a discussion with my friend and colleague Harry M. Johnson. For further readings cf.:

T. Parsons, An outline of the social system. In: T. Parsons et al., *Theories of Society*. Vol. I. Glencoe, Ill. 1961: 30 - 84.

T. Parsons, An approach to psychological theory in terms of the theory of action. In: S. Koch, *Psychology: A Study of a Science*. Vol. III. New York, 1959: 612 - 711.

CHART II.

SPORT IN THE ACTION SYSTEM

Subsystems

Culture
(including the culture of sport in general and of particular
sport disciplines)

Social System   Outlined in Chart I
(including many types of sport "groups," such as sport fed-   for the example of
erations, associations, clubs, teams, a contest of teams)   a small sport group,

Personality System   such as a team
(including the specific personality system of participants
in sport)

Behavioral Organism

* * * *

Physical-organic Environment

Any social system — and also a small sport group — is intimately part of a more general action system, consisting of culture, the social system (including all types of sport groups and associations), the personality system and the behavioral organism as outlined in Chart II. In turn the general action system is related to the physical-organic environment, most directly through the behavioral organism. According to the theory, the four systems composing the action system are arranged in a hierarchy of control ranging from culture to behavioral organism, and a hierarchy of conditioning in the reverse direction.

As Chart II suggests any sport group is part of a much larger set of social systems and is "controlled" by the general culture, which itself may be thought of as having many subsystems. Factors such as age, sex, social class, and skill are partly environmental, but they may be the focuses of rules of the sport group, arising in part from the overall concern for such broad values as competitive achievement and fair play. A role such as that of coach is a role in a social system larger than the "team" narrowly defined, as in a different direction the football "squad" is larger than the "team." Again, a referee isobviously a role-specialized participant in a social system having still different boundaries.

The complex interrelations roughly indicated in the charts raise many problems for research and will help clarify many open questions in persisting results. Many of the distinctions made are also treated in other theoretical schemes, but some point to particularly neglected areas in small group research. This theory applies well to systems as large as a society and as small as a game of tennis singles. Indeed the small group studies of Bales (1950, 1953) had, at one period, considerable influence on the development of Parsons' theory, including the discussion on functional problems. Moreover this theory provides a framework for systematically relating cultural, social-system, personality variables and even those of the behavioral organism. In the field of sport we have hardly begun to analyze the problems connected with these fundamental distinctions.

We might mention that the common allegation that this theory implies too much concern for the static, rests on rather fundamental misundersanding of the theory itself. Conflict, exchange, and structural change all find a place in the theory. This does not mean, of course, that many problems in the study of small groups may not be well handled by other theoretical approaches, such as those of Bales, Blau, Homans, the field-theorists or the newly emerging mathematical theorists. Yet not all of these approaches lend themselves easily to the study of sport groups since they have been partially designed for the study of discussion groups, therapeutic groups, or groups in laboratory settings.

We have been talking so far about the sport group in regard to its analysis from the point of view of sociology. This question may now well be: Is there no hope for physical education and social practice in sport? This is a legitimate question. And as far as the area of small group research is concerned, a question that can easily be answered. Yes, there is hope and not only on the basis of more theoretical insight into this area. Results, whether they are obtained on the level of psychological studies of individuals in social situations or on the level of an approach that we have emphasized, namely sociological studies concerned with groups, will very often have an immediate payoff for teaching of physical education or coaching of athletics. A review of the main results obtained so far in the area of small group research will make that quite explicit.

There have been a number of studies focused on conditions of individual and group performance in sport or physical skill. Effects of audiences on performance which earlier did not lead to significant results in a number of studies (cf. Kenyon and Loy, 1966) have shown recently, when separating the phase of learning and performance, a facilitative effect of audiences in a motor task (Martens, 1968). Competition with other groups seems to result in an increase in performance only when competing against potentially similar groups, while the performance of potentially weaker groups matched against stronger ones decreases (Start, 1966). Positive interpersonal relations in rifle teams showed an effect on performance (McGrath, 1962, yet a sociometric and participant observation study of rowing teams did not confirm, that harmony of team members was a condition of high team efficiency. Quite to the contrary strong internal conflict correlated with a consistent increase in level of performance (Lenk, 1965). Investigations of basketball teams seem to indicate that the formal organization of the team is a crucial variable. Moreover, the very general result concerning conflict and efficiency seems to need more qualifications. In the study of Klein and Christiansen, the strength of the opponent was found to have an influence on relations between liking and efficiency. Moreover, interactions were observed to occur more with the most liked and disliked (1966).

The motivation of a group of mountain climbers was found to be inversely related to certainty of outcome. In case of optimistic prospects communication between team members carried pessimistic statement and vice versa (Emerson, 1966). Achievement as an independent variable was set in field experiments with physical education classes. The reinforcement of the achievement value showed less effect in highly structural classes (Hammerich, 1966) and resulted in changes of ranks, yet opposite to the hypothesized changes, since the groups under study seemed to balance the experimentally created imbalances out (Lüschen, 1966).

The surrendering of defensive layers in situations of high pressure was studied in a sociodramatic experiment and showed in a baseball team loyalty to the team the most important layer, which was surrendered last (Charnofsky, 1966). A more recent study with rowing teams confines the result, and in general, shows, however, in the sequence of surrendering layers the determination of groups by situational factors. In a potential championship team winning over rivals was given up later than in the college baseball team (Lenk, 1968).

Following the general interest in leadership studies since the early work by the Lewin school, Fiedler found psychological distance of leaders positively correlated with team effectiveness (1960). More recently leadership was found to be curvelinearly dependent on a number of situational variables: relation between leader and followers, task structure and the power of a leadership position. As a general result of a number of studies one may state that leadership is more determined by situational factors than was anticipated earlier. Thus, good leaders may well turn out to be bad in different situations. A recommendation to adjust the situation to the leader and not vice versa may thus be well based (Myers and Fiedler, 1966). Field managers in baseball were, in another study, found to have less effectiveness on teams than is generally believed (Grusky, 1963). In situations of crisis, however, they are functioning as scapegoats (Gamson and Scotch, 1964).

The studies cited so far, are concerned primarily with structural properties of single groups, often only individuals in social situations. Only in a few cases have systems of two interacting, competing teams been analyzed. Yet, these units seem to be of primary importance and small group studies in sport should definitely expand to these systems of interaction of small units, which are joined by a third party, the referee. The two studies that could be mentioned in this regard are first, the Sherifs' *Groups in Harmony and Tension* (1953) in which the increase of hostility of competing groups of boys in a camp is analyzed. The second one, is that by Elias and Dunning on the dynamics of sport groups in which they try to explain the configuration of two opposing football teams (1966). The problem brought up by them is of quite some prominence for the theory of conflict. Whereas, cooperation and competition had so far been studied e.g., in their separate influence on group structure, the problem occurs now as one, where the structural relationships between both orientations in groups have to be studied. Gumpert, Deutsch and Epstein (1969) report on findings with the prisoner's dilemma game. Cooperation in a competitive situation occurred more likely under conditions of symbolic rewards, where one was rewarded for good performance by points. Cooperation was absent under conditions of reward with money. Results of one of our earlier studies (Lüschen, 1961) showed a high prominence of values of affiliation in sport. The higher the level of performance among athletes, the more values of affiliation were expressed. One may thus state the hypothesis, that the more symbolic the rewards, the more likely cooperation will be displayed in a competitive situation; one of the reasons being, that the system of interaction and the conditioning rules for reward have meaning only for those involved and depend on mutual consent (cf. Homans, 1961; Anderson and Moore, 1960). This is an old problem (Simmel, 1923). Yet the theoretical explanation is open. The study of sport groups in contest could make a definite contribution to that needed insight and into the study of conflict in general (cf. Lüschen, 1968).

The discussion of results in the study of small sport groups has made the casualness of research findings quite obvious. Yet, even these casual results have shown potentialities for the study and theoretical insight of groups and interaction systems in general, and moreover, the applicability of those results for theory and social practice in physical education and athletics.

RELATED LITERATURE

A. R. Anderson and O. K. Moore, *Autotelic folk models.* Sociological Quarterly, 1960, 1: 203-216.

K. W. Back, T. C. Hood and M. L. Brehm, The subject role in small group experiments. *Social Forces,* 1964, 2: 181-187.

R. F. Bales, *Interaction Process Analysis.* Reading, Mass., 1950.

R. F. Bales, The equilibrium problem in small groups. In: T. Parsons, R. F. Bales and E. A. Shils, *Working Papers in the Theory of Action.* Glencoe, Ill. 1953: 111-161.

P. M. Blau, *Exchange and Power in Social Life.* New York, 1964.

D. Cartwright and A. Zander, *Group Dynamics.* New York, 1968.

H. Charnofsky, Die Aufgabe von Verteidigungsschichten in Drucksituationen. In: G. Luschen. 1966, 237-250.

M. Deutsch and R. M. Krauss. *Theories in Social Psychology.* New York, 1965.

N. Elias and E. Dunning. Dynamics of sport groups with special reference to football. *British Journal of Sociology.* 1966, 4: 388-402.

R. M. Emerson, Mount Everest. In: Lüschen. 1966. Also in: *Sociometry,* 1966, 3: 213-227.

F. E. Fiedler. The leader's psychological distance and group effectiveness. In: Cartwright and Zander, 1960.

E. Goffman, *Encounters.* Indianapolis, 1961.

P. Gumpert, M. Deutsch and Y. Epstein, Effect of incentive magnitude in cooperation in the prisoner's dilemma game. *Journal of Personality and Social Psychology,* Jan. 1969, 1: 66-69.

K. Hammerich. Leistungsforcierung im Sportunterricht. In: G. Lüschen, 1966, 224-236.

A. P. Hare, *Handbook of Small Group Research.* New York, 1962.

G. C. Homans, *The Human Group.* New York, 1950.

G. C. Homans, *Social Behavior : Its Elementary Forms.* New York, 1961.

G. C. Homans, Bringing man back in. *American Sociological Review,* 1964.

G. Kenyon and J. W. Loy. Soziale Beeinflussung der Leistung bei vier psychomotorischen Aufgaben. In: G. Lüschen, 1966, 192-202.

M. Klein and G. Christiansen. Gruppenkomposition, Gruppenstruktur und Effektivitat von Basketballmannschaften. In: G. Lüschen, 1966, 180-191.

H. C. Kozman. *Group Process in Physical Education.* New York, 1951.

H. Lenk, Konflikt und Leistung in Spitzensportmannschaften. *Soziale Welt.* 1965, 4.

H. Lenk, Aufgabe von Wertbindungen bei Hochleistungsruderern. *Soziale Welt.* 1968, 1: 67-73.

G. Lüschen, Leistungsorientierung und ihr Einfluss auf das soziale und personale System. In: G. Luschen, 1966.

G. Lüschen. *Kleingruppenforschung und Gruppe im Sport.* Koln 1966.

G. Lüschen, Cooperation, association and contest. Paper at AAAS-meeting, Dallas, Tex. 1968.

G. Lüschen. The Sociology of Sport. Trend-report with annotated bibliography. *Current Sociology,* The Hague and Paris, 1968.

A. Malewski. *Interaction and Behavior (in Polish).* Warsaw. 1964.

R. Martens. Ph.D. Thesis, University of Illinois, 1968. The Effects of an Audience . . . A Complex Motor Skill.

J. E. McGrath. The influence of positive interpersonal relations on adjustment effectiveness in rifle teams. *Journal Abnormal Soc. Psychology.* 1962, 6: 365-375.

T. M. Mills, *The Sociology of Small Groups.* Englewood Cliffs, N.J. 1967.

W. Moede, Der Wetteifer, seine Struktur und sein Ausmass. *Zeitschrift fur Paedagogische Psychologie,* 1914, 15: 353-368.

W. Moede, *Experimentelle Massenpsychologie.* Leipzig, 1927.

J. L. Moreno, *Who Shall Survive?* Beacon, 1953.

A. Myers. Team competition, success and the adjustment of group members. *Journal Abnormal Soc. Psychology.* 1962, 5: 325-332.

A. E. Myers and F. E. Fiedler. Theorie und Probleme der Fuhrung. In: G. Luschen, 1966: 92-106.

M. S. Olmsted. The Small Group. New York, 1959.

T. Parsons. Levels of organization and the mediation of social interaction. *Sociological Inquiry*. Spring, 1964.

J. Piaget, *The Moral Judgement of the Child*. New York, 1965.

W. E. Schafer. Die soziale Struktur von Sportgruppen. In: G. Lüschen, 1966, 107-117.

M. Sherif and C. W. Sherif, *Groups in Harmony and Tension*. New York, 1953.

M. Sherif, *Intergroup Conflict and Cooperation: The Robbers Cave Experiment*. Norman, Okl. 1961.

G. Simmel. The number of members as determining the sociological form of the group. *Am. J. Sociology*, 1902, July: 1-46, Sept.: 158-196.

G. Simmel. Der Streit, In: Simmel. Soziologie, Berlin, 1923.

K. B. Start. Wettbewerb und Geschicklichkeit im Sport. In: G. Lüschen, 1966, 203-208.

R. M. Stogdill. Team achievement under high motivation. *Business Research Monograph*. Ohio State University, 1963, 113.

G. P. Stone. Bergriffliche Probleme in der Kleingruppenforschung. In: G. Lüschen, 1966, 44-65.

S. A. Stouffer et al., *The American Soldier*. Vol. I, Princeton, 1950.

M. Triplett. The dynamogenic factors in pacemaking and competition. *Am. J. Psychology*. 1898,4: 507-533.

W. F. Whyte, *Street Corner Society*. Chicago, 1943.

REACTION TO LÜSCHEN PAPER — John W. Loy, Jr.

As the hour is late, and since I know that several of you have questions which you wish to address to Professor Lüschen, I will dispense with the sheaf of notes in my hand and confine myself to making a few very broad remarks.

First, I would like to congratulate Dr. Lüschen for his excellent job of outlining the problems and prospects of small group research in the sport situation. He covered a lot of territory in a short space of time.

In large measure I find myself in nearly full agreement with the various positions Professor Lüschen took in his paper. I especially support his statement that although several hundred small group studies have been conducted, there has been correspondingly relatively little development of micro-social theory and the empirical findings themselves have not always been the most conclusive. My special fear is that things are likely to get worse before they get better. Since the study of small groups is such a highly developed subfield in sociology; and as physical education students prefer the concrete to the abstract; and since quantitative theses rather than qualitative theses are currently the norm, I expect to see as many white sophomores and white rats in small group laboratories as are now found in exercise physiology and motor learning laboratories. It is evident in physical education that the several thousand empirical investigations in exercise physiology and motor learning have not produced a very large body of theoretical knowledge. Hopefully, students pursuing small group research in the sport context will produce profound as well as profuse studies.

I suggest that one way of assuring better research is for the interested student to pay careful heed to the insightful admonitions given by Professor Lüschen. Specifically, I make reference to Dr. Lüschen's discussion of the neglect of socio-cultural variables in past small group work. He states, and I think rightly so, that studies are needed: (1) which place greater emphasis on culture and social structure rather than personality; (2) which examine small groups as micro-social systems or subsystems of larger and more encompassing macro-social systems; and (3) which consider "real" rather than "contrived" groups.

As somewhat of an aside I note that one manner of getting sport out of the laboratory and to correct the three oversights pointed out by Dr. Lüschen is to study sport groups as subcultures. Although experimental control may be admittedly lost, many theoretical insights might be gained regarding sport involvement when sport groups are studied from this suggested perspective. Two analyses of "deviant" sport subcultures have recently been made which could provide useful models for the interested student. Marvin Scott has examined behavior at the race track from a dramaturgical perspective and presents his findings in a book just out, titled *The Racing Game*. Similarly, Ned Polsky, by means of participant observation has studied the subculture of the pool room and records his observations in a recent text titled *Hustlers, Beats and Others*.

Professor Lüschen's call to "bring the group back in" leads me to make a counter call to "bring sport back in." For it seems to me that Dr. Lüschen stresses the potential importance of sport situations for testing sociological theories; whereas I wish to argue for the importance of studying sport as a social phenomenon. In short, I think there is a fundamental difference between the individual who is trying to explain a phenomenon and draws upon sociological theory to do so, and the individual who has a theory in hand and seeks a situation in which he can test its implications.

However, I believe both Professor Lüschen and myself concur in the importance of using the sport context as a medium for developing social theory. It strikes me as surprising that social psychologists and sociologists have virtually ignored sport teams in their analyses of small groups. I think that they have missed the boat because sport teams as small social systems can be viewed as microcosms of larger social systems, including society itself. They present in miniature such societal features as a division of labor, a code of ethics, a government, means of communication, prestige rankings, ideologies, myths, and even religious practices.

Some of these features of sport teams as social systems were presented by Dr. Lüschen in his interesting Parsonian paradigm of the sport group. His taxonomy is an effort to delineate the overall structure of the sport group and to suggest the functional problems a given group must resolve in order to maintain itself as an ongoing social entity. I am not clear as to how Dr. Lüschen proposes to use his paradigm in the development of social theory, but believe that his taxonomy may have some merit as a didactic service. In fact, I employ a similar Parsonian paradigm in my undergraduate class when discussing the possible implications of Bales' small group research in the analysis of leadership roles among athletic teams. I specifically use my taxonomy to illustrate the fact that in sport groups one may often find the two complementary leaders, i.e., a task leader and a social-emotional leader, that Bales found emergent in his laboratory analysis of small discussion groups.

Since my own paradigm is similar to that of Professor Lüschen's I'll present it for those who wish to compare the two. Although my paradigm lacks some of the teutonic characteristics of Professor Lüschen's it features the same functional problems and similarly stresses the external and internal dimensions of a sport group as a social system. In addition, however, I emphasize the instrumental and expressive dimensions of a sport group and am solely concerned with the question of leadership roles. Thus, I indicate that one may find Bales' two types of leaders both within the collectivity of players and the collectivity of coaches. In my class I typically make reference to the Green Bay Packers of "old" with Bart Starr at quarterback as the task leader of the team, and Paul Hornung at halfback as the team's social-emotional leader. Well, since we have gotten somewhat removed from Dr. Lüschen's paper I'll conclude my own remarks at this point and throw things open for questions from the floor for Professor Lüschen.

EXTERNAL CULTURAL DIMENSION	INTERNAL SOCIAL STRUCTURAL DIMENSION	
Adaptive Problem—winning games from other teams	*Decision-Making Problem*—relating of team members to each other to reach and carry out group decisions	MEMBERS AS MEANS
Leader role—coach as technical expert and executive leader	*Leader role*—team member as task leader	INSTRU-MENTAL DIMENSION
Pattern maintenance and Member Recruitment and Retention Problem—acquisition, training and control of group members	*Integrative Problem*—relating members to each other to "get along" with each other	MEMBERS AS ENDS
Leader role: coach as educator and morale leader	*Leader role:* team member as social-emotional leader	EXPRESSIVE DIMENSION

DISCUSSION

CHARLES H. PAGE: I'm very much tempted to make a speech. I've been talking too much today, but every time I'm confronted with an effort to use Parson's social systems scheme which Dr. Lüschen used in order to make more sense out of a concrete area, an area of reality, I get increasingly confused and sometimes furious. I think the utilization of highly abstract categories, to use a technical word, which are analytical and not at all concrete categories, to bring order — and this is the presumed purpose of such a scheme of categories — to bring order and to make more sense and to learn more about the reality itself, I think it's extremely difficult when we try to apply the system of Parsons to any concrete small group area such as certain kinds of sport teams or sport organizations and so on. Therefore, I was very pleased when John Loy flashed on the screen essentially the same scheme so far as the categories are concerned but in a much more simplified manner. I'm not sure, however, that any of us can learn more about the world of sports by applying a scheme which has been designed in my judgment not for the purpose of learning about reality but for developing sociology. Parsons, who incidentally is an old friend of mine, is a man who is deeply concerned with sociology, but, I don't know how concerned he is with society. His schemes are of use in the chess-like ratiocinational, theoretical activities of people who are interested in the development of abstract sociological theory. Similarly, people who are interested in applying theory to sport are apt to be less interested in sport — I was glad to hear Mr. Loy's call for bringing sport back in — than in seeing whether or not their highly theoretical schemes can be applicable. And, of course, they can be if you go through certain verbal exercises, and thus we have the sociology of everything, the Parsonian sociology of everything, if you want to make the application. But I'd call for looking at this thing in a reverse fashion. Look at sports as a concrete area of activity and then, as I think Mr. Loy was beginning to suggest when he all too briefly described his paradigm, see what more we can learn about reality by applying certain distinctions, such as Bales' distinction between task and morale leadership and perhaps even Parson's basic functional problems of all social systems, which are the four categories that Dr. Lüschen outlined and also appear in Loy's paradigm; but I'm really disturbed by this effort unless I see it done in black and white where I can struggle with it for about ten hours. I don't know how the rest of you feel, but I thought I'd say that as a sociologist, which I am, who is interested I think in sport more than I am in sociology.

LÜSCHEN: I would completely agree with you that my primary interest was in developing sociology, exactly that. I see the merits of the Parsonian approach in this way. Although you may not want to buy the theoretical insights provided by this rather abstract systems approach, I would say it will at least get your thinking organized. I know, of course, quite well the opposite point of view; that as of today, I think is held by Andre Malewski. He couldn't care less about Parsons, and thinks that theory should be developed within the realm of small testable hypotheses. You may hold this point of view, but still fail to come up with the anticipated results. As a case in point, the theory of which recently he has claimed, has led him into all types of difficulties although at the first glance it seemed to be quite easy.

PAGE: I should qualify my own comments, and then I'll be quiet, and that is, I certainly agree with you, Dr. Lüschen, that one of the merits of this system, or a less complex system, is that it does call the attention of people who are seriously interested in a field such as this, to all of its possible aspects; that is, it calls for an inclusive kind of search. With a theoretical scheme of this sort you are guarded to some extent against missing things that you might otherwise miss. That I agree with. I think this is one of the advantages. But I'm not sure how helpful it will be when actually analyzing what goes on in fact.

GREGORY STONE: I just want to make a brief comment. This sort of "taxonomics game" may not facilitate our vision, for another reason. If we look through lenses or maybe a better word would be prism, there may be certain types of light filtered out. I think that we are being overly generous to talk of Parsons and others of that ilk. I'm not sure this is the way to develop any science — to sit down and build elaborate boxes and then find out where the world fits into them. For me the important part of science is the problem, the question. I think that this kind of taxonomy avoids the matter of problems. The history of science, I think, is typically a graveyard of theory. It's the problems that live in the science and the least interesting part of the science, I think, are the answers. Once you have an answer, that's it, for a while anyway, until somebody comes up with another question that throws the earlier answer into doubt. For example, one of the schemes of Parsons is essentially a static scheme. The emphasis is upon integration and upon equilibrium; consequently, matters of historical change in this case, in sport, don't fit anywhere in the box. The whole matter of rules, or, for example, Riesman's very beautiful little essay on the emergence of American football out of British rugby primarily because Americans have problems in knowing what a scrimmage was. This kind of problem was stated so well by Riesman that I don't see where it fits in the scheme at all. I kept wondering where the water buckets were in the box or the sports equipment, which are very important parts, I should think, of performance in sport. I wondered what a non-symbolic reward was as opposed to a symbolic reward in terms of Dr. Lüschen's hypothesis. In other words, I think such a scheme blinds us and buries questions. I think in any kind of a scientific endeavor the important matter is the matter of the question; so if I were going to pull the gown off the sociology of sport, I think I would lay out a set of problems trying to be as concrete as possible, and then having these questions, begin looking for the sorts of hypotheses that might be incorporated into carefully designed research, although I'm beginning to worry also about carefully designed research. It seems to me the more tightly designed the research, the more trivial the results of the research and this bothers me very much in sociology generally. So I share Professor Page's concern with this particular approach in sociology of sport. I could go on, but I become overly emotional.

LOY: Do you wish to respond, Professor Lüschen?

LÜSCHEN: Problems of, for instance, change of the rugby into the American football game would perhaps be treated only as functional problems in this scheme. I am well aware of the problems of change. However, Parsons would claim that you can do it this way and has worked on that considerably in the last five or six years.

STONE: Supposing you take changes in basketball. What's the matter with basketball now? It's boring — this parade up and down the court. The concern in changing the rules has to do with speeding it up, much as wrestling has been speeded up in college and high school, to make it more appealing to the spectator. I don't see the explanation of this kind of change in that diagram. And that's a very important part of the sociology of sports — to know how the rules change.

LÜSCHEN: Well, you know of the work in this area by Elias and Dunning who could, in a way, explain this situation based upon the problems of integration and equilibrium. In this way they concluded that since there was disequilibrium, the system or the rules had to be adjusted again.

STONE: You can say that basketball has achieved such a monotonous state of equilibrium and integration that something has got to be done to shake it up.

LÜSCHEN: Yes. But you are thinking now in terms of the team. The overall system must, of course, also consist of the spectators and thus there may be quite a bit of disequilibrium insofar as, for instance, the interest of the audience fades completely.

STONE: Or because of the box office.

HARRY WEBB: Why does it? I feel like Charles does, if I don't like it, I get mad as hell. What seems to be involved really is the question of how best to get at the social information, information about social process. So, I want to make two points. First of all, there is some variation on the so-called structural-functional approach, which isn't that bad I suppose, in sociology. With some alterations in it, it is possible to produce some beautiful kinds of information. On the other hand, I think you can demonstrate fairly clearly that the structural-functional approach leads not only to an inability to deal with change, but leads to a real conservative attitude towards everything proper and so the change is not going to get you anywhere. Of course in sport, as sport develops in our kind of society, the change is very much in the operation. You cannot examine sport from that kind of an approach.

The most ambitious example of the application of this kind of approach to real phenomena is Smelser's theory of collective behavior. Smelser takes the baggage and dispenses with a good deal of it conservatively by setting up a hierarchy of those four components; values, norms, the way in which people are rewarded as they operate in interaction, and the facilities which they employ, and he attempts to rank these in order from highest to lowest. He attempts to explain social change, revolutions, this kind of thing, down to and including panics. In other words you reorganize the way a component itself is organized. Once he has started that, he sets up these components and values and norms and down to facilities. In the change of facilities process he says you explain the relationship that exists between these different kinds of components — for example, revolution includes panics. This points to a beautiful model. It's very, very interesting. It says, strain appears at these lowest levels where social action is actually going on and it reorganizes some things; it organizes the aspects of these things at the very top which are abstract. Now an interesting thing occurs here, because you get a direct line between what is abstract and what is concrete. Recall for a minute, this business about the difference between the real and the ideal. The real thing is this thing that we do in real life. We talk about this in terms of the terms that we use. For example, the way in which terms get meaning is that the first cycle that is read and the second cycle that is read refer to some abstract assigned time. Now the nature of this relationship is never identified but it is by participating in that assigned time that they retain similarity of meaning. This problem goes on for a very long time. What is the relationship between the abstract and the ideal? Finally, philosophers throw it our entirely. The sociologists don't know because they don't even know the problem exists. They certainly don't recognize it as a philosophical one. But what you get in Smelser, an otherwise brilliant theorist, is an attempt to show a relationship between what is not real and what is real on a step by step basis. In other words operating across a continuum. That simply cannot occur. The abstract and the real are qualities and there is no connection between them. So at that point Smelser runs into a lot of trouble, but what does he do with the internal organization of his component? He throws it out and does not use it, in the rest of the book which is a brilliant attack on social problems. He has to get rid of the very theoretical framework which he introduces at the beginning to get to the problem. What kind of lesson does that provide? It provides the problem, the kind of thing which Charles mentioned earlier and that is by taking the large view you control things that you otherwise might miss. But until the stone floats out and you get down to the concrete, the nitty-gritty, if you like, you haven't got anything that's worth listening to or looking at. The acceptance of such problems cannot provide that kind of insight, concrete insight, into the way in which people interact. They are absolutely useless.

I'm not sure, and I agree with Page. There is a very little difference between the small group studies that are reported and the format that is identified at the beginning. I mention this and feel strongly about it because there is a drive in sociology today to force the large group — the hedgehog thinkers — that's the way he puts it — out of the world and to introduce the fox. Once you introduce the fox, the small minded myopic kind of thinker, the possibility of ever getting to the big problem is enormously diminished, as you can see. The value again of that approach is that larger concerns remain and the things that you finally develop are worth looking at and maybe employable.

I'm now going to give you an example of how this thing can operate. If you get rid of the baggage and take the structural forms alone and ignore the business about constitution and function, boundary making, this kind of thing, you can examine the way structures in society are organized. You can then take a look at the more dominant ones and watch the way their values and their system of operating filter over into others and this comes back to the basketball example that you just gave. Over a long period of time it finally develops and it's a sufficient labor process because of the increasing sophistication in the measurement of time. You can always correlate the development or the measurement of units to the increasing rationalization of the production process itself. What goes on in sport? Sport develops as an alternative way of providing tensioned release in a system which is closing it off in other areas, the community type kinds of things. The time then comes in in the economy where sport develops only in industrial life of the large scale merging societies. It does not occur anywhere else but in sport. It then comes to be a popular kind of development to the extent that it reflects kinds of structural organization and the values that occur in that dominant situation in the economy. Time is one of those elements. You can then go back and examine those activities most popular. What are they? Those that are most crucially limited by time factors — for example, football in which each play is set up on a time basis. It's interesting to note that the excitement of the game increases at the end of both halves where the competition with time as a major factor is always greater. The same thing happens in a basketball game. Everybody is apathetic as hell but at the last moments, or the last moment, of each half it becomes an interesting game as production of units constantly competes with time. You can see this process, you can also read the paper about the subject. You can see this process in piecework units and shots. The same thing operates there. To the extent these activities themselves are more or less greatly rationalized, they are more or less popular. So you take the two components, rationalization of activity on the one hand and time dimension on the other. Those activities emphasizing most of both are the ones that are most popular, as in football. The extreme rationalization of the fact that a kid starting at any position at fourteen, winds up as a guy who runs back and punts exclusively on a **professional** team. Introduce the time unit as well and you've got the popular activity. In that sense you can demonstrate what kinds of activity for example become popular in terms of structural elements existing in the larger and more dominating institution and the ones in which more people participate as they get older. This is essentially true.

The point, finally, to get this thing out of the way — I'm sorry that I got wound up — but the point finally is that we must avoid destruction of the hedgehog because he's got a good deal to say, where the fox is capable only of analyzing the kinds of things that the hedgehog produces. If you lose one-half, you lose it all. That's why it's important to protect this kind of approach and at the same time it is also important to very much learn of the difficulties.

CYRIL WHITE: The sociologists are talking all about sports, something that the sociologists are not supposed to be doing, whereas the sports men are arguing about sociological theory, something that they know nothing about, and so we have a type of conflict at the moment. We should look to what Doctor Lüschen is saying, something that he's said to me many times. I'll try to do this in my own way. Deal with the social realities that you know, like sport, and use what methods of understanding, and use what tools of understanding, seem to give the best result. I think this is what he's saying. Instead, we have been taking the view that Parsons is the answer to the maiden's prayer as far as sport is concerned, or any other prayer. I am interested in sociological theory, but in my work, which I mentioned this morning, Smelser's theory seemed to be the best for my purposes. I think this is what we must try and do if we want to make progress and not get back at the rather absurd situation where the sociologists argue about "Let's have more sport" and the sportsmen argue "Let's have more sociology."

BRIAN SUTTON-SMITH: I can draw an analogy as to what is happening — perhaps it may be out of order — but there are certain things happening in the field of education, not only in the sociology of sport, like people who are trying to dream up schemes about what is inclusive and what is exclusive, what you can fit it in, and where certain parts of the whole business ought to be replaced; and then we come up with a big taxonomy something like sociology. Oftentimes in an effort to make the things fit we tortuously try and shove things closely together but in so doing we distort. The danger is that we should not be trapped by system, and I think that is what our two sociologists were trying to tell us in essence and we have to be quite careful about that. Let's uilize system but don't let's be trapped by it and I think we have to be careful in our instruction about that.

LÜSCHEN: Well, I would like to mention that, of course, I knew what I would get into here, since I knew my colleagues, and the reason why I applied this system is that it is for the time being the most conclusive system that we have, the most conclusive theoretical system I think there is. I don't think anybody would disagree.

On the point brought up by Mr. Webb, that it does not meet reality and that indeed it can be compared with a kind of Platonic approach, people who strongly oppose Parsons very often would, however, make the remark that it very well fits reality. I may just mention Mr. Homans who says Parsons doesn't know anything about theory, but he is a very good empiricist, and indeed for a number of instances his taxonomic system fits reality. I would claim that. However, I am well aware of certain things I cannot explain and can't get out of, and I think Parsons himself couldn't get out of. Certain boxes have not a very strong explanatory power. The problem is, of course, always a conflict, whether you want to explain certain problems in a particular frame of reference on the one hand, or whether, on the other hand, you would just like to study the plain facts which, of course, would have meaning only if you apply certain models from the very beginning. So there is no way of avoiding certain theoretical systems in any type of research. The distance here between reality and the theoretical system may be quite high, I give you that, and I think it is definitely a problem here.

One more point, the problem of equilibrium, for which Parsons has, of course, been quite strongly criticized and most strongly by my fellow countryman Ralf Dahrendorf, who even earned a prize with an article he wrote for the *American Journal;* the thing is, if you read Parsons as far as I understand him, he will always claim that this is some kind of an assisting model, a model that would help you to organize your data, but that you should, of course, always be aware that it actually is a consistent problem, a consistent stage of disequilibrium. Blau, of course, stating it more strongly, has said "I had better do away with the equilibrium problem and start with the disequilibrium problem," but implicit in that is some kind of equilibrium notion. So I think that Parsons himself would not die for the equilibrium model, but as you may have observed many of his followers would. Thank you.

Gerald S. Kenyon

5. Sport Involvement: A Conceptual Go and Some Consequences Thereof

On the assumption that those interested in the social nature of sport seek to achieve more meaningful descriptions and more powerful explanations, a necessary and obvious prerequisite is a viable conceptual system. If well formulated, it will, in all likelihood, consist of both unique and borrowed terms, and serve as the basis for formulating propositions which in turn, should facilitate inquiry and enhance communication.

As we seek to improve our understanding of sport we have a wide array of concepts and frames of reference from which to choose. The choice will depend upon, among other considerations, whether we are concerned with sport as a social system, as a vehicle for the occurrence of social processes, or as a cultural product. If we are primarily interested in the actions of persons in sport situations a concept which may be of some use is that of *involvement*. Certainly the currency of the concept in the serious literature on games and sport seems to be increasing; probably the most familiar example is its appearance in the work of Roberts and Sutton-Smith (Roberts and Sutton-Smith, 1962; Sutton-Smith, et al., 1963) in conjunction with their conflict-enculturation hypothesis.

Recently, a sub-committee of the International Committee for the Sociology of Sport has been in the process of planning a cross-national study of involvement socialization. After hearing the term being used in differing contexts by those participating in the planning workshops, I came to the conclusion that all may not have been using it in quite the same way. Moreover, having already employed the concept in some of my own work I have developed certain reservations about the manner in which I have been using it. I believe, therefore, that before we go any further, we need to do some conceptual spade work, which should result in either developing a more definitive and useful construct, or rejecting the term altogether. Thus, with this objective in mind, I would like to report the results of what at times was a most perplexing journey through a semantic labyrinth, in which vagueness and ambiguity were the major source of illumination. More specifically I would like to present a conceptual schematic, if you will, of the concept *involvement,* and then explore how such a system might be used; first, to describe and explain human action in sport, and second, to discover the consequences of human action in sport. In each case I will illustrate with what I hope are plausible propositions. However, I would like to stress the point that what I am proposing is not an explanation of sport, but rather a tool that might be useful in the pursuit of explanations.

THE CONCEPT OF INVOLVEMENT

The problem, as I view it, is to find a better way to talk about what people do and what people feel when confronted with sport. Insofar as the term *involvement* might be useful for such purposes, it behooves us to say what we mean when we employ such a concept, particularly in a research context. Casual observations reveal that the word enjoys widespread use in the English language. Its shades of meaning are several, ranging from getting involved *in something* to getting involved *with someone,* both of which are of no small significance. However, if we consult an unabridged dictionary, we may find something useful, although dictionaries probably make greater contributions to supplying us with information on word origin, pronunciation, and syllabification, than on word meaning. In any case, the lexicographer for the new *Random House Dictionary,* as might be expected, provides fifteen definitions (in the verb form), including "to bring into difficulties," and "to swallow up, engulf or overwhelm." Although such definitions are obviously inadequate for our purposes, others show more promise, including "to combine inextricably," "to engage the interest or emotions or commitment of," and "to preoccupy or absorb fully." Reading on, the following synonyms were suggested: "complicated," "knotty," "tangled," and "perplexing." Interestingly, the sole antonym was "simply," a definition which I came to accept most readily.

Dictionary definitions at least partially aside, it seems to me that in general, when we speak of being involved, we are talking about an actor's relationship with one or more manifestations of sport. Thus, involvement becomes *social action related to some manifestation of sport.* However, it consists of more than active participation in sport situations. In addition to its *behavioral* dimensions, there are *cognitive* and *dispositional* dimensions. I would like to elaborate a little, by treating each separately.

Involvement As Overt Behavior

There are two basic *modes* of behavioral involvement. *Primary* involvement refers to actual participation in the game or sport as a player or contestant, while *secondary* involvement refers to all other forms of participation, of which there are several, including participation via the *consumption* of sport and participation via the *production* of sport. One consumes at any point in time in one of two ways — *directly,* through attendance at the performance of others (those who are primarily involved), or *indirectly,* by exposure to one of the several forms of mass media which permits people to be involved secondarily.[1] The *producer,* on the other hand, is responsible for bringing the spectacle up to expectations.

Obviously, people can behave in sport situations in several different ways. While doing so they are playing one or more *sport roles.* Those associated with primary involvement are, of course, the *athlete* or *player.* These, in turn, may be *winners, losers, first-stringers, substitutes, superstars, etc.* Roles reflecting secondary involvement are both consuming and producing. The *spectator* represents the *direct* consuming role, while the *viewer, listener,* and *reader* represent *indirect* consuming roles. Producing roles are of three kinds: leadership roles — *instructor, coach, captain, cheerleader,* or *manager;* arbitration roles — *referee, umpire,* or *scorekeeper;* and entrepreneurial roles — *promoter, manufacturer, wholesaler, retailer,* and *concessionaire.* Figure 1 shows the various modes of involvement together with representative roles.

Cognitive Involvement

The cognitive world of most people includes sport. The amount of sport information made available to persons in most countries makes it almost impossible to avoid learning something about it. It seems to be knowledge

MODE	PRIMARY	SECONDARY				
		CONSUMER			PRODUCER	
		direct	indirect	leader	arbitrator	entrepreneur
contestant		spectator	viewer	instructor	member of --sports governing body	manufacturer
athlete			listener	coach	--rules committee	promoter
			reader	manager	referee	wholesaler
player				team leader	umpire	retailer
					scorekeeper	
					other officials	

(ROLE axis label at left)

FIGURE 1

SOME SOCIAL ROLES ASSOCIATED WITH PRIMARY AND
SECONDARY MODES OF SPORT INVOLVEMENT

[1]The distinction between direct and indirect consumption may be appreciated better when we consider that the spectator is a part of the sport situation and may have some immediate and spontaneous effect upon the event, while this is not the case for other consumers. Indeed, they may consume at an entirely different point in time (relevance of time and place).

of two kinds: on the one hand, people acquire information on the major features and requirements of a sport contest, and the situation in which it occurs; while on the other hand, persons acquire a knowledge of the outcomes of sport contests. At this time, little is known about the level, variability, and source of such knowledge. Suffice it to say that this is a most fertile field for research, particularly in view of the attention paid today to the field of linguistics and the nature and function of mass communication. Despite this state of affairs it seems obvious that the playing of sport roles, whether they be primary or secondary, producer or consumer oriented, depends upon the nature of the role player's cognitive system pertaining to sport in general, and to the sport situation in which he finds himself in particular.

Involvement Dispositions

Whether a person is overtly involved in sport at a given point in time is not a necessary condition for harboring certain feeling states or dispositions toward one or more manifestations of sport. Even without actually engaging in sport actors may become deeply involved in an emotional sense. Just as sport becomes a part of most people's congnitive systems, these same people have likely acquired various values and attitudes, general and specific, relevant to sport as the social object.

Drawing upon Campbell's "residues of experience," or what he calls "acquired behavioral dispositions" (Campbell, 1963), it is possible to characterize dispositions toward sport, like all others, into two dimensions: *acquired means* of behaving and *acquired goals*. Acquired means include acquired behavioral routines, programs or sequences of response, and schedules for behavior. For the most part these are akin to the previously discussed cognitive elements of involvement. Acquired goals, or end concepts, include acquired drives, motives, purposes, needs, need-dispositions, and cathectic orientations (Campbell, 1963, pp. 136-137).

One of the more frequently studied dispositions associated with sport is *attitude*. Again, as is the case with any other social object, the possessing of attitudes toward sport does not imply observable behavior in sport situations. In other words, one could develop favorable dispositions toward involvement in sport but never be *overtly* involved. However, although a disposition toward involvement does not imply behavioral involvement, behavioral involvement in most sport situations is a function of one's disposition to be involved. This is not particularly profound since most conceptions of social action have a motivational or normative element (e.g., Parsons and Shills, 1951; Smelser, 1962). Although I have divided the two for analytic purposes it behooves us to recognize their linkage.

A CONCEPTUAL MODEL: WHAT IS THE PAYOFF?

Having had a go at conceptualizing sport involvement, it remains to be shown what the consequences might be of using such a conceptualization to pursue our goal as stated at the outset — namely, a better understanding of sport and related phenomena. Basically, there are two possibilities from which to choose. It seems to me that we can either seek to improve our understanding of the phenomenon *per se,* or, in a more general sense, seek to improve our understanding of other social phenomena through the study of sport involvement. Stated in another way, the first approach employs involvement as the dependent variable, while the latter approach employs it as the independent variable — the means ends dichotomy.

Whichever approach is chosen we are, for the most part, still at sea — having considered involvement in much of a vacuum. What is needed is a broader frame of reference, within which we can begin to formulate and test propositions. One way (but obviously only one of several) of achieving this, I suggest, is to view involvement from a *temporal perspective.* This will allow us to consider involvement in three stages: *becoming involved, being involved,* and *becoming uninvolved.*[2]

First, let us consider becoming involved, or in more familiar language *involvement socialization.* If we set as our goal the understanding of sport involvement *per se,* at this stage we are asking how people become involved or more specifically, how do people learn to play sport roles. How does one become an athlete? How does one become a member of the International Olympic Committee?

Although role theory is not well developed, we should be able to identify the major situational and personal factors that prepare someone to play a particular role. For example, if we adopt Kemper's reference group approach (1968), wherein he argues that roles are learned and levels of achievement reached through the acting together of three types of reference groups; namely *normative, comparison,* and *audience groups,* then the most effective socialization should occur as a result of considerable exposure to all three. For an athlete, we would expect normative groups, such as his family, and certainly his coaches, to set high standards of performance. There would need to be present a comparison group made up of attractive role models, such as national sport stars and superstars, or even the players of the next higher level of ability. Finally, there would be an audience, known and unknown, who themselves play various secondary involvement roles. Although not particularly profound, in propositional form, we might have the following:

> In part, effective involvement socialization is a function of exposure to, interaction with, and reinforcement from members of normative, comparison, and audience groups who play other sport roles within both primary and secondary modes of involvement.

---

[2]Although the time at which an actor may enter each stage may correspond roughly to stages of his life cycle, it is also possible for the passage through all stages to occur early or late in life or somewhere in between.

Some limited support for such a proposition comes from data acquired from 110 track and field athletes who participated in the final trials for the 1968 U. S. Olympic Team. Based upon a preliminary look at the data, most of the group reported that all during their career, they have subscribed to high ideals, reinforced by a variety of reference groups from the family to girl friends, were provided with plenty of role models whom they could identify by name, and finally depended heavily upon audiences both immediate and remote, including family, peers, and consumers of mass media.

So much for involvement socialization. As more work is carried out in this area, we should be able to formulate many more propositions capable of explaining the process in a more complete way.

I turn now to the second stage of involvement, that is, having become involved, some persons continue to relate to sport through *persistent patterns of action* (Moore, 1963, p. 3). But not all people persist in the same way. Thus we have the proposition that:

Sport involvement is pattern-like, but differential.

Although at the moment there is little empirical support for such a proposition, McPhee (1963) has put forward an "addiction model" wherein he postulates various "paths of consumption" of sport or leisure pursuits. He has labeled such patterns as "explosive," "chronic," "divergent," "normal," "abortive," and "aversive." The McPhee model is based on the assumption that if we examine the involvement behavior of a large group of persons primarily involved in a particular sport or physical activity we could expect to find different patterns of involvement over time, that is, not everyone would participate with the same frequency or at the same intervals. For some persons involvement would be on a rather regular basis and well-integrated into the life style. Other persons may play a few games separated by a period of inactivity or, in other words, be involved on more of a cyclical basis; while still others become involved in an activity only to find the time required for it increasing exponentially or in McPhee's words, ". . . carried away toward consumption ever rising beyond any bounds and without return, for example, drinking to unconsciousness and then hospitalization" (McPhee, 1963, p. 194). Here at Wisconsin, we have recently tried to fit some time series involvement data to stochastic models, which permitted us to test the "patterns of involvement" hypothesis (Kenyon and Schutz, 1968). The results, based upon relatively short term play in two sports, suggest that some order is present in data generated by observing persistent involvement.

Although patterns of persistent *secondary* involvement may exist, I know of no empirical work that has investigated same. However, the findings may be less rich than those from primary involvement, as sport situations facilitating secondary involvement may impose more limitation on the actor by virtue of their more rigid structure. While he can choose when he will play golf or tennis, at least to some extent, he can only attend football games (or sell programs there) when his team plays at home, and can only read *Sports Illustrated* once per week.

It is conceivable that some success may be had in efforts to *describe* persistent primary and secondary involvement, but *explaining* the discovered patterns presents us with a much more formidable task. However, since we are dealing with an aspect of social behavior, and insofar as there are common elements among many manifestations of social behavior, the efforts of social psychologists and sociologists in their quest for understanding more general social phenomena might be helpful. For example, within the context of Festinger's Cognitive Dissonance Theory we might generate propositions such as:

> Actors secondarily involved as partisan spectators are more likely to attribute a loss by their team to factors unrelated to overall team ability than are non-partisans.

Moving to the third stage of involvement, namely *becoming uninvolved,* we find few if any attempts, either theoretical or empirical, to deal with processes of withdrawal and termination. It is conceivable that the description of withdrawal could be accomplished using concepts found suitable for describing involvement persistence. When it comes to explanation, however, I would suspect we might consider theories of social change.

THE OTHER SIDE OF THE COIN

I would like to pause a moment to remind you that in examining involvement from a temporal perspective, thus far my examples were oriented toward involvement phenomena as dependent variables. It also is possible to look at the other side of the coin, raising questions about sport involvement as the independent variable. This leads to a consideration of a variety of consequences of involvement, for individuals, social systems, large and small, and for sport itself.

Taking involvement stage by stage and considering *involvement socialization* first, it seems reasonable to expect an array of consequences as sport roles are learned, particularly for such institutions as the family and the school — witness the role of games in enculturation during childhood as shown by Roberts and Sutton-Smith. *Persistent involvement,* that is the enactment of sport roles over time, likely has implications, though not clear at the moment, for achieving and maintaining status within various social systems, for explaining certain instances of social mobility and perhaps for achieving some measure of identification with family, school, community or nation. The third stage, namely *withdrawal,* can't help but have some impact upon one's life style, and in turn affect other groups and institutions for example, the economy.

To illustrate involvement as an independent variable consider the following proposition:

> Identification is a function of group related persistent secondary sport involvement.

Although for purposes of analysis I have suggested that involvement could be either the dependent variable or the independent variable it would be well to point out the naivete´ of assuming a clear cut distinction here. Clearly, the results of any well formulated research project should have implications for both sport and the situation within which it exists. However, whether it would be fruitful to consider developing a theory of involvement remains a moot point. A decision to inter-relate confirmed propositions concerning involvement in sport would no doubt await the time when more than a few have been established. Of first consideration, however, will be whether or not to simply incorporate these verified propositions into existing social theory explaining social action in general, or whether or not to make some effort to develop a more modest theory explaining sport itself. One might expect the person whose primary interest is in sport would choose the latter route; while he whose first interest is in what is common to social systems in general, might prefer the former approach. In any case the two are mutually compatible.

SUMMARY

On the argument that before one can study anything seriously, he needs to have a way of talking about that which concerns him, it has been my purpose this afternoon to look at a concept frequently used in the study of sport phenomena — namely the concept of *involvement*. Although my intentions were honorable, it should be clear that the task is far from complete. In any case, the degree to which my characterization of involvement will prove useful will depend not only upon further logical analysis of sport phenomena, but upon the utility of such a scheme when used in empirical inquiry.

REFERENCES

Campbell, Donald T. "Social Attitudes and Other Acquired Behavioral Dispositions" in S. Koch (ed.), *Psychology: A Study of a Science*. New York: McGraw-Hill, 1963, Vol. 6, pp. 94-172.

Kemper, T. D. "Reference Groups, Socialization and Achievement." *American Sociological Review*, 33 (February, 1968), pp. 31-45.

Kenyon, Gerald S. and Robert W. Schutz. "Patterns of Involvement in Sport: A Stochastic View." Paper presented at the Second International Congress of Sport Psychology, Washington, D.C., 1968.

McPhee, W. N. *Formal Theories of Mass Behavior*. New York: Free Press, 1963.

Moore, W. E. *Social Change*. Englewood Cliffs, New Jersey: Prentice-Hall, 1963.

Parsons, T. and E. A. Shils (eds.). *Toward a General Theory of Action*. Cambridge, Mass.: Harvard University Press, 1951.

Roberts, John M. and Brian Sutton-Smith. "Child Training and Game Involvement." *Ethnology* I (1962), 185-199.

Smelser, N. J. *Theory of Collective Behavior*. New York: Free Press, 1962.

Sutton-Smith, Brian *et al.* "Game Involvement in Adults." *Journal of Social Psychology*. 60(1963), 15-30.

REACTION TO KENYON PAPER — Walter Schafer

I will begin with my own reaction to the paper and then open the floor for your comments and questions. I would like to congratulate Dr. Kenyon for doing a good job at what he set out to do, namely, to clarify the definition and meanings of the concept *sport involvement*. However, I have some questions about the merit of what he set out to do, and I would like to organize my comments around five different points.

My first point is that clear, well defined concepts are necessary. I think there can be no disagreement about that. What is a concept? A concept, very simply, is a name attached to a category of phenomena. It is a name which is an abstract name, a name which we apply to a category of things, and it contrasts with a name which we attach to a concrete phenomena. The term "boy" applies to a category of concrete entities, in contrast to "Johnny," which is a name for a particular concrete entity. Clearly, concepts are necessary in order to direct our attention to categories of phenomena which we anticipate studying, whether the particular phenomenon is a cause or effect. Also, we need clear definitions of concepts, so that the reader and future investigators will know what the boundaries are around the categories of phenomena which a particular investigator is looking at. If he says he is studying A or B it is necessary to know what A or B consist of, what is included and not included in those categories. The lack of precision of definitions is a real problem in all the social sciences. It's a real problem perhaps more in sociology than in some other sciences, particularly the physical and natural sciences, but it is a real problem, and it's a problem which we should be aware of in developing this new sub-area of the field of sociology.

This brings me to my second major point, however, which I'll state in the form of a question: How are we to achieve, to quote Mr. Kenyon, "a worthwhile conceptual system"? How are we to achieve a consensus as to how concepts should be defined? I would suggest two general strategies for accomplishing this task, which will be a never-ending task, by the way. One is to develop a conceptual system before their use, to develop concepts and definitions of concepts before we actually use them in research. That is what Professor Luschen was attempting yesterday and in part, is what has been attempted here. A second approach, however, is for investigators to create their own definitions and then use their definitions in concepts. In other words, not to develop abstract conceptual systems beforehand, but for investigators to decide on their concepts and meanings and then through time be refined and adopted as they are judged to be useful. In other words this second approach is a process approach. It's a process whereby independent investigators do independent work, create independent concepts and then use them and through time other investigators determine themselves which are useful and which are not useful concepts. How do we decide whether to adopt a definition of a concept? I would suggest we don't do it on an *a priori basis*. We do it in terms of whether a definition is useful or not; that is, whether it designates a boundary around a set of categories which is a useful boundary or not useful. That's how we determine whether to adopt a definition and that is how we arrive at a consensus. We arrive at a consensus as to a conceptual system, a definitional system, as we arrive at a consensus of what is useful and not useful, and I would argue the only way to determine the utility of definitions is to use them. I would agree then that we need clear definitions but the way to arrive at them is by using them rather than developing conceptual systems and definitional systems in the abstract. I think that a purely conceptual type of paper of this kind is useful, however, but I think it is not useful laying out ideal definitions. I think it is useful for pointing attention to categories of phenomena which we need to be studying. It is useful for identifying sport phenomena to study, either as independent or dependent variables. For example, the types of involvement which were outlined on the screen I think do represent categories of participants or people who are involved to which we give much attention. I think the discussion of reference groups was useful for directing attention to the fact that there are three different kinds of reference groups to which we should give attention. So, I think it is useful, but for a different reason than perhaps Professor Kenyon intended, which brings me to my third point.

I would argue that efforts to develop definitional systems in isolation from research take us away from concrete phenomena, away from the level of analysis in which we would be operating into a semantic labyrinth and into the very vagueness and ambiguity which Professor Kenyon was seeking to avoid. Let me cite some examples. Early on in the speech the statement was made, "I consider behavioral involvement to be social action related to some manifestation of sport." Well, must behavioral involvement in sport be social? Cannot an individual be involved on an individual basis? When I ski, I'm involved in action but it's not necessarily social action. And furthermore, what does "social" mean? There are many definitions of that concept. It depends. What does "manifestation of sport" mean? Well, I'm not entirely sure and I'm not sure that it is necessary as part of the definition. My general point, then, is that by developing this definition in isolation from a specific research problem we are led into ambiguities and abstractions which are unnecessary. Or to cite another example, the term "involvement dispositions"; I'm not entirely clear on what this means. Does it mean attitudes? At one point that is suggested; on the other hand, in another sentence "acquired goals, or end concepts, include acquired drives, motives, purposes, needs, need-dispositions and cathectic orientations." In other words, the general concept "involvement dispositions" apparently includes a whole category of concepts and I'm just not sure how useful it is even if we do come to a consensus as to what it means. Why not talk about the specific concept which we are going to use — goals, or attitudes, or needs or whatever, or drives or goals. So again I would suggest that we may be getting into more trouble than we are avoiding by developing a highly abstract concept with an ambiguous definition. Or to cite just one other example, using the proposition: "Sport involvement is pattern-like but differential." In the first place, we defined sport involvement at such a high level of abstraction that one cannot be sure here as to what kind is meant. Furthermore, I would suggest that both the terms "pattern-like" and "differential" are unnecessarily abstract and jargonish; that we could say the same thing just as simply by saying that there are both differences and similarities in how people participate and spectate, and perhaps we would identify more precisely what we are talking about.

On to the fourth point, then, and I would really like here to underscore a point which Professor Kenyon made, "Developing a conceptual system does not direct us to questions by itself." Developing a conceptual system does not lead us to questions. We raise questions because of some concern we have, concern with a practical question, a practical problem or a concern about a gap in knowledge or a theoretical problem, and I would suggest that the attempt to identify and clarify definitions themselves may be dangerous if it diverts us into thinking that we are discovering new knowledge, because we are not. It may be a useful step along the way, and I don't mean to contradict anything Professor Kenyon said. He made this point. I would like to underscore it. But I would like to call attention to another proposition which was stated. Correct me if you did not give it in this exact form: "In part, effective involvement socialization is a function of exposure to, interaction with, and reinforcement from members of normative, comparison, and audience groups." Now I would suggest that this may or may not be a valid proposition. It's a highly general proposition which includes many specific ones within it, but my immediate question is, where does the proposition come from? How do we arrive at a proposition of this kind? Do we just pull it out of the air? The analysis of concepts by itself does not lead us to formulate propositions. We formulate propositions on the basis of some theory from existing research or existing theories at a higher level of extraction.

This brings me to my fifth and final point. As sociologists of sport, we should be drawing on more general sociology in two ways. First of all, we should be drawing concepts which have already been developed in other areas of sociology. We should not begin from scratch in coming together here. There is nothing very new about sport or nothing very unique about sport. Rather we should ask what specific aspects of sport have in common with other social phenomena and draw on more general sociology or subdisciplines in using concepts. We should use those which have already been shown to be useful. I was chatting with Professor Demerath, a sociologist here at Wisconsin, and he made the point that this is a frequent error in his view in the development of new interests. He pointed out that the same thing is happening as sociologists come together with ministers and theologians. They essentially begin all over again and we don't need to do that, I would suggest.

I would suggest that a second way in which we should draw on general sociology is in the formulation of propositions or in the formulation of hypotheses. We should draw on more general propositions as a source of specific hypotheses. For example, there's already been a tremendous amount of work done on leadership, on the consequences of different leadership patterns. We don't need to start from scratch in sport. We should be paying attention to that specific body of knowledge within social psychology for the consequences of various kinds of participation for individuals. Yesterday I suggested that we need not approach the question of athletic participation and deviancy entirely from scratch. There is already a body of knowledge which leads us to the formulation of specific hypotheses in this specific area. Perhaps I can illustrate what I have said under this fifth point by drawing a simple diagram (see Figure 1). If we use the two large circles

FIGURE 1

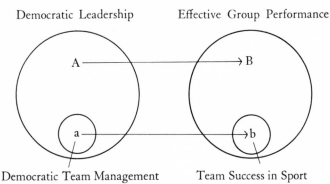

to represent concepts and the arrow to indicate cause at a general level, then we can see perhaps that democratic leadership tends to contribute to effective group performance. If we are concerned about the same question in sport, we should view leadership in sport as a particular type of this general phenomenon. Then, to establish or test casual relationships within this more general context, we may come at it with a primary interest in developing knowledge about sport phenomena themselves or we may come at it out of the interest of developing general knowledge about social phenomena. Well, in whichever case, I think we should begin whenever possible by drawing on or placing sport phenomena within the context of more general categories of phenomena.

So much for my remarks. Although I think the paper has been useful, I think its usefulness is somewhat limited and I think perhaps a more fruitful approach is to use the concept of involvement with respect to particular investigations recognizing that particular types of involvement may be parts of more general categories of phenomena in other spheres of social action.

DISCUSSION

SEYMOUR KLEINMAN: With regard to the last point I can see where we could draw on prior knowledge in order to establish the hypotheses to investigate certain areas, but I suggest to you the possibility that perhaps sport or any particular phenomenon which you are investigating socio-logically, psychologically, or even philosophically, may indeed be a unique phenomenon; and the uniqueness of each particular phenomenon and the way you approach that uniqueness must depend upon the development of a particular kind of scheme or the development of a particular kind of framework with which to attack the individual study. So I can see your point in one sense, but in another sense I think there is a great deal of uniqueness in each particular phenomenon which we are investigating. I wonder, then, whether it is wise to sort of put our eggs in one particular basket, which I don't know whether you are doing or not, but you might be.

WALTER SCHAFER: Yes. I don't think I would disagree with you. I don't know what your comment would be, Gerry. I don't think I would disagree with you, but I would suggest that we should first of all ask whether we can receive guidance from more general sociology in understanding this particular phenomenon and ask, looking at the literature, is this similar to other relationships in other settings from which we can then draw on insights in the formulation of hypotheses. If not, then we should formulate concepts and causal propositions which may be unique. That's my own reaction. Do you want to comment on that, Gerry?

GERALD KENYON: By virtue of our labeling of a phenomenon and using that label differently from labels attached to other phenomena, we imply that there must be some uniqueness, although often we discover later that what we thought was unique wasn't as unique as we might have originally supposed. But, I would like to feel that sport must have at least one unique element — at least sport as a social phenomenon — to justify separating it from other social phenomena. Now I'm not sure whether you are ready to say that there is absolutely no difference between sport as a social phenomenon and any others.

SCHAFER: No, I clearly wouldn't. I clearly wouldn't but I would like examples. I'm sure there are characteristics of this situation which existing concepts in sociology and social psychology are not at all useful, but I'm having difficulty in my own mind thinking of examples.

CHARLES PAGE: I'd like to follow up the question of Mr. Klein-man's and your answer to it, and Gerry's answers, and refer to Jay De-merath, to whom you have referred because shortly after your conversation with him we spent an hour and a half together, using part of that time to discuss this very question that's been raised. Whereas as a student of some sort of sociology I must go along with your fifth point, that certainly one of the very important things to do is to utilize both the concepts and the theories of sociology for the generation of possible hypotheses with respect to any concrete field that we are investigating. At the same time I think in the case of the illustration that you cited, namely, religion and religious behavior, Demerath's chief field of interest, and perhaps in the case of sport, that for a good many of us who are sociologists by trade one of the difficulties in applying our sociology to the substantive and concrete areas is that we know so darn little about the areas themselves. I think one of the dangers for the sociologist is to go into a new field knowing little about it. I know that this is a very important danger in the case of the sociology in religion. There is no question about it. There is publication after publication in this area, and I'm not referring to Demerath's work, where the sociologists absolutely don't know enough about religious behavior, religious belief, indeed about theological doctrine, to make the assertions they often make about the field. Now this may hold for some of us who are sort of marginal sport buffs and sociologists too. We may not know enough, and this goes back to the question of uniqueness, of course. Is there something about the world of sport or sport behavior or something that should be known intrinsically? I don't want to be a kind of phenomenological intuitional sort of guy who says you have to grasp understanding of this by doing this or that, but I think that there is a danger here, that a beautiful didactic exercise of the kind you just went through which I would love to have my introductory students experience, sometime blurs over a bit.

BRIAN SUTTON-SMITH: In psychology, of course, we have a problem, by which I mean that for years we have been looking for the one set of laws of learning or the one learning paradigm. But over the years it cannot be said that we have been particularly successful in finding one system which will apply to all classifications of learning. So now you have anything from one to eight different systems and more recently various contentions that you really have to think of these laws relative to all the other capacities of a particular species that you are dealing with, if it's a cross species contrast, and if it's a human being, you have to think of the particular laws as they interact in the developmental stage, which the child has arrived at. So, in a sense one system is impossible. There are some general parameters but they are not really of much use except as you see the interaction effect of these parameters operating with the attention capacity or symbolic capacity or whatever it is of the organism you are dealing with. So I would feel you have to go both ways.

SCHAFER: Yes, clearly.

SUTTON-SMITH: You start with your general. Sociology is obviously one thing relevant to sport, but only one thing. But insofar as you are doing the sociology of sport, you come in with the frames you have and then you study the specific situations and try to find out how general parameters are modified in this particular case and whether there are new dimensions you have never thought of before that seem to come in that have to be taken into account and what effect that has on the general system. But that is sort of self-evident. I would say, and I'm very impressed again in psychology with the fact that we start off so often with a hypothesis and then we find that what looked like a fairly simple paradigm explaining the relationship between two variables turns out to be complicated by variables unique to the instructions we have given to the character of the experimenter who happened to be there and we didn't even think about him for thinking we had him controlled, and so on. So just in the general way psychology has gone I would certainly expect not only have you got a few unique things in sport, you've got thousands of them. But I liked your final point. It would seem to me I would almost rather sit down and have people who are in sports giving me anecdotes about sports. I really think that is more valuable than all this conceptual stuff that is going on, really.

WALTER GREGG: I might be exposing a considerable amount of ignorance here and I might be casting us into something you don't want to get into, but one of the simple ideas about instruction is that we want to instruct so that the individual will come to participate, be a participator, not just go through our classes and so on but be a participator. And, we might say well one way to do this is to really get him hooked on a sport or one can say that he has developed skill enough so that he actually wants to participate, wants to use it. Another thing we are saying also now is that, "well, that's important, but maybe understanding and getting him to come to see that means certain things to him is more important than the skill." Now is this what we are talking about, investigating these kind of things?

SCHAFER: Well, I would put that specific problem in a more general category of learning theory, I suppose, at a general level. I'm kind of doing this off the top of my head although I think I could go to the literature and support it. You stated two propositions, the greater the active participation in an activity the more positive the motivation toward that activity, right? Or, to state another one, the more active participation in a learning activity the more effective the learning.

GREGG: The more skill one has the more apt he is to participate regularly, that is, take it on.

SCHAFER: Okay, that could be cast, and I mean you have just cast it, in general terms and abstract terms not specific to sport at all. It might relate to all kinds of activities including other than motor activities. Well, I would suggest that that general proposition probably is valid in the psychology of learning literature, and probably has been tested. Perhaps Professor Sutton-Smith can answer that better than I. If that's true then why not begin if you wanted to test that out in the specific context of physical education, why not begin by drawing on that more general literature to formulate the specific hypothesis. On the other hand, perhaps there is something specific about physical activities which may be unique, and which these propositions don't apply to. Perhaps other types of relationship of the individual to the activity facilitate continued participation or rate or amount of learning, and that has to be discovered.

GREGG: What you are saying is if we are going to study these kind of things there are already ways of doing this.

SCHAFER: Yes, I'll say usually that's the case, but not entirely. I would agree with Professor Page that there may well be unique characteristics of sport activity and sport organization. Perhaps we can't completely include all sport phenomena within our concepts and I'm sure that we can't derive all specific relationships between phenomena from existing theories in behavioral science, but I would suggest that a major number of the specific problems that we are all concerned with are really part of a more general set of phenomena which we have already done related research on in other settings. We have already done all kinds of research on political behavior, religious behavior, family behavior, and many other kinds, and I would suggest that there may be commonalities here with those other areas. But I would agree that that is not entirely the case.

SUTTON-SMITH: But you are arguing that so as not to begin with new general abstract conceptual systems. You can also play the other equally treacherous game of doing verbal translation exercises where you take the leadership thing and all you do is talk about the possibilities of leadership in sports and don't actually study it and that is almost equally useless.

SCHAFER: Yes, that's right. I would not argue for that, because that's what I was criticizing too.

SUTTON-SMITH: You want to come back to more specific translations.

GUY REIFF: I have two questions and the second is dependent on the first. When we are talking about sports involvement how are we defining sport? Is this organized participation in a skill which may be related to physical activities, such as running, bicycling, walking, this type of thing?

KENYON: I think the definition of sport is much more difficult to manage than the definition of involvement in sport which is obviously bad enough.

REIFF: When I said that I didn't mean the definition in its most literal sense. I mean as we were using it here in the title.

KENYON: Yes, I understand. In this situation I am drawing upon Loy's characterization of sport where he talks about it as an institutionalized game whose outcome is determined by some form of physical prowess. I know he could express it more eloquently than that, but I think that if you analyze each of those terms, and it takes a while, as he has demonstrated, then I think you can characterize sport in such a way allowing you to include certain forms of activity and exclude others. Now insofar as there is competition associated with it as there is in game forms, and insofar as it's been organized sufficiently to set up some rules, a governing body, regularly scheduled events and the like, then it begins to approach sport. But, insofar as it's a random physical activity, and we can list thousands of those, I'm not sure it is very useful to include it in the realm of sport.

REIFF: That satisfied the first question so, which tells me it's all right to pursue the second one. As I know you are aware, for the last four or five years at Michigan, and at Wisconsin, Minnesota, and Penn State, we've been chasing the Holy Grail of activity as related to coronary heart disease and so forth. We identify high and low risk groups and try to get these people to exercise, in other words take part in some sport which usually consists of jogging, walking, bicycling or any other form of activity they want to do, and after four or five years of fruitless endeavor to try to get them as far as what is referred to as an adherence rate, to get people to stay with it — and when I say people I'm talking about people who are really old people, over 35 — I realize this is a social psychology function and in terms of the conceptualization of what makes people get involved in these things, and I would be interested in some answers as to the proper approach to get people to take part. We have tried everything and none of it works, and I'm talking about a high risk coronary group that has been isolated, and identified as such, and knows it.

KENYON: Well, I think this is certainly an example of where I think we might be able to draw upon concepts from sociology and social psychology to explain behavior, if that's what you are really getting at, or in this case you are talking about the lack of behavior. I don't have the answers except I think I can rule out one that has often been put forward, and that is, it has been argued that for one reason or another people are not active in physical activities because they don't have the right attitude, or they are not sufficiently motivated, or they don't support the idea that sport is a good thing. We have been collecting data on attitudes for three or four years now and have sampled a number of populations, both adolescent and adult, and it seems quite clear that whether or not people engage in physical activities seems not to depend upon the attitude they hold for physical activity because in almost every case people possess rather high positive attitudes toward physical activity and sport no matter how you characterize it. And certainly if you characterize physical activity in some instrumental way, which is the sense of your present concern, that is as contributing to the development of health and physical fitness, it's like motherhood. People just don't knock it, they are in favor of it. They express positive attitudes towards it. So that is not an explanation.

REIFF: A positive attitude does not do it.

KENYON: I don't think so, not in and of itself. But if you get into the rewards that are afforded to the person who engages in physical activity and who does not, then I think you can begin to explain some of it.

SCHAFER: I wonder if I could follow that up first with another comment. It strikes me that there are perhaps at least four different theories of behavior change — and that's really what you are talking about — which might be useful. There has been research on mass persuasion and its relationship to change in behavior. I think, and again this isn't really my area, but I think I've had enough acquaintance with it to suggest that this research has been rather negative, that it's not very effective to tell people or try to persuade people through the mass media or through lectures or other means of this kind. Or another area is theory of normative influence. There is a lot of research in all kinds of contexts suggesting that an effective way of bringing about change is to expose people to group pressures that will lead them ultimately to internalize the merit of doing whatever the activity is.

REIFF: That, by the way, is the one that works the best, the peer status impression. If you get three or four guys to do it, and set up a routine, then he can do it. Lots of times they told me they didn't feel like it, but they'd rather do it in a group. But it doesn't work across the board.

SCHAFER: Well, then, one would want to ask what is it about that variable, not done intensively enough, or over a longer period of time or perhaps there is something unique about this activity. Perhaps the dependent variable, physical exercise, requires such a strong commitment in time and effort that a more potent independent variable is required.

REIFF: Well that's the thing that really concerns me, because we already have a ready made group of consumers and we don't have any problem with them. It is the non-consumers that we have been involved with. Changing that type of behavior is a sticky wicket.

KENYON: A person on our campus that's been very close to this same program, that is, dealing with older faculty, is Professor Stoedefalke. I'm not sure that he would like to react to this but the impression I have is that they have met with considerable success at taking persons who may be what, fifty and fifty-five years of age who really haven't seen much activity if at all in their lifetime, certainly not for twenty years, and you've been at it now for over a year and they're still coming back. Is that true or not?

KARL STOEDEFALKE: That is true, and I yield to John Pooley who leads the activity and he might be interested in speaking to the concept of having a good time or enjoying the activity. Our adherence rates I believe are extremely high and not accurately reflected when our data are pooled with Penn State, and Minnesota.

REIFF: Is this a university community you are talking about?

STOEDEFALKE: Yes. But they are not the problem that the real world is though. I don't have any trouble getting the professors to cooperate. It is the real world that you are trying to get out.

REIFF: Yes. Well, the real world is not the university campus.

STOEDEFALKE: They're a lot easier to get than someone out here running a shoe shop, or an insurance man.

JOHN POOLEY: It's true that we do have a captive audience. One of the observations that may be of benefit here is that many of the members of the faculty who are involved say that this is the first time they have ever been exposed to physical activity or physical education. In other words, what they are saying is that probably because their skill level was not of the highest standard in high school or junior high, they were left to one side and they developed a resentment for activity. The types of activity based upon sheer enjoyment, and fun, have sort of captured their imagination or their interest and many of them, of course, now have got to the stage where they wouldn't for almost any reason at all consider not coming to one of the classes held three times a week, unless they were out of town. So it may well be a question of the type of activity that we present to them and possibly overlaid with the enjoyment factor. This was particularly true at first. At the end of forty-five minutes, they were coming out of the gymnasium or off the field perspiring very heavily, not really having known that they had worked, but they'd had a lot of fun doing it. This is the approach that we have used and I think our retention figures are something to the extent of well over 90 per cent from the time we started over eighteen months ago. So the main problem is to get them in some way motivated to come for two or three sessions and then, of course, depending I suppose on the instructors that you use, then you either keep them or else you shoo them away.

SCHAFER: This brings me to my third theory which is the reward theory, that people repeat those things which they find rewarding, very simply, and maybe what you are saying is that one should know what the meaningful rewards are for a particular group of people. In this case it's fun. Particular kinds of activities seem to result in a greater reward of that kind than others.

POOLEY: It's interesting too, that they are able to see over a period of time an improvement in psysiological parameters too. Naturally, tests are given at fairly regular intervals; we hope not too frequently because this might put them off, but they see an improvement in blood pressure and in heart rate. Their recovery rates come down and many of them relate experiences where clearly their whole outlook upon their work is attributed to the program. So that several men quite spontaneously will come up and say, at the beginning of the program or shortly after it was begun, "We are able to do much more work. We are much more productive than we have ever been before."

STOEDEFALKE: One last point, and that is in the program which has now run for sixteen months not one single session of calisthenics has ever been led and there has never been, to my knowledge, a push-up, a sit-up or a side straddle hop, which I think is unique to a physical activity program. As to the question of what would drive you away from the program, the answer is "Calisthenics."

KLEINMAN: I think this is an interesting discussion but I want to get back to some of the points made in regard to the paper concerning the development of conceptual schemes. I have a tendency to agree that the development of conceptual schemes does not help us; we have to operate from another starting point. However, just one point in defense, and that is, in a sense the development of conceptual schemes doesn't come out of a vacuum. I don't think Professor Kenyon developed his conceptual scheme in a vacuum; it came from somewhere. He saw things going on. He saw other events going on in the world from which he decided to develop a particular kind of scheme of things and raise some questions as a result of the conceptual schemes or the framework that he came up with. In your response, however, you said perhaps a better way to begin would be to begin with the development of a definition and go from there, instead of developing a scheme. But I would suggest that even that perhaps isn't the way to get at the thing in a sense. I'm not as reticent as Professor Page to talk phenomenologically — I would not want to apologize for that! I would say, perhaps a good way to get about things and goings on in the world is to go on out there and look and see and get descriptions and ask people. So, I think your example was a good one. Yes, go on out and ask them what's going on, just like this guy on the bus tells you. This gives you a great deal more insight in the development of conceptual schemes or in the development of simple definitions.

SCHAFER: Well, I'm sorry. I think I was misunderstood because what I was saying is what you are saying, that the need is to begin with specific problems, as specific as possible, specific research problems, and to develop definitions in relation to those specific problems. I mean maybe even the problem of exercise programs and, if it's possible, draw on more general concepts and to define them, but if not, begin by developing even lower level and more concrete definitions. My point was that we should develop definitions in relation to specific problems which we are studying rather than in the abstract, which at some later point in time someone else will use.

SUTTON-SMITH: Can we come back to your third point because we have a nice illustration here. One of the problems, it seems to me, in jogging and exercising with people who need this, is that you usually start off with calisthenics. But, in John's program, I just asked him, he gets a reward in there real fast. The reward is usually to do this damn thing and afterwards you feel great. Then it's too late. What's putting you off is the pain in the beginning. John apparently plays a minor ball game. I think he ought to tell us a little more because this is an attempt to get the reward in there quickly, and it's one of the ways of changing.

POOLEY: I started off naturally by going in with certain ideas of low structured ball games and activities using paddle bats, frisbees, occasionally medicine balls, but usually in game type situations of two a side, three a side, and perhaps up to six a side. I should say that these groups are mainly in the region of eight or nine or fifteen or sixteen. I find that I go in and try to react spontaneously to the situation and utilize an area; for example, we might find that there are two sets of goalposts, football goalposts, standing in the particular part of the field. Well, let's try to use these in some way or another. So I simply started them running in and out of these goalposts, obviously trying to keep away from the posts and keep away from each other by passing a ball and keeping them going the whole time, keeping them going. Then I introduced another one, and as a result with about five or ten minutes of activity that, for anybody, it can be a lot of fun and, of course, it's eminently simple. I would go from an activity like that where another type of skill might be involved using a paddle bat or a tennis ball or mush ball and then after I was able to observe the group from the outside, for perhaps ten minutes, then I would change the activity again and introduce another type of apparatus and it might be a more formally structured game like German handball, which we have found to be extremely interesting to them. We simply modify the rules according to the ability of the people concerned. The only rule we have is that you don't run with the ball. It's only passing, and in order to get everyone involved with five or six a side, for example, everyone must touch the ball before you can score. Then you obviously get people involved.

PAGE: From what Mr. Pooley has said I suspect as an outsider that this program at the university of Wisconsin has a not-so-secret weapon involved and that is excellent leadership, which I should think in this type of program would be very important.

REIFF: Leadership is really the key to the whole problem. And the other problem, I was talking about the real world and a university or a bunch of professors are not what you deal with when you get out, as you all know, in the community.

PAGE: I'm interested in your comments about professoria. I suppose one of the most obvious things about us is that many of us have more knowledge of the relationship between exercise and health to begin with than people who haven't read a book or two or listened to colleagues such as yourself on these matters. That's one thing, and I think another thing is that, and this gets back to a point that was talked about yesterday, that the range of activities with which fun can be associated is much greater for the educated, the formally educated, than for the less educated. That is, we can get fun out of more things. So your people can run around the goalposts doing this silly business of passing a ball or whatever. They are doing it and actually get fun out of it with a greater expectation, whereas your guy down there in the shoe store or selling shirts, wherever it is, doesn't have the psychological expectation. He is much more apt to associate fun with about three or four types of activity only; sex, booze, maybe some game that he once played when he was younger, or looking at the television screen, thus, a fairly small range.

REIFF: It's hard to replace those with activities.

PAGE: It's easier for us to find fun. It's even fun being a sociologist for a few people.

SCHAFER: One of the points you made was that when people were involved in formulating the activity and the rules they were more positively motivated to it, which is in common with Professor Gregg's point earlier.

KLEINMAN: Could you give us your fourth theory?

SCHAFER: Oh, I'm sorry.

PAGE: You had two, I think.

SCHAFER: No, I think I've given three, mass persuasion, exposure to social norms, and reinforcement theory. I'll give five. The fourth one is involvement in decision-making, and a fifth is group discussion, and really this is very close to the social pressure theory. There is a wide body of literature in social psychology suggesting that one effective means for bringing about change or especially commitment to a new behavior or belief, is by involving people, potential converts, in group discussion about the activity. Well, whether or not it would be relevant or a useful predictor in this particular case, I'm not sure, but those are five possibilities.

KENYON: As the clock approaches the closing hour, there is always a great effort to get in the last word. I'll try to be brief. I feel somewhat caught in a sense because I'm usually ready to identify with the empiricist camp and consequently I don't really want to get bogged down in matters of definition or conceptualization. However, in reference, Mr. Schafer, to your second point, which I'm not certain you really wanted to say in that way, you suggested that we can't really talk about anything *a priori;* in other words, we can't formulate a concept, we have first to investigate. I guess I would have to argue however, that we must somehow, even if only intuitively, have some idea of what it is we are looking at in the first place. For example, we were talking about how we might get a better insight into sport phenomena and one suggestion, which happened to be raised by two or three persons, was that we might simply watch these little things that occur in sport situations and perhaps have people relate their various experiences to us. I think this would provide us with a rich source of material. Yet, coming back to involvement I think the difficulty with this approach is that first of all, there are certain aspects of involvement that are quite obvious — that we are all well aware of, particularly in the overt sense. There is no great need any more to wonder about these things. The problem remains however, of how we can talk about them in unambiguous ways both in describing various aspects of involvement *per se,* and in relating involvement with other sociological phenomena. Thus, I think we are forced now to take these obvious phenomena and do something with them, so that we can talk about them in a way that is mutually understandable. So I think that while there is much to be learned about the intricacies of relationships among players, spectators and the like by looking at the anecdotes that they can provide us, I think that we can get started on conceptualizing some aspects of involvement almost immediately because it is just simply so obvious. Certainly the process of scientific inquiry is such that you are really not doing science, or you haven't completed the job until you've been able to express what you have been observing in terms that will find a degree of consensus, at least among those persons who have been studying the phenomena in question.

SCHAFER: Okay, let me make just one quick comment. My point is that I agree that definitions have to be formulated beforehand. That's necessary in order to know what it is you are studying and what it is you want to measure. But my point is that it is most useful to develop definitions of concepts in relation to specific problems, specific studies, so that when one goes about studying a particular kind of involvement then we will formulate a definition about that particular kind of involvement, rather than attempting to develop a definitional system in isolation from particular studies. That was my point.

GREGG: You may have answered what I was going to ask. Gerry, are you using the term "concept" as the same as the term "proposition" or "hypothesis"?

KENYON: No, I'm not. A proposition is a formulation made up of a combination of two or more concepts, while a concept is a single generalization of particulars. As an aside I think it is interesting that in the world of curriculum development we now have the "conceptual approach." Here, however, what they are talking about are really propositions. I think this introduces some confusion in the system, unfortunately, but if we subscribe to what most philosophers of science and of social science say about concepts, we are talking about something more specific. In fact, a concept is not interesting until it gets into a proposition.

John W. Loy, Jr.

6. The Study of Sport and Social Mobility

Much has been said about the American Creed, the American dream, and the United States as a land of opportunity with an "open" class system. As Leonard Reissman has observed:

> The belief in social mobility holds a strategic place among American values. It is a hub around which much of what Americans believe revolves, whether it is shouted as a platitude or cynically rejected. The creed of egalitarianism means not only that we are social equals, though not economic equals, but even more to the point, that the class structure is open and available. The positions at the top are open to those who have the talents, aptitudes, and whatever else it takes to reach them. At the same time, of course, we must be prepared to accept the corollary: Those who do not reach the top do not deserve to. Americans of all classes have held to this belief and have made it legend. The honor roll is filled with the names of heroes who give substance to the legend, and in every period there is always a fresh example of someone who has gone from rags to riches. The legend continues to remain alive and real, to the cynics as to the patriots (1959, pp. 293-294).

The rags to riches myth occupies an especially prominent place in the world of sport, for every major sport has its heroes who were recruited from humble social origins and rose to unimagined heights of social success. Thus, we have the rags to riches stories of such sport figures as Willie Mays (Smith, 1954), Mickey Mantle (1967), Bill Russell (1966), Bob Cousey (1961), Johnny Unitas (1965) and Althea Gibson (1958). These stories and others like them have played a major role in sustaining the American dream. But are these individual illustrations of social mobility in sport the exception rather than the rule? In short, to what extent does sport involvement facilitate upward social mobility? This rather simply stated question is an exceedingly difficult one to answer, as a number of problems both theoretical and methodological are associated with it.

101

PROBLEMS

Dimensions of Mobility

A major reason for the difficulty in determining the degree to which sport participation enhances social success lies in the fact that social mobility is a most complex, multi-dimensional phenomenon. Conceptually, one can account for the sources of variation in social mobility in terms of seven basic dimensions (See Tumin, 1967, p. 88).

First, there is the dimension of *direction*. As Sorokin long ago (1927) pointed out, "There are two principal types of social mobility, *horizontal* and *vertical*" (1958, p. 133). Horizontal mobility is the transition of an individual from one social position to another across one or more social strata, either upward or downward. Although both dimensions of mobility are important, this paper will address itself largely to the matter of vertical social mobility.

A second dimension of social mobility is that of *distance*. Past research has tended to emphasize total mobility, and only recently has there been a deliberate stress on measuring the degree or distance of mobility (Svalastoga, 1965, p. 123). We have some information concerning the total volume of sons of blue-collar workers who become white-collar employees, but we have little knowledge regarding how far they ascend within the white-collar ranks or what percentage rise even higher.

A third dimension of social mobility is that of *time*. Attention can be centered on *intra*generational mobility, or it can be focused on *inter*generational mobility. In either case, one may ascertain the amount of time it takes an individual to move from one social position to another. Furthermore, one can measure the degree of mobility per unit of time.

A fourth dimension of social mobility concerns the specific kind of *status change*. For instance, one can be primarily concerned with occupational mobility, educational mobility, prestige mobility or some combination thereof. For both theoretical and empirical reasons, most investigations of mobility patterns have emphasized occupational changes, but other status changes might be equally relevant in the sport situation.

A fifth dimension of social mobility is the *unit* of analysis. Does one, for example, study the mobility patterns of individuals, families, peer groups, age cohorts or even larger social groupings?

A sixth dimension of social mobility "concerns the distinction between *objective* and *subjective* changes in status" (Tumin, 1967, p. 88). A change in salary as measured by annual income is an example of the former; while an internally perceived change in psychic gratification as a result of increased salary exemplifies the latter. Objective changes in status have typically received most research attention due to their relative ease of measurement.

Finally, a seventh dimension of social mobility has to do with the social *mechanisms* underlying it. We, of course, are concerned here with sport involvement as a major mechanism of mobility. It is obvious, however, that successful participation in athletics might facilitate upward mobility in a variety of ways. Therefore, analyses of the mobility patterns of sportsmen should attempt to isolate the predominant means of facilitation for given groups of individuals; and if several ways are considered in combination, then some attempt should be made to assess the direct and indirect influences of each.

Measurement of Mobility

The preceding discussion of the several dimensions of social mobility reveals the conceptual complexity of the phenomenon. Moreover, it indicates that its measurement is also a very complex matter. Tumin (1967) observes that in order to simplify the problems of mobility measurement at least eight choices must be made:

(1) *Which aspects* of mobility shall be measured, e.g., economic, educational, or occupational prestige? (2) *Whose experiences* shall be analyzed, e.g., individuals', families', and strata's? (3) *Who* shall be *compared*, e.g., fathers with sons, groups of sons with each other, or groups of persons at one time vs. the same persons at another time? (4) What *starting points* shall be taken, e.g., first job, "best job," job at age 30? (5) What *termination points* shall be taken, e.g., best job, last job, job at a certain age? (6) What *classifications of jobs* or of other factors, and how many divisions should be employed, e.g., census classifications of occupations; three, four or five divisions of income; blue collar vs. white collar; three, four or five educational levels? (7) If several aspects of mobility are to be measured, e.g., education, income, occupational prestige, etc., shall these be put together into a *combined index* of mobility, and if so, how? (8) Shall the analyses include *objective* and *subjective* dimensions of mobility? If both, how shall mobility be reckoned, i.e., how can different rates of objective and subjective mobility be accurately combined? (p. 89).

Ideally, the choices associated with measurement problems should be made on the basis of some theoretical rationale; but this is easier said than done. Blau and Duncan (1967) have noted, for example, that "the design of mobility research is not suited for the study of the problems posed by stratification theory, for it centers attention not on the institutional differences between societies but on the differential conditions that affect occupational achievements and mobility within any one" (pp. 3-4). In general, measurement choices in past research have been largely made on pragmatic grounds associated with the factors of time, money, assistance and availability of subjects. Hopefully more attention will be given to theoretical issues in future research.

PATTERNS

A Model Study

As a model, the interested investigator of social mobility would not go wrong in referring to the recent work of Blau and Duncan, titled *The American Occupational Structure* (1967). Their inquiry is based on a representative sample drawn in 1962 of over 20,000 American men between the ages of 20 and 64 (p. 1). In addition to its sample, the study is notable for its use of quantitative multivariate techniques. As noted by Blalock, "the Blau-Duncan study provides the first really major empirical application of path analysis to sociological data" (1968, p. 297). Blau and Duncan clearly spell out the major conditions underlying occupational success, show the relationships between family and occupational life, outline the historical changes in the occupational structure, and comment on the causes of social mobility in contemporary society. Perhaps most importantly for the investigator of athletic mobility, they provide normative mobility standards with which results of smaller scale studies of selected groups can be compared.

Some Studies of Mobility Related to Sport

Although no definitive study of social mobility in the sport context has been conducted, numerous social scientists have commented on the role of sport as a mechanism of mobility for lower class youth. Hodges (1964) states in his text on social stratification that "college football has functioned as a highly effective status elevator for thousands of boys from blue-collar ethnic backgrounds" (p. 167). Surprisingly, Hodges provides not one shred of evidence to support his rather striking statement.

In a similar manner, other social scientists have made rather broad generalizations on the basis of only a modicum of empirical data. For instance, Havighurst and Neugarten, on the basis of a case study, assert that "Athletic prowess combined with education often provides a very good base for mobility in a lower class boy" (1957, p. 45). And Riesman and Denney, on the basis of their cursory examination of early All-American football listings, write:

> There is an element of class identification running through American football since its earliest days, and the ethnic origins of players contain ample invitations to the making of theory about the class dimensions of football. Most observers would be inclined to agree that the arrival of names like Kelley and Kipke on the annual All-American list was taken by the Flanagans and the Webers as the achievement of a lower-class aspiration to be among the best at an upper-class sport (1951, p. 310).

An exception to these expository accounts is Weinberg's and Arond's study of professional boxers (1952). Drawing upon empirical data, they show that nearly all boxers are recruited from low socio-economic backgrounds. They also show that although a number of successful boxers experience a rather quick economic ascent at a young age, their punitive sports career typically results in an equally swift economic descent.

Other sociological studies of professional athletes, while not directly concerned with mobility patterns *per se,* do, nevertheless, provide some data from which inferences can be made. Information regarding the income and educational levels of major league baseball players, for example, is contained in the works of Gregory (1956), Andreano (1965a, 1965b), and Charnofsky (1967). Moreover, a comparison of the three studies is indicative of changes in the social characteristics of professional ballplayers. As an example, Charnofsky's data when compared with that of Andreano may indicate ". . . an important trend toward increasing college education for major league baseball players" (p. 8). On the basis of data collected from 75 major league players in the summer of 1965, Charnofsky found that ". . . only 3% of the sample failed to graduate from high school, and whereas only 17% managed to earn a college degree, 58% had attended college . . ." for one semester or more (p. 8).

Findings from the few studies of professional athletes, while giving some indication of the social status of certain sportsmen and a hint of their social origins, do not provide a firm basis for generalization concerning mobility patterns; nor do they show the linkage between sport, education and the broader occupational structure of society. Regretfully, research studies regarding the relationships between participation in collegiate athletics, college graduation, and consequent upward mobility are also few in number. On the one hand, a couple of large scale surveys have been made which illustrate the occupational success patterns of former college athletes in several sports, but they fail to report where the athletes began their social ascent. On the other hand, largely in the form of master theses in physical education, there have been a few studies which indicate the social origin of athletes in several sports, but they fail to show what social heights the athletes have risen to in later life. An early example of the former type of study is the survey made by the National Biographical Society in 1927 and presented in the volume titled *Who's Who in American Sport* in 1928. Questionnaires were mailed to more than 32,000 contemporary or former sportsmen in America, and over 12,000 responded in whole or in part. Data concerning present occupation, educational achievement, and past athletic records are reported for 4,000 of the individuals who returned their questionnaires. In order to gain some small historical insight into the occupational trends of selected sportsmen, the speaker has coded the data for these 4,000 individuals and placed it on edge-notched punch cards to be hand-sorted and analyzed in the near future. Admittedly, the analysis is not likely to produce important findings, since the social origins of the sportsmen are not given in their biographical sketches.

A more modern survey of some scope is that made by the Assistant Athletic Director at the University of Pittsburgh in 1961. He located 1,678 former Pitt lettermen whose performances date from 1900 to 1960. A questionnaire was mailed to each of these former athletes and 1,391 or 83% returned them. The former Chancellor of the University of Pittsburgh, Dr. Edward H. Litchfield, presented some of the findings of the survey in an article written for *Sports Illustrated* with Myron Cope in 1962. They cite several exemplary cases of personal success and report that 37% of the sample had earned advanced degrees. They also record what percent of athletes in each of seven sports (tennis, baseball, golf, track, swimming, football, and basketball) have succeeded in each of eight professions (medicine, law, engineering, education, management, entrepreneurs, sales, and dentistry). A predominant number of golfers were found to have gone into sales work, swimmers stressed engineering, baseball players were prominent in education, and there was ". . . a clear affinity between football and dentistry. Only 8% of former lettermen [had] gone into coaching, of whom three-quarters [were] also teachers" (p. 67). Again, no data were given as to what was the original socio-economic background of the athletes in the various sports.

An example of an investigation explicitly designed to determine the socio-economic background of college athletes is that of McIntyre (1959). He set forth two hypotheses: "(1) Differences in socio-economic levels are characteristic of persons engaging in various types of sports, and (2) individuals who participate in contact or combative type sports, such as football and wrestling, are more likely to have been brought up in a lower social setting than those athletes who participate in non-combative sports" (p. 66). McIntyre tested his hypotheses by determining the socio-economic background of varsity athletes participating in football, basketball, gymnastics and wrestling at Pennsylvania State University in the 1958-59 academic year. In brief, he found that ". . . football players are characterized by a constellation of socio-economic factors which are not typical of other athletes"; and "wrestlers seem to fall into a socio-economic background pattern very similar to that of basketball players and gymnasts" (p. 68). A specific finding underlying his general conclusions is the fact that 69% of the fathers of football players had not completed high school as compared to 35% of the fathers of basketball players and 31% of the fathers of gymnasts and wrestlers (p. 26). Where the athletes of McIntyre's sample are now located in the social structure is, of course, an open question; suggesting that longitudinal studies of athletic mobility are needed.

At this point in the paper I wish to note that all of the guest speakers at this symposium have examined in some manner the relations between sport and social stratification; and three of the speakers have systematically studied aspects of social mobility of sportsmen. Professor Webb (1968a, 1968b), at the National Convention of the American Association for Health, Physical Education, and Recreation held in St. Louis last March, reported his research regarding the social backgrounds and success patterns of college athletes. Professor Schafer and his colleagues have recently presented findings concerning relationships between athletic participation and academic achievement in the *American Journal of Sociology* (Rehberg & Schafer, 1968) and *Transaction* (Schafer & Armer, 1968). In brief, the combined findings of their investigations show a positive relationship between participation in interscholastic athletics and high school grades, completion of high school and college plans (Schafer, 1968, p. 7). A particularly striking discovery of their researches is the fact that ". . . A greater percentage of athletes than non-athletes expect to complete four years of college among working-class rather than middle-class boys; among boys with less, rather than more, parental encouragement; and among boys in the lower rather than the upper half of their graduating class" (Schafer & Armer, 1968, p. 61). They conclude:

> It would seem, then, that interscholastic athletics serves a democratizing or equalizing function. It represents a vehicle for upward mobility, especially of those otherwise not likely to complete college. And the data suggest that, at least as far as participants are concerned, athletics fosters rather than interferes with the educational goal of sending a maximum number of youth to college (Schafer & Armer, 1968, p. 61).

One of the most substantial studies reported in the literature regarding social mobility among sportsmen is that of Professor Lüschen (1963). In an investigation of a sample of 1,880 youth in German sports clubs he found that 14% were upwardly mobile and 7% were downwardly mobile. Moreover, he discovered a number of characteristics which differentiated the two groups of sportsmen. Lüschen found, for example, that approximately half of the upwardly mobile sportsmen occupied leadership positions in the clubs, while not a single important office was held by downwardly mobile sportsmen. Another interesting finding of his study is that sport seems to be an important means of instilling middle class values in upwardly mobile lower class youth. A third point of interest is that the lowest status sports in Germany appear to be cycling and boxing followed by soccer, wrestling, and field handball. Finally, it is noted that Lüschen found that downwardly mobile sportsmen showed a preference for boxing and hockey while upwardly mobile athletes preferred sports like track and rowing. These latter findings have certain parallels with findings reported by Meyer (1951) in America.

Meyer attempted to identify certain characteristics related to success in the human relations aspect of work-group leadership. He administered a battery of tests to approximately 200 first line supervisors in a large utility company. Meyer established a criterion of leadership ability and classified supervisors rated in the upper and lower 27 per cents on the criterion measure as good and poor supervisors, respectively. Regarding the differences between the two groups, Meyer reports that:

> The most conspicuous of all the differences found was probably the fact that many more of the good supervisors had participated in sports than had the poor supervisors. In twenty-one of the twenty-five activities listed, more of the good supervisors indicated that they then did or that they had at one time participated in the activities than did the poor supervisors. For most of the popular sports, such as tennis, golf, football, softball, swimming, track, and bowling, the differences were significant at at least the five per cent level of confidence.
> . . . [However] more of the poor supervisors had participated in boxing and wrestling than had the good supervisors (p. 22).

The preference shown for combative sports by poor supervisors raises an interesting problem for the psychologist as well as the sociologist. Two other findings of Meyer which might be of interest to the student of personality are: (1) ". . . poor supervisors indicated that they were more fond of their mother than of their father . . ." (p. 26), and (2) although the poor supervisors of manual workers participated more often in card playing, pool and billiards than did the good supervisors, a greater proportion of the poor supervisors indicated that they never made wagers on their games (p. 26). In conclusion, Meyer states that ". . . the poor supervisors were evidently somewhat defensive about admitting the possession of any reprehensible characteristics" (p. 26). His several findings bring to mind the research of Coopersmith (1967, 1968) and Rosenberg (1965) on self-esteem. It may be recalled, for instance, that Rosenberg discovered that ". . . adolescents who report close relationships with fathers are considerably more likely to have high self-esteem and stable self-images than those who describe these relationships as more distant" (p. 44).

Mobility Mechanisms of Sport

In summary, the several studies cited are suggestive of at least four ways in which involvement in sport as an active participant might facilitate upward mobility. First, early athletic participation may lead to the high development of selected physical skills and abilities which permit entry directly into professional sports. For example, adolescents may become boxers, jockeys or even professional baseball players with a minimal amount of formal education.

Second, athletic participation may directly or indirectly enhance educational attainment. Participation in interscholastic athletics may foster better grades, increase the possibility of graduation, and/or lead to an athletic scholarship from a given college or university. Collegiate sport competition, in turn, may influence the attainment of academic degrees and/or the acquisition of marketable sport skills.

Third, as spelled out by Schafer (1968, p. 3), athletic participation may lead to various forms of "occupational sponsorship." Thus, a successful street fighter may acquire a promoter and be groomed for the Golden Gloves Tournament which in turn may lead to a professional boxing career. Or a wealthy alumnus may sponsor a college sport star through such means as summer jobs and upon graduation give the athlete a position in his corporation. Or the successful athlete may marry into wealth by using his popularity to establish courtship relations with well-to-do coeds (see, e.g., Annarino, 1953).

Fourth, athletic participation may possibly facilitate upward mobility by the fact that sport competition may lead to the development of attitudes and behavior patterns valued in the larger occupational world. For example, Meyer's study suggests that sports experience may conceivably foster leadership ability via the acquisition of human relations skills.

Negative Arguments

A word of caution is perhaps in order at this point. Since the major emphasis of this paper is on sport as a means of upward mobility, we may do well to suggest that in certain cases sport may act as a negative mobility mechanism. Coleman, in his book *The Adolescent Society* (1961), makes the case that athletic participation is detrimental to educational attainment, in that, it discourages stress on scholarship, and encourages a diversion of school resources, parental support and student energies away from the mission of academic excellence. Even if one accepts the criticism of Coleman's conclusions by Schafer and his colleagues (Schafer, 1968; Schafer & Armer, 1968; Rehberg & Schafer, 1968) and their counter findings, there is still the question of whether athletic participation is additive in nature. In short, is there a linear relationship between athletic participation and degree of social mobility? An interesting problem for investigation would be to study the mobility patterns among a cohort of outstanding high school athletes who complete a college education but who differ among themselves in the fact that some discontinue athletic participation while others remain involved. A first look at the problem has been made by Sage (1967). He examined the differences between eighty-five undergraduate male college students who had been outstanding high school athletes but forty-three of whom elected not to participate in college athletics. Sage found that the nonathletic subgroup achieved better college grades, were less likely to be fraternity members, and were occupationally oriented rather than socially oriented to their college environment.

Finally, on the negative side of the ledger we mention the most interesting investigation made by Pooley (1968) which examined the question of whether involvement in soccer clubs by immigrants and certain minority group members facilitates or inhibits their assimilation of the core values of American culture. His general conclusion was that sport involvement acts as an inhibiting agent. If the assumption is granted that conformity to the core values of a culture is important for social achievement, then it may be inferred that immigrants and minority group members who retain allegiance to certain ethnic subcultures via sport involvement may limit their chances for upward mobility.

PROSPECTS

Even assuming that over-all sport acts as a positive mechanism of mobility, there is still the largely unexplored area of social stratification and mobility within sport. First, information is needed about the status hierarchy of sports in America at both the amateur and professional levels. A worthy thesis problem would be to establish a NORC scale or to develop a Duncan status index for sport. Second, knowledge is needed concerning the differential effects of participation in various sports on upward mobility. Do participants in the higher prestige sports, for example, experience greater mobility than participants in the lower prestige sports? Third, information is needed regarding social mobility within a given sport. Are professional quarterbacks, for instance, more likely to become coaches or general managers than tackles? Fourth, knowledge is needed about the extent to which individuals' social and ethnic backgrounds inhibit or facilitate entry into and mobility within given sports. Brief mention will be made of a few studies which touch on these problems.

On the basis of his analysis of Negro athletes in professional baseball, Blalock (1962) has set forth thirteen theoretical propositions concerning occupational discrimination. It is suggested that the application of his propositions to different professional sports might in large part account for the differential rates of discrimination found in various sports.

A highly interesting investigation of differential sport participation as a function of social background is Eggleston's (1965) study of Oxbridge Blues. For the benefit of the "Yankees" in the audience, the term "Oxbridge" denotes the joint consideration of Oxford and Cambridge, while the term "Blue" corresponds in the main to our concept of a varsity letter. Eggleston investigated the relationship between secondary school origin and the awarding of Blues in soccer, rugby and cricket at Oxford and Cambridge over a ten-year period (1953/4 to 1962/3). Analysis of the awards granted showed that ". . . the ex-pupils of the maintained grammar schools are at a disadvantage to ex-pupils from the public schools in cricket and rugby, both absolutely and relative to their total representation in the university population" (p. 241). In translation, boys entering Oxford and Cambridge from private secondary schools were more likely to earn varsity letters in cricket and rugby than were boys admitted from public secondary schools.

As concerns mobility within a sport, reference is made to the work of Grusky (1963). He argues that the type of position an individual occupies within an organization greatly influences his acquisition of varying role skills; and further argues that the possession of key role skills is highly related to an individual's chances for assuming a leadership position in an organization. Specifically, Grusky hypotheses that high interactors are more likely to obtain leadership positions than are low interactors. High interactors are characterized by their occupancy of centrally located positions, performance of dependent tasks, and high rates of interaction with their workmates. Grusky obtained confirmative support for his proposition by finding in the context of professional baseball that high interactors (i.e., infielders and catchers) are more likely to become field managers than are low interactors (i.e., outfielders and pitchers). Loy and Sage (1968) in an extension of Grusky's work found that interscholastic baseball captains are more likely to be from the ranks of high interactors rather than low interactors.

Grusky's work and its extension by Loy and Sage illustrates the usefulness of theory in empirical investigations of changing social statuses among sportsmen. Moreover, although general theories of social stratification have been held to be too abstract for dealing with social stratification and mobility problems at the micro-level, it may, nevertheless, be possible to make certain worthwhile transformations and applications of general theories to specific situations.

The speaker, in conjunction with a colleague, is presently trying to apply Lenski's theory of social stratification (1966) to professional football. Lenski contends that *prestige* is largely a function of *power* and *privilege*. He defines *privilege* as "the possession or control of a portion of the surplus possessed by a social organization" (p. 45); and defines *power* as "the probability of persons or groups carrying out their will even when opposed by others" (p. 44). Two types of institutionalized power are recognized by Lenski: (1) *Authority,* which he defines as "the enforceable right to command others"; and, (2) *Influence,* which he defines "as the ability to manipulate the social situation of others, or their perception of it, by the exercise of one's resources or rights, thereby increasing the pressure on others to act in accordance with one's own wishes" (p. 57).

It should not be too difficult to get actual or vicarious football participants to rank, say, the various offensive positions of a team in terms of perceived social prestige. The variance associated with given prestige ranks could then be accounted for in terms of power and privilege. Privilege could be considered in terms of the portion of the economic surplus of the organization possessed by an individual; and thus operationally measured by average annual salary according to team position. The concept of power, however, poses more difficult measurement problems. With respect to authority it is obvious that the quarterback has the greatest legitimate right to command others, but the rank order of other team positions as concerns authority is open for debate. And the amount of influence associated with a given team position is even more difficult to objectively assess.

Since power within a social system is largely associated with the set of structures and processes related to goal-attainment and decision-making, perhaps influence could be examined in terms of the probability of a given player influencing the call of a quarterback. Thus, the suggestion of a halfback is likely to carry more weight than that of a tackle. Alternatively, one might determine the average number of opposing players an offensive player is likely to influence in the course of a typical play or the duration of a game. Thus, a center usually keys on only one or two defensive men, whereas a guard may come into contact with several opposing players. This latter approach to the assessment of influence brings to mind the concept of "territorial control" made so prominent of late by Ardrey in his work *The Territorial Imperative* (1966) (see also Browne, 1968). But let us turn from speculation to summary.

Albeit superficially, I have attempted: (1) to show the conceptual complexity of the phenomenon of social mobility, (2) to indicate the problems associated with its measurement, (3) to suggest a model study as reference for the interested investigator, (4) to review some research related to the mobility patterns of sportsmen, (5) to outline some of the ways in which athletic participation may facilitate upward mobility, (6) to suggest that in certain cases sport involvement may negatively influence mobility, and (7) to illustrate how social mobility might be studied within sport as well as outside it.

The major generalization which can be made from the discussion to this point is that not much is really known about the extent to which athletic participation facilitates upward mobility, if in fact it does. This over-all conclusion in conjunction with what has been said herein suggests that at least three basic kinds of studies need to be made. First, we need to determine what in fact are the social backgrounds of athletes in various educational institutions in America at the present time. Second, longitudinal studies of athletes, using appropriate control groups, are needed to determine the effects of athletic participation on their future social and occupational careers. Third, since athletes yesterday may not be similar to athletes today and since changes in the social structure may have differentially affected mobility rates of sportsmen, studies of the mobility patterns of former college athletes are also needed. In the time remaining at my disposal I wish to share with you some preliminary findings of a recent exploratory investigation related to this third type of study.

UCLA Study

As previously pointed out, the major weakness of research bearing on the problem of mobility patterns of college athletes is the fact that investigations have either focused on social backgrounds or on success patterns and have not considered initial and termination points of mobility simultaneously in a given study. In view of this fact I recently made an effort to examine both the social backgrounds and success patterns of a selected sample of college athletes. Specifically, I attempted to ascertain the social origins and present social status of Life Pass holders at the University of California, Los Angeles. In order to obtain a Life Pass, an athlete must have competed at the college level for four years and have earned at least three varsity letters. According to records of the Athletic Department of the University, 1,386 men had received a Life Pass as of last spring. Addresses were obtained for 1,097 of these men, and a six-page questionnaire concerning past and present social statuses was mailed to each individual. Thirty-three questionnaires were discounted because of wrong addresses, in fifteen cases the individual was deceased, and in twenty-eight cases the Life Pass was found to be honorary rather than earned. Thus, 1,021 former Life Pass holders were eligible for response; and of this group 845 or 83% returned their questionnaire. The survey data was coded this past month and is presently being transferred to punch cards to facilitate analysis. Although a full analysis of the survey will not be completed for some months, a peek at the data for purposes of this paper has revealed some interesting findings.

Social Backgrounds. In order to get a general idea of the social backgrounds of athletes in different sports an effort was made to determine the socio-economic status of their fathers' occupations, the percent of their fathers in blue-collar jobs, and the percentage of their fathers who had less than a high school education. The mean occupational prestige scores of fathers measured by the Duncan socio-economic status index are shown in Table 1. For purposes of illustration the sports are arbitrarily grouped into six categories. As is evident from the Table, the lowest status score is recorded for fathers of wrestlers, followed by scores for fathers of boxers, football players and baseball players. It is interesting to note that three of the four sports placed in the lower-lower and upper-lower categories are combative in nature (i.e., contact sports). In the lower-middle category are found the status scores for fathers of athletes who competed on soccer, rifle, rugby, track and handball teams. While in the upper-middle category are occupational prestige scores for fathers of team managers, gymnasts, volleyball players and basketball players. Within the lower-upper category are found status scores for fathers of fencers, swimmers, tennis players, cricket players, hockey players and oarsmen. Finally, in the upper-upper category we find the sport of golf.

TABLE 1

MEAN OCCUPATIONAL STATUS SCORES OF FATHERS OF
FORMER ATHLETES IN TWENTY COLLEGIATE SPORTS

SPORT	N	STATUS SCORE	CATEGORY
Wrestling	(27)	43	Lower-Lower
Boxing	(12)	47	
Football	(192)	48	Upper-Lower
Baseball	(89)	49	
Soccer	(32)	51	
Rifle Team	(12)	51	
Rugby	(16)	52	Lower-Middle
Handball	(6)	53	
Track	(119)	53	
Team Managers	(34)	55	
Volleyball	(3)	55	Upper-Middle
Basketball	(91)	57	
Gymnastics	(33)	58	
Fencing	(5)	60	
Crew	(64)	62	
Ice Hockey	(9)	62	Lower-Upper
Cricket	(17)	63	
Swimming	(78)	64	
Tennis	(50)	64	
Golf	(19)	74	Upper-Upper

A number of the figures in Table 1 should not be accorded too much significance since they are based on very small numbers of respondents. The only apparent anomaly in the status hierarchy, however, is the sport of ice hockey. It is noted that the sport has not been played since World War II, and all Life Pass holders in the sport were born prior to 1917.

TABLE 2

PERCENT OF FATHERS IN BLUE-COLLAR OCCUPATIONS
ACCORDING TO SPORT

SPORT	N	% BLUE-COLLAR
Wrestling	(27)	48.1
Baseball	(90)	36.5
Football	(192)	34.6
Track	(119)	30.5
Soccer	(32)	26.3
Gymnastics	(33)	26.3
Basketball	(91)	16.4
Swimming	(81)	13.3
Tennis	(50)	13.3
Crew	(64)	10.4

Table 2 shows the percent of fathers in blue-collar occupations when their sons entered college. As is evident from the Table, nearly half of the wrestlers came from blue-collar homes as did approximately a third of the football

TABLE 3

PERCENT OF FATHERS NOT COMPLETING HIGH SCHOOL
ACCORDING TO SPORT

SPORT	N	% NOT COMPLETING HIGH SCHOOL
Football	219	51.59
Wrestling	28	49.99
Baseball	94	49.98
Track	131	43.50
Gymnastics	34	38.21
Basketball	107	37.38
Swimming	81	27.15
Tennis	54	25.91
Crew	67	23.87
Soccer	35	22.85

players, baseball players and trackmen. About a quarter of the soccer players and gymnasts came from blue-collar homes; while less than a fifth of athletes in basketball, swimming, tennis, and crew came from blue-collar backgrounds.

A somewhat similar rank order is found in Table 3 which presents the percent of fathers having less than a high school education. As can be seen from the Table, approximately half of the fathers of football players, wrestlers and baseball players. On the other hand, approximately seventy-five percent of the fathers of tennis players, swimmers, soccer players and oarsmen finished high school.

Success Patterns. In order to obtain a general idea of the over-all mobility patterns of athletes, the mean occupational prestige scores of their first job upon leaving college and of their present job as of the Spring of 1968 were compared with that of their fathers. Table 4 portrays the differences among

TABLE 4

A COMPARISON OF FATHERS' OCCUPATIONAL STATUS SCORES
WITH THOSE OF SONS' FIRST JOB AND SONS' PRESENT JOB

SPORT	FATHERS' MAIN JOB	N	SONS' FIRST JOB	N	SONS' PRESENT JOB	N
Wrestling	43	(27)	70	(24)	77	(27)
Football	48	(192)	63	(192)	74	(206)
Baseball	49	(89)	64	(90)	75	(91)
Soccer	51	(32)	74	(33)	79	(36)
Track	53	(119)	67	(120)	77	(121)
Basketball	57	(91)	69	(92)	77	(100)
Gymnastics	58	(33)	67	(33)	80	(33)
Crew	62	(64)	69	(52)	78	(65)
Swimming	63	(78)	67	(80)	78	(81)
Tennis	64	(50)	70	(51)	75	(55)

fathers and sons associated with a given sport. As concerns present job, there is not much of a difference in occupation status scores among the various groups of athletes. Moreover, the majority of former athletes are employed in occupations having relatively high socio-economic status. Perhaps the most striking aspect of the Table, is the great degree of social mobility achieved by athletes whose parents had the lowest socio-economic status.

Table 5 further illustrates the success patterns of college athletes. For example, nearly forty-four percent of all athletes were found to have earned an advanced degree.

TABLE 5

PERCENT OF ATHLETES HOLDING ADVANCED DEGREES
ACCORDING TO SPORT

SPORT	N	% OF ATHLETES WITH ADV. DEGREES
Gymnastics	34	61.75
Soccer	35	54.28
Wrestling	28	50.00
Track	131	45.79
Swimming	81	45.67
Basketball	107	43.91
Tennis	54	40.72
Baseball	94	37.22
Crew	67	29.85
Football	219	29.21

Average = 43.84

TABLE 6

PREFERRED PRESIDENTIAL CANDIDATE OF ATHLETES
ACCORDING TO SPORT

SPORT	N	% PREFERRING A REPUBLICAN CANDIDATE	% PREFERRING A DEMOCRATIC CANDIDATE
Wrestling	28	60.71	25.00
Football	219	55.70	21.91
Crew	67	55.22	20.89
Basketball	107	54.20	22.42
Swimming	81	53.08	29.62
Gymnastics	34	52.94	26.47
Track	131	51.90	29.77
Baseball	94	46.80	23.40
Soccer	35	42.85	42.85
Tennis	54	42.59	31.48

Consequences of Mobility. In summary, the preliminary analysis has resulted in a number of findings which are indicative of the social mobility patterns of college athletes. It is hoped that further analysis will provide firmer ground for generalization. But even assuming that some information is acquired about the past and present social statuses of athletes, there still remains the very important issue of what are the consequences — both positive and negative — of social mobility for given groups of athletes. In short, how are the *life-styles* and *life-chances* of athletes affected by upward mobility?

Although our survey of former athletes cannot directly answer this question, the questionnaire used did contain a number of items related to the matters of *life-style* and *life-chances.* For example, regarding political preference which is an aspect of life-style, we asked each former athlete whom he intended to vote for in the coming presidential election. Table 6 shows the percentage of athletes in each sport favoring a Republican or Democratic presidential candidate. It is clear from the Table that the majority of athletes favored Republican candidates.

Finally, as an example of a finding related to an aspect of life-chances, the percent of former athletes who have been divorced at least once are shown in Table 7. Over-all the divorce rate of former athletes is relatively low.

TABLE 7

PERCENT OF ATHLETES WHO HAVE BEEN
PREVIOUSLY DIVORCED

SPORT	N	% DIVORCED
Tennis	54	16.66
Track	131	16.03
Gymnastics	34	14.70
Football	219	14.61
Soccer	35	14.24
Crew	67	13.43
Baseball	94	11.70
Basketball	107	11.21
Wrestling	28	10.71
Swimming	81	9.87

In conclusion, I hope that this paper will in some small way stimulate several students in the audience to conduct as part of their graduate work, research related to the problem of sport and social mobility.

REFERENCES

Andreano, Ralph. "The Affluent Baseball Player," *Trans-action* (May/June 1965a) 2(4): 10-13.

Andreano, Ralph. *No Joy in Mudville.* Cambridge, Mass.: Schenkman, 1965b.

Annarino, Anthony A. "The Contributions of Athletics to Social Mobility," *56th Annual Proceedings of the College Pysical Education Association.* New York, 1953.

Ardrey, Robert. *The Territory Imperative.* New York: Dell, 1966.

Blalock, Hubert H., Jr. "Occupational Discrimination: Some Theoretical Propositions," *Social Problems* (1962) 9(3):240-247.

Blalock, Hubert H., Jr. "Book Review of Peter M. Blau and O. Dudley Duncan, *The American Occupational Structure,*" *American Sociological Review* (April 1968) 33(2):296-297.

Blau, Peter M. and O. Dudley Duncan. *The American Occupational Structure.* New York: John Wiley & Sons, 1967.

Browne, Evelyn. "An Ethological Theory of Play," *Journal of Health, Physical Education and Recreation* (Sept. 1968) 39(7):36-39.

Charnofsky, Harold. "The Major League Professional Baseball Player: Self-Conception versus the Popular Image," Paper presented at the Annual Meetings of the American Sociological Association, August 29-31, 1967 in San Francisco.

Coleman, James S. *The Adolescent Society.* New York: Free Press, 1961.

Coopersmith, Stanley. *Antecedents of Self-Esteem.* San Francisco: W. H. Freeman, 1967.

Coopersmith, Stanley. "Studies in Self-Esteem," *Scientific American* (Feb. 1968) 218(2): 96-106.

Cousy, Robert. *Basketball Is My Life.* Englewood Cliffs, N. J.: Prentice-Hall, 1961.

Eggleston, John. "Secondary Schools and Oxbridge Blues," *British Journal of Sociology* (Sept. 1965) 16(3):232-242.

Gibson, Althea. *I Always Wanted To Be Somebody.* New York: Harper & Brothers, 1958.

Gregory, Paul M. *The Baseball Player: An Economic Study.* Washington, D. C.: Public Affairs Press, 1956.

Grusky, Oscar. "The Effects of Formal Structure on Managerial Recruitment: A Study of Baseball Organization," *Sociometry* (1963) 26:345-353.

Havighurst, Robert J. and Bernice L. Neugarten. *Society and Education.* Boston: Allyn and Bacon, 1957.

Hodges, Harold M., Jr. *Social Stratification (Class in America).* Cambridge, Mass.: Schenkman, 1964.

Lenski, Gerhard. *Power and Privilege (a theory of social stratification).* New York: McGraw-Hill, 1966.

Litchfield, Edward H. with Myron Cope. "Saturday's Hero Is Doing Fine," *Sports Illustrated* (July 8, 1962) pp. 66-80.

Loy, John W. and John N. Sage. "The Effects of Formal Structure on Organizational Leadership: An Investigation of Interscholastic Baseball Teams," Paper presented at the 2nd International Congress of Sport Psychology, November 1, 1968 in Washington, D. C.

Lüschen, Günther. "Soziale Schichtung and Soziale Mobilitat Beijungen Sportlern," (Social Stratification and Social Mobility Among Young Sportsmen), *Kolner Zeitschrift fur Soziologie und Sozialpsychologie* (1963) 15(1):74-93.

McIntyre, Thomas D. "Socio-Economic Background of White Male Athletes from Four Selected Sports at the Pennsylvania State University," (M.Ed. thesis, Pennsylvania State University, 1959).

Mantle, Mickey. *The Education of a Baseball Player.* New York: Simon & Schuster, 1967.

Meyer, Herbert H. "Factors Related to Success in the Human Relations Aspect of Work-Group Leadership," *Psychological Monographs* (1951) (No. 320) 65(3):1-29.

Pooley, John C. "Ethnic Soccer Clubs in Milwaukee: A Study in Assimilation," (M.S. thesis, University of Wisconsin, 1968).

Rehberg, Richard A. and Walter E. Schafer. "Participation in Interscholastic Athletics and College Expectations," *American Journal of Sociology* (1968) 73(6):732-740.

Reissman, Leonard. *Class in American Society.* New York: Free Press, 1959.

Riesman, David and Reuel Denney. "Football in America: A Study in Culture Diffusion," *American Quarterly* (1951) 3:309-319.

Rosenberg, Morris. *Society and the Adolescent Self-Image.* Princeton, N. J.: Princeton University Press, 1965.

Russell, Bill. *Go Up For Glory.* New York: Coward-McCann, 1966.

Sage, John N. "Adolescent Values and the Non-Participating College Athlete," Paper presented at the Southern Section CAHPER Conference, December 2, 1967 at San Fernando Valley State College.

Schafer, Walter E. "Athletic Success and Social Mobility," Paper presented at the National Convention of the American Association for Health, Physical Education, and Recreation, March 30, 1968 in St. Louis, Missouri.

Schafer, Walter E. and J. Michael Armer. "Athletes Are Not Inferior Students," *Trans-action* (Nov. 1968) 6(1):21-26, 61-62.

Smith, Ken. *The Willie Mays Story*. New York: Greenburg, 1954.

Sorokin, Pitirim A. *Social and Cultural Mobility*. New York: Free Press, 1959.

Svalastoga, Kaare. *Social Differentiation*. New York: McKay, 1965.

Tumin, Melvin M. *Social Stratification (The Forms and Functions of Inequality)*. Englewood Cliffs, N. J.: Prentice-Hall, 1967.

Unitas, John. *The Johnny Unitas Story*. New York: Grosset & Dunlap, 1965.

Webb, Harry. "Success Patterns of College Athletes," Paper presented at the National Convention of the American Association for Health, Physical Education, and Recreation, March 30, 1968a in St. Louis, Missouri.

Webb, Harry. "Social Backgrounds of College Athletes," Paper presented at the National Convention of the American Association for Health, Physical Education, and Recreation, March 30, 1968b in St. Louis, Missouri.

Weinberg, S. K. and H. Arond. "The Occupational Culture of the Boxer," *American Journal of Sociology* (1952) 57:460-469.

WEBB: Loy's paper is essentially a report on the sometimes interesting and sometimes not so interesting studies that have been done before, particularly with respect to mobility among athletes with some, of course, introductory cautions regarding the definitional and empirical difficulties involved in doing such investigations, but the upshot of the reports is that participation and upward mobility appear to have some connection about which not much is really known. He then mentions two studies which he has underway, the first dealing with the distribution of authority among team members, an interesting problem, given the high degree of rationalization of some activities, but less interesting if that degree is low. He did not cover that part of his paper but it's related to Lenski's distinction between power and privilege and the fact that prestige produces both of them.

Lenski in a sense, takes this from Weber's distinction between class and status, class based upon occupational background, and status being something which is achieved in a community setting; and that, of course is a reply to Marx's earlier emphasis on the fact of occupation as the major basis on which different kinds of attitudes and opinions are formed. In that sense, participation in the economic structure not only influences the way individuals think, but the way society is developed too. It's in that sense, as well, that he says that social consciousness is a direct result of social existence. The one then tends to produce the other. Weber, goes on in the *Protestant Ethic* and demonstrates — demonstrates brilliantly, I think — the fact that the two are related and possibly in the other direction; and he points out the very great importance of the Protestant influence, the Protestant ethic, in the development of the capitalistic economy.

In any case, from Weber, Lenski makes this distinction between power and privilege based on prestige and, of course, these are institutionalized particularly in terms of power — in terms of authority and influence; and Loy is interested in investigating the degree of authority, the degree of influence, based upon position on an athletic team. He contrasts the way in which, for example, a halfback and a tackle have differential influence in getting the quarterback to take up a certain kind of play. Well, that kind of focus is interesting and productive only so far as the activity itself is rationalized; that is, it has considerable division of labor and so on, to some ranking of the men on the team in terms of the position they play. In other words, distribution of authority is based on the presumed contribution they make; presumably the contribution of the quarterback is greater than that of the offensive guards and the tackles who are protecting them. Ordinarily the quarterback believes it too. Take a look at Joe Namath: he was up there in training camp, it was before he had ever played professional ball, and he had picked up some $600,000 in the process and the people were around in an effort to get his signature on pieces of paper and bar bills and everything else, and he was giving it out and he told them that he was very sorry that he had to leave because it would be too bad for them, they wouldn't be able to get any more signatures, you know, passing it around and saying they had known Big Joe. Well, the emphasis on this is the sense in which the tackle has less confidence in himself in that respect than a guy like Namath, but it in turn depends on the degree of rationalization of the sport itself.

The second piece of research mentioned is the one dealing with the "fact" of upward mobility of athletes. There are some difficulties with which we should talk about. First of all, Loy claims that 83 per cent is a good figure on the return. Well, 83 per cent is a good figure on the return if the people in the remaining 17 per cent do not differ in any major respects from those obtained, for example, in age. Also, the fact that the nature of the economy over those periods of years has changed quite a deal as he tried to point out, and it would affect the way in which these athletes develop their mobility levels, means, or medians or whatever. The 3 per cent of cases lost because they couldn't find an address, seems small, but they still constitute 3 per cent. And when you're operating in terms of relatively high levels of confidence, for example, .05, there is a possibility that the lost 3 per cent could influence the result. But they don't bother me half as much as that 17 per cent of non-returns does. The fact is, aside from the questions of reliability and validity, survey research must take into consideration the kinds of people who don't answer these questions. That is, who are the lost 17 per cent? For example, are they upper-class people? Probably not. They are very likely the people at the bottom. In a study of this kind of thing, based on my own experience, you run into a lot of trouble with guys who haven't made it, and they don't want to reply. Why should they? They have been losers in a system which places an awful lot of emphasis on not only competition but, more important, on getting there, getting the success, and lacking it they don't reply. It's my even bet that the guys who have not replied are the guys who have not succeeded and it's precisely those guys that we are most concerned with. So it would seem at the very best that a genuine effort be made to pick these people up, and that is of course aside from the fact that there is this real question, very serious question, about what that large number of years has done to affect those results and these are a couple of the kinds of things that should be taken up.

I was going to mention that I wanted a more clear-cut emphasis on that question of conservatism and liberalism too; that should be better qualified, as Page points out. Wallace would make a difference and the intention to vote for a man in May in an enormously confused political situation is not a very good indication of what might have been developed there. The other thing, of course, is guess who those guys are? Are they all kids? We really don't know who they are on the basis of age and that's not a criticism because this kind of analysis has not been made yet, but there is a tendency for people as they get older to become politically more conservative and that would mean that if he has older people in that sample, that this would affect the amount of people, the number of people, voting Republican rather than Democratic. This kind of thing would have to be controlled as well. Since, of course they have all been upwardly mobile themselves, at least from what it looks like there, they would also be expected to be more conservative since that is related as well to education levels on the first hand, occupation next, and income level next, so these kinds of things will have to be handled if the study is to develop what Loy would like it to.

The other kind of thing that is difficult to get at, the thing that substantially contributes to mobility, is whether or not the guy has a college degree. A lot of athletes don't make it, and you have already skewed your results in an obvious direction if you take only those guys who have got degrees. Clearly they are going to succeed as it seems is indicated by those figures. Four years, of course, in college and three years of getting letters is bound to produce a degree — there is a very high level of correlation based on my own work between number of letters achieved and the likelihood of degree — it's about 0.90. So these guys have got degrees and that assists them in this upward drive. The fact that they seem to achieve at about the same level is difficult, of course, to speculate on, because of the things that we have already mentioned, but the difference between father's occupation and son's occupation, that is if all these guys were drawn from a current population, that kind of result could reasonably be expected. The reason for that is because of the change in the occupation market from predominantly blue collar and agricultural to one in which there is a great deal of emphasis on white collar activity and you can get there with a high school degree. The occupation variable is not a very good discriminator.

Now if you want to know the difference between these guys, for example, team athletes as opposed to individual athletes on occupation as defined today, that's one thing. But if you want to test the difference between father's occupation in 1920 and somebody else's occupation in 1940, and somebody else's again in 1960, that's very difficult to do, because of this change in the occupation market. Bureau of Census and Bureau of Labor Statistics show that on a conservative estimate some thirty-two or thirty-five thousand jobs a week, blue collar jobs a week, are being dealt out of the economy because of cybernation; that is, the computer control of productive processes has been affected, in addition, by the fact that there has been a hell of a lot of job retitling going on in our society. In a system which emphasizes success, defined by the kind of occupational status the man has, you can do a lot to level that by simply retitling jobs. So, for example, the girl who works as a secretary and makes fifty-five bucks a week in New York is called a "gal Friday." There are at least 300 such listings in the New York Times each Sunday for gal Fridays. What does that imply? Well, she is the big man's right-hand girl, and without her he cannot operate effectively. So she goes off, pretends she's gal Friday and makes $55 a week. The assistant manager, so-called, in a loan company will make $90 to $110 a week and live in a community like East Lansing next to the professor who is making sixty, seventy, eighty thousand — not really of course, but who is making substantially, $15,000 and up: but they can live in the same homes because of the way the economy has changed as well. Instead of purchasing things, we buy them on credit. Houses can be purchased on 30-year mortgages and he can buy the same house that a man much higher in status and in income has. The status levels are roughly the same. There is no distinction in that sense. Now, as I say, if you want to compare them then, because of these changes over time within a specific time, that's one thing. But one thing that compounds the difficulty of inter-generational mobility is the change in the occupational market itself. The way things have worked you can expect some increase in job status or occupational status over every generation in spite of things like education and in spite of things like background, that is, as averages, so these are additional kinds of problems. As Loy points out, it's important that more research be done; but it is, as he has also pointed out, difficult to do that research and so far as his own particular research is concerned there are some additional kinds of things he will clearly have to do if these results are to be accepted.

But since we are interested in this thing and it's difficult to get at information, it just so happens, folks, that between the shirts in my suitcase I discovered some of my own data; and so I would like to present some of that to show that there are some similarities between what Loy has got and data obtained elsewhere.

The data that I have is on some three hundred odd, Michigan State athletes. This is part of a brief synopsis of the two papers that were presented in St. Louis this last spring,* neither of which, like everything else I've done, is published. In any case there were some 300 athletes, and they were all on tenders; which means what? Which means they are the best damned athletes money can buy. So that this business of ability is controlled. These athletes came into Michigan State with tenders and they cross a four or five year period: there were just a few that came in '57, but they run from '58 to '62. The last bunch is supposed to be out by '63; so in other words these computations, which have been made very recently, involve athletes who have been out of school for at least five years. Their classes have graduated five years ago, so the time is controlled, athletic ability is controlled and other items as well. There are differences, of course, as you cross the country from the PCC to the Big Ten, and to the Ivy League, and those differences should be investigated as well. They also may skew results, as you might expect. In any case they operate at a very high level of point production, time diminution, you know, in terms of the mile and so on — they have some first rate athletic teams on the Michigan State campus as Wisconsin is well aware and so that one kind of thing is controlled.

Let's take a look just at what some of these background factors are in terms of occupational status, income and so on. The argument is that ath-

---

*Research Symposium on the Sociology of Sport, AAHPER National Convention. March, 1968.

letes come disproportionately from disadvantaged families; as Table 1 demonstrates they clearly do not. If you take total family income by fifths (in 100's of dollars), for all U. S. families in 1960, as obtained from the U. S. Census, you find twenty per cent of American families earning less than

TABLE 1

ATHLETES' FAMILIES AND U. S. FAMILIES*
COMPARED ON GROSS INCOME

	TOTAL FAMILY INCOME (in 100's of dollars)					
	0-27.9	28-47.9	48-64.9	65-89.9	90+	
U. S. Families	20**	20	20	20	20	100
Athletes' Families (n = 253)	6.7	23.3	28.5	29.6	11.9	100
	Chi square = 52.91			p < .001		

*Data from U. S. Census of Population: 1960, Final Report PC (1)-1C, General Social and Economic Characteristics, p. 1-226, Table 95. If a "one sample, goodness of fit," test is applied to a distribution of athletes' families on gross income (expected distribution being on fifths as for U. S. families) then X^2 = 52.91   p < .001.

**per cent.

$2790, and twenty per cent earning over $9,000; in addition, but not included here, less than 5 per cent were over $15,000; so for those of you who think there has been a great deal of income redistribution, at least according to government figures, it hasn't happened. In any case when athletes' families are compared with all U. S. families, you can see that very few of the athletes come from that bottom fifth and not many of them come from the top fifth either. They are middle income kids and they come from middle level, at least as far as income is concerned, backgrounds. Chi-square for this distribution is greater than 52, which, friends, I can tell you, gives a probability of somewhat less than .001. In other words, athletes come, not from the poorest or the richest fifths, but from the middle income levels.

Well you say, the hell with that, man, you know — you skewed it, really it's team athletes we are talking about because we know about those guys that are playing fencing, tennis and golf: but if you do the same thing with team athletes only, the argument fails; the same thing happens. (Table 2). The percentages are roughly the same in both cases, 8.4 at the top, 5.4 at the bottom. And if then you say "I didn't mean them at all, I meant the football players": the same thing follows, (Table 3), these guys come from middle income levels. Well, that's going to affect mobility already, isn't it? When sport type alone is contrasted on income, it's clear (Table 4)

TABLE 2

TEAM ATHLETES' FAMILIES AND U. S. FAMILIES
COMPARED ON GROSS INCOME

	TOTAL FAMILY INCOME (in 100's of dollars)					
	0-27.9	28-47.9	48-64.9	65-89.9	90+	
U. S. Families	20	20	20	20	20	100
Team Athletes' Families (n = 166)	5.4	24.1	28.3	33.7	8.4	100
	Chi square = 51.53		p < .001			

TABLE 3

FOOTBALL ATHLETES' FAMILIES AND U. S. FAMILIES
COMPARED ON GROSS INCOME

	TOTAL FAMILY INCOME (in 100's of dollars)					
	0-27.9	28-47.9	48-64.9	65-89.9	90+	
U. S. Families	20	20	20	20	20	100
Football Athletes' Families (n = 111)	4.5	27.0	28.8	31.5	8.1	100
	Chi square = 35.62		p < .001			

TABLE 4

SPORT TYPE AND FAMILY INCOME

	TOTAL FAMILY INCOME (in 100's of dollars)					
	0-27.9	28-47.9	48-64.9	65-89.9	90+	
Team (n = 166)	5.6	24.1	28.3	33.7	8.4	100
Individual (n = 87)	9.2	21.8	28.7	21.8	18.4	100
	Chi square = 8.84		p < .07			

that athletes in "individual sports" are overrepresented at the top and bottom fifths, the latter because of track athletes.

GREGORY STONE: Are those averages again that you are dealing with?

WEBB: No, this was clearly based upon categories, no mean or anything else is involved here: the first category includes those families earning less than $2800. At this point chi-square equals 8.92 which gives a probability level slightly higher than .05 which means that you cannot accept or reject the hypothesis but it's quite close as you can see. What is surprising, the team athletes are the kids who are supposed to be from the poor families relative to individual athletes and that does seem to be the case except for the differentiation at the bottom of the category where about 10 per cent of the individual athletes originate and about 7 per cent of the team athletes. That may be due to Negroes in track. At the top level roughly 20 per cent of the individual athletes are up there compared to less than 10 per cent of the team athletes. If you then use something like Kruskal-Wallis analysis of variance and get what would amount to the median on each one of these things — analysis of variance is not the distinction between means but calculates a mean or a central tendency for all groups being compared. It's used, of course, when you are comparing more than two groups and then it examines the amount of the variation around that calculated tendency. You can take the scores for each group and rank them and, although this is mentioned somewhere else in the paper, if you were to do this on the basis of calculating means on, in this case, income, the correlation between what's achieved by this and by the other more powerful statistics is something like .9; it's very, very high. In any case at

TABLE 5

SPORT RANK ON GROSS INCOME*

1. Fencing	7. Basketball
2. Wrestling	8. Gymnastics
3. Baseball	9. Football
4. Swimming	10. Track
5. Golf	11. Hockey
6. Tennis	

*Kruskal Wallis H = 23.27 for these data, significant at .009 level, indicating a significant income variation between the sports, which tends to hold on a Team-Individual basis, as above. (n = 263)

Rank sums for each value are divided by n for that value and the results are then ranked. This seems to be an effective method when employed on gross income and then compared with the ranking by means on gross income, Spearman Rho = .94 (p < .01). The mean, of course, may only be used with data of at least "interval" level of measurement, and thus not with "occupation."

the bottom in terms of income are track, hockey, football, and gymnastics. At the top you might expect fencing and baseball. Wrestling is surprising. It may result from the fact that wrestlers' blue collar fathers earn more money as you can see in Table 5.

In terms of father's occupational status, again this is significant. You have got the explanation of the rank. Sums are divided by "n" for that value and the results are then ranked. This seems to be an effective method when employed on gross income and then compared to the ranking by means of gross income. In any case the ranking remains relatively the same. At the top you get an idea of where these kids come from; 33 per cent of

TABLE 6

SPORT TYPE AND FATHER'S OCCUPATION

	Father's Occupation					
	Prof-Tech	Cler-Sales	Trades	Labor	Not Home	
Team (n = 178)	10.1	12.4	30.9	32.6	14.0	100
Individual (n = 85)	32.9	17.7	22.4	16.4	10.6	100

Chi square = 25.77   p < .001

TABLE 7

SPORT RANK ON FATHER'S OCCUPATIONAL STATUS

1.	Golf	7.	Gymnastics
2.	Fencing	8.	Track
3.	Tennis	9.	Hockey
4.	Swimming	10.	Football
5.	Baseball	11.	Basketball
6.	Wrestling		

Kruskal-Waylis H = 50.82, p < .001 (n = 268)

them are from professional technical backgrounds, compared with 10 per cent of the team athletes. At the other end of the scheme about 33 per cent of the team athletes are from labor backgrounds compared with about 16

TABLE 8

TEAM AND INDIVIDUAL ATHLETES BY MAJOR SPORT
ON GROSS FAMILY INCOME

	Total Family Income					
	0-27.9	28.47.9	48-64.9	65-89.9	90+	
Major Team (n = 148)	6.7	22.2	26.3	35.1	9.4	100
Major Individual (n = 63)	11.1	22.2	28.5	22.2	15.8	100

Chi square = 5.00   p > .20

TABLE 9

TEAM AND INDIVIDUAL ATHLETES BY MAJOR SPORT
ON FATHER'S OCCUPATIONAL STATUS

	Prof-Tech	Cler-Sales	Trades	Labor	Not Home	
Major Team (n = 151)	10.6	12.6	30.5	35.1	11.2	100
Major Individual (n = 61)	31.2	13.1	23.0	21.3	11.4	100

Chi square = 14.65   p < .01

per cent of the individual athletes. Not-home proportions are roughly the same, because of divorce, or the old man took off, and so on. If you consider team and individual athletes in only major sports on gross family income, these proportions remain roughly the same, although there is some diminution of differences, and the same thing of course goes for comparison on the father's occupational status. Roughly 30 per cent of them stay at the top, about 35 per cent of the major team athletes at the bottom, so these guys originate in different backgrounds but backgrounds which are dissimilar only at the top and the bottom levels of the income levels of the rest of the population. They tend to come from the middle income ranks.

There is the question then, given what we know about the background; what happens to them when they come to school? What are their success patterns in school? And that was part of that second thing; the fact is first that — let me come back to this for just a minute — what you would like to do, of course, is predict mobility based on some criterion. One of these, of course, is getting a degree. It's difficult to say whether the kid, if he leaves Michigan State, goes somewhere else to get a degree. Roughly 70 per cent of the kids entering Michigan State, based upon the best figures we can get, graduate. It may be somewhat higher than that. Based on a study done I think down in Ohio three or four years ago, reported in the *American Sociological Review,* the figure goes up to about 75 per cent for all kids entering college. Well, 75 per cent of them graduate, but they don't graduate with their class. Many of them take two or three years in addition to get out of school. But most of them, that is, roughly three quarters of them, get degrees; but in any case at Michigan State about 70 per cent get a degree.

The first part, that is the background, is based upon information obtained from the Big Ten. The parents had to fill out these financial statement forms to make sure the kids could get the dough and then the second part, the business on how well he makes out in school is not asked of him but is obtained from records in the Michigan State vaults (which by the way are very difficult to get). The third part of the study which is under way now is an attempt to find out how well these kids have done, what are they doing today, and then, of course, contrast this with that occupational background with the same qualifications and conditions that I have mentioned before which apply to this work as well as to Loy's or anyone else's. So, just to see how some of this makes out, here are some other tables (indicating). This contrasts five years later what's happened to these kids; 49 per cent of the team athletes have gotten degrees in Michigan State, roughly 51 per cent have not; 60 per cent of individual athletes have gotten degrees, roughly 41 per cent have not. Now if you include in that sample, which you can see down here at the bottom (indicating) 161 and 143, those kids who were not at Michigan State more than two years, that is, they were there less than two years, they had grade point averages at Michigan State of 1.5 out of a four point system or above — (that means F+ or above), they also sent at least one transcript to another school, which we get from the records as well — of course, they are in the records — and they were at least in the top 70 per cent of their high school graduating class. In other words those kids if they went some place had some bare chance of getting a degree. You have 42 such kids. You add that and get the proportions at the bottom; 67 per cent of all athletes graduate, and the way this manipulation of material operates, 33 per cent did not.

Team athlete success is determined by number of letters, degree obtained or not obtained, race, white and negro, and grades. A negro kid coming to Michigan State is supposed to really have an opportunity; man, he's going to make it. What's Harold Lucas, who was an All-American at Michigan State, an All-American Tackle, and who later played a little professional ball and then dropped out, what's he doing today? He's working in a factory in Detroit. There are several cases of athletes that I can give like this where the success in athletics has been very great in terms of the number of letters and athletic honors won. What happens to them in terms of getting a degree? The percentages are at the bottom; 56 per cent of white athletes get degrees, 38 per cent of negro athletes get degrees, five years after this group has left school. I think it should be clear that the likelihood that the negro kid is likely to get that degree later on is much less than that of the white boy.

The following are for white boys only, and here fathers' occupation is related to whether or not the degree is obtained. Professional and technical, kids coming from that group, 49 per cent of them graduate, 46 per cent from white collar groups, 56 per cent of the kids from blue collar groups and 70 per cent from the families where the father's absent. That would indicate that athletics provides opportunity for lower class whites. Of course, this business might not fit with lots of schools as well, it has to be taken into mind, and they are likely to get degrees somewhere else. But for those kids at Michigan State five years later the effect of occupations seems to be clear on getting that degree, and that degree is the ticket of admission to white middle level kinds of occupations and middle level income levels. The kid at the bottom level is making it. He clearly is from these figures.

Of course, there's the fact that he's bound to stay at Michigan State too. He is dependent on his athletic financial support. How about the wealthier kid? He can take off because he doesn't need that money. In fact, his folks, based upon upper occupational level income, can afford to pay his way at another school. So this has to be considered as well when you have a look at that figure. Now if you just take the bottom 40 per cent, then control also for blue collar origin against white collar origin, you get a definition of lower class and upper class, taking whites only. Sixty-four per cent of those white kids at the bottom are getting degrees, contrasted with 52 per cent of the kids in the upper income and occupational groups. When sport type at the lower level is compared, 68 per cent of team athletes compared with 50 per cent of the individual athletes obtain degrees, which may mean that the team athletic business ties the kid tighter, more tightly into operating in an associational unit which provides some varieties of support and this may be an explanation of the difference in effect. The individual athlete type on the other hand is operating in strong competition with other kids and if he's not so successful the likelihood of his dropping out, of course may be much greater.

And then finally come the term categories, and this is the thing that would or could affect the information already presented. This gives for the lower class kids and the upper class kids the number of terms they spent at Michigan State — one to three, four to six, seven to nine. We're on the term basis, so that would be less than a year, one year, two years, three years, four years, and five years. Twenty per cent of the lower class kids have been at Michigan State five terms or less, contrasted with 36 per cent of those upper class kids so that there is a tendency based upon occupational background to leave and that, of course, is probably based upon this difference in effect of parent's ability to support the athlete elsewhere. The kid with the higher occupational background because he's independent financially can do that.

Well, there are a great many other things that have to be investigated. One of the things that should have been done here and was not — it hasn't been done because I haven't had the time — is control of that term business, how long these kids are actually in school. In other words, of those kids who are there for four years or more, how many are getting degrees in terms of white — negro differences and team-individual ones. But the larger question is the possibility of doing this kind of thing beyond the kinds of things we can get from records, where there is very little bias, and that involves questionnaires, going out and asking questions about mobility, you cannot get away from it — and the differential interest in answering those questions based upon the degree or the amount of lack of success, so that those questions remain. I suppose with very tight follow-up systems some of them might to some greater or lesser extent be controlled. In any case the area is an important one and Loy is beginning a contribution in that area.

DISCUSSION

DAN LANDERS: Did you say roughly 50 per cent of the athletes at Michigan State did get a degree in '57 and with Loy about 49 per cent had advanced degrees?

WEBB: Loy, don't forget, has guys who have been there for at least four years, they have got three letters, that means that they were there for four years, and as I pointed out there is a very high correlation between getting a degree, and number of letters earned: the higher the number of letters the greater the probability of getting a degree. I have everybody, whether they actually got any letters or not, they came to Michigan State and left because they couldn't really make it or they didn't think they could make it. It was that kind of thing.

JOHN ALBISON: I'd like to refer to John Loy's remark on the response to the question asking about letters earned. We recently did a survey of 275 of our graduates at the University of Michigan, interviewing 65 per cent of them and surveying the rest with a mail questionnaire. One of the things we asked them was what they did in high school. We went back and checked high school annuals and found out it didn't turn out that way. Also, we asked the people teaching what professional organizations they belonged to (both by interview and on the questionnaire) and we got a great number of organizations. I sent names to the appropriate organization and on reply it turned out that even with professional people there was a significant difference between the organizations they reportedly belonged to and the ones they actually belonged to. Moreover, there was no difference between the questionnaire and the interview responses, they were consistently lying. I think it's an indication of something we have to watch in any kind of a questionnaire. If you can get it some other way, you will be better off.

WALTER SCHAFER: I'd like to first of all congratulate both Mr. Webb and Mr. Loy, because the study of this has been virtually nil until now. Just one further question which I'd like to direct to Mr. Loy. I think we have to be cautious with regard to comparing the athletes' occupations with their fathers' occupations, I think we have to be cautious about concluding anything about an unusual contribution of athletics to occupational outcome. If you looked throughout the country you would find that the average status range of occupations now to be substantially higher because the whole economic structure has moved up. You could take account of that however, as Duncan did by looking at the descriptions of occupations in 1950 compared to 1925.

LOY: That's a point well taken. I carried out the study last spring with limited funds which ran out in June. Thus, the data reported here were analyzed by hand. However, when I submit my data for computer analysis later this year, I shall attempt to control for the factors you mention as well as several brought forth by Harry. I shall likely use the recent work of Blau and Duncan as a model for my final data analysis. Although I was not familiar with their text when I began my project, I fortunately asked a number of questions identical to those included in their survey. Thus, I can make use of their findings for comparative purposes.

SEYMOUR KLEINMAN: It might be an interesting paper in itself.

LOY: There is no doubt about it. The thing which really needs investigation, however, is the reasons for the extreme secrecy practiced by athletic departments and what means might be the most effective in obtaining relevant materials from athletic files. For example, a number of athletic departments of major universities have carried out their own extensive studies in recent years regarding such matters as grant-in-aids, academic achievement, recruitment, etc., but these studies are difficult to come by. The major problem in my own study was obtaining a list of names and addresses of former athletes at UCLA. I spent a great deal of time discovering that there was such a list and still more time obtaining permission to use it.

JOHN POOLEY: Although in part you've tried to answer the questions just a moment ago by saying that you haven't had sufficient time to look at the data in the way which you would wish, I wonder if you see any indication of possible ethnic background of some of these students. Bearing in mind the paper by Riesman and Denney, there may be some difference according to interest. And a second question, are there any studies going on in any other country that one might compare, or might be relative?

LOY: I obtained information regarding an athlete's religious background, the national origin of his parents and grandparents, whether a language other than English was spoken in the home, and similar questions. Thus, I am sure that I will find ethnic differences among sport groups, but I hesitate to suggest what these might be until I have had a thorough look at my data. However, regarding national origin, I recall that 60 per cent of the fathers of soccer players were foreign born and I know that athletes of Japanese descent were most often found in baseball and wrestling. With respect to religion, I was struck by the fact that a third of the gymnasts came from Jewish families, while athletes from Catholic homes were most prominent in football. One odd finding which I recall is that one-third of the grandfathers of cricket players were Russian born.

As concerns your second question about comparative studies, I must reply that the only work which I am aware of is the study I cited conducted by Dr. Lüschen in Germany and the investigation of Eggleston in England.

KLEINMAN: I think the point he has made, is that the Russians invented cricket!

GREGORY STONE: Just a brief observation. I was impressed with what seemed not to be a close fit, but some sort of a fit between some of my data on spectators and the background of these people in your study. I'm just wondering if you can make some wild inference about the socialization process here.

LOY: I, too, was struck by certain similarities between my data, your own results and the findings of Dr. Lüschen. I don't really know what to conject, however, regarding a socialization process. There does seem to be a relationship between contact sports, such as boxing, wrestling, and football and low SES. This fact might be related to past research which reveals that football players and wrestlers tend to come from large families and that boys from large families tend to have higher pain thresholds than boys from smaller families. However, I am not sure how to tie these odd empirical bits into a theory of socialization.

STONE: I don't know what this means, but there must be some sort of a socialization process. I can't go so far as to think of caste development in sports — I don't dare say that — but it's interesting, the similarity.

CHARLES PAGE: You cannot marry the girl when you are in the movies looking at her.

LOY: My cursory analysis of the returns has led me to form a number of hunches about several aspects of sport, stratification and socialization, but I had best remain silent until I've had a closer look. I can't wait to really get at the data, however.

Brian Sutton-Smith

7. The Two Cultures of Games*

INTRODUCTION

In this paper I wish to take the role of historian rather than the more familiar one of psychologist. Some recent research on children's play seems to suggest that children's imaginative play is not universal. When this is put together with an earlier finding of Roberts and mine, that competitive games are not universal, it leads to some basically new notions about the role of play, games and sports in society.

Let me highlight the significance of these contentions by pointing out that we are just emerging from the era of "universality" in games' scholarship. The systematic study of games at the end of the last century, for example, was devoted largely to demonstrating the universal character of play and game forms throughout the world. Whether games were said by anthropologists to be diffused from some centers of civilization, or to have been autonomously invented, their parallelism was not in doubt. Again when games were studied as survivals of earlier customs, as in folklore, the devolutionary scheme was unilineal. In child psychology, likewise, children's play sequences were said to be atavistically reminiscent of the single evolutionary history of mankind. While each of these grand schemes in anthropology, folklore or psychology subsequently fell into theoretical desuetude, the habit persisted nevertheless of taking it for granted that, at least on the empirical level, children's play and children's games would be in most places much the same. Child psychologists continued to write about the language of play as if there were no foreign languages, while comparative psychologists sought for universal laws of exploration and playful behavior amongst varied species, paying little attention to the implications of species-specific differences. "Universalism" thus persisted as an empirical habit even though the theoretical superstructure had been discredited. Of

---

*Also a University Lecture sponsored by the University of Wisconsin Lecture Committee.

course, the assumed triviality of the whole subject-matter made it difficult for most serious scholars to rise to new theoretical heights without some functional justification (Sutton-Smith, 1968).

Nevertheless, an erosion of this older point of view has been going on apace over recent years. The fundamental import of Huizinga's *Homo Ludens: The Play Element in Culture* (1938), for example, was that the dualistic premise behind the older studies was no longer tenable. Huizinga set out to show that the play element permeates all of culture — that men, in law, business, war and politics act much of the time as do players at their games, with rules, with spatio-temporal confines, with secrecy, with intensity, with voluntariness and with a sense of difference. Which implied that the older view of games and sports as the cast-offs of culture was no longer relevant and had been sustained by the underlying puritan distinction between the serious and the non-serious, between the real and the unreal, between the important and trivial. Games and play could be vestiges only in a culture which degraded such expressive experiences. Huizinga's work implied that men had always been playing and gaming even when they did not recognize it. More recent studies by Szasz, Haley, Berne and Goffman which in various ways illustrate the permeation of gaming strategies throughout social behavior are an implementation and specification of the Huizinga viewpoint. An illustration is Goffman's recent statement that a game is a place where you can test out your courage, your gallantry, your integrity, your composure and your stage confidence without too great a cost. You can keep up your character as society demands, but without ruinous trial and error (1968).

Paradoxically, although Huizinga heralded a new era in thinking about play and games, in which their forms were treated as realities coeval with those of work, he still dealt with them primarily as universals. And it is this assumption that I most wish to protest in this paper.

PLAY AND GAME DEFICITS

In our cross-cultural work Roberts and I had reached the conclusion that the basic forms of competitive games with which we dealt, those of physical skill, chance and strategy and their various combinations were not universal (Roberts and Sutton-Smith, 1966). We found, indeed, that only in the most complex cultures were all forms present — and as these post-neolithic cultures were those that had been the chief focus of Western History and Scholarship, it was natural that some games would have been assumed to be universal. On the other hand if one dealt with less complex cultures, as we had, there were some which had no such games, some which had only games of physical skill, and some which had mixtures of physical skill and chance, or physical skill and strategy. Furthermore these differences seemed to make sense in terms of the many correlates we were able to establish for them. The cultures with no competitive games, which were mainly Australian and South American, were kin homogeneous and very simple. There appeared to be few distinctions in small group life around which ludic contest could profitably develop. The groups with games of physical skill on the other hand were groups in which contesting over hunting and fishing skills were a part of the cultural pattern. The ludic contest seemed related to this function. Again groups with games of chance were nomadic and faced with considerable survival uncertainty. They used religious procedures for decision making (divinatory) purposes. Games of chance were an exercise of the same sort. Groups with strategy were more complex than all the others. There was both advanced technology and class stratification. The games appeared to have been a part of the learning of social diplomacy and military skills amongst the military or priestly elite groups. We saw the games as buffered models of power (character contests in Goffman's more recent terms), within which the child could acquire some of the basic performances required by the adult culture.

Whether or not our various analyses were correct in detail, I think we presented strong evidence for the view that games were cultural inventions (not biological universals). Given the circumstances of mankind their development may have been ethologically probable but it was, nevertheless, not essential. What this meant was that we were required to account for the presence of games in terms of the accidentals of learning, rather than the universals of biology and ecology.

In a way there was nothing strange in this. We are used to thinking of individual differences in play and sports habits and preferences. Yet we have paradoxically tended to combine this recognition with the older one, that play and games are yet universal in form throughout humanity.

My sense of the importance of the finding that games were not universal has been heightened by a new work published this year entitled *The Effects of Sociodramatic Play on Disadvantaged Pre-School Children* by Sara Smilansky (Wiley, 1968). For some time various psychologists working in Head Start programs have been pointing out that such children tend not to play imaginatively. Their play is dominated by sensory-motor and kinetic activity. Smilansky working in Israel with immigrant groups from Asia and North Africa has now documented this fact with these groups. Unlike middle-class children, these children do not indulge extensively in role playing, dramatic play, or imaginative activity. They proceed from motor play to rule games without the symbolic activities which have usually been assumed to mediate between these. So, not only are competitive games not universal, it now appears that imaginative play is not universal either. This is quite a shock. Though we should add that the Smilansky's findings need to be treated with tentativeness until further data are in hand. Questions have been raised about their generality.

In the rest of this paper, I would like to construct a hypothetical picture of what I have termed here the games of two cultures. From the work we have already done on physical game cultures, chance game cultures and strategy game cultures, it will be realized that I should actually be talking about the games of many cultures. I am opting for simplicity at this point, however, because I think there is something very important to be learned by so doing. We are at a point in history when two major cultural game schemes interpenetrate each other with considerable scholarly confusion as attempts are made to reduce one to the other.

ASCRIPTIVE GAME CULTURE

There is one type of game culture, which is the one we read about in Philippe Aries: *The Centuries of Childhood*, which I will, following sociology, label as the ascriptive game culture. Here, as Aries describes, children are not separate from the surrounding adults. Life is always living in a crowd. The families tend to be extended rather than nuclear. The group is dominated by the arbitrary power and control of its leading individuals. Parents tend to give instructions and exact demands without reason or explanation ("Go get the bread. If you aren't home in five minutes I'll murder you." "Don't ask questions.") They expect the children to fight their own battles in the streets.

In these groups, if we can follow Smilansky, when children have grown beyond sensory-motor play (about the ages of two and three years), they imitate the activities of their adults. But their imitative play is not imaginative. They use realistic toy representations (rather than improvised ones), to imitate in very circumscribed ways the behavior of their parents. If they play together it is usually in terms of one child bossing the others. When the others refuse to be the subordinates, the play breaks down. Or the play is in parallel terms in which each child with the same toy does the same thing. In addition their play is strongly object-related; they cannot readily shift to something else, or improvise without the toy. Their spoken language tends to be power oriented or manipulative of others (bring me this, take that away). Words are act and object-oriented. Laughter is aggressive and has a ridiculing function.

Once we get to the age of five to nine years, then we can rely on the record contained in folklore, because the materials that were collected by Newall (1883), Gomme (1894) and the others as survivals of an earlier cultural state, were actually current expressions of this ascriptive cultural state which was being followed by ever fewer people. In this folklore record we find the play of this age period for girls preoccupied with ritual dramatic games in which, with song and dance, the girls enacted the practices of marriage, death and the working life. The majority of these games were central person games. Although rule games, they were not the games of players who were equal before the law, but of a group of players contesting against the ascribed power of the central person. Most customarily the power of the central person consisted in her ability to choose or to exclude the others as marriage partners, the next central player and the like. In parallel fashion the central person games of hiding, chasing, capture and attack played by the boys, centered on the special powers of a central person, to call the player he would chase, to immobilize him, etc. Players were defended from the dangers of identification with this aggressor through counting-out formulae. Around the middle years, 9 through 12, these games gradually transformed into those where the central person could maintain his centrality only through a real exhibition of power (as in King on the Mountain or Bull in the Ring) and later in early adolescence there developed in addition, central person games in which the central figure was a scapegoat to be tricked and made a fool of at the very moment he was being made a King. In an old New Zealand game of the 1890's called the King of the Golden Sword, the new boy who was appointed King, sat on a special perch, was blindfolded, given the duty of knighting his followers; was told to draw the sword through his hand with a flourish and then touch each warrior. Unbeknown to him the sword had been dipped in the latrine. "The Dozens" as played amongst Negro children is an excellent example of the same form.

At about ten years of age also there arose those games of physical skill which were the most widespread of all games throughout the variety of human cultures of which we have record; which means everything from marbles, pitching, athletics, knife games, to spear throwing and racing. As we move back over the past hundred years, however, we do not find the team games as we currently know them (Strutt, 1801). There were team games but they were diffuse teams with few differentiated roles, and with sometimes a powerful leader on each team. They looked like central person games transformed into two teams. Amongst children the games might involve one group attempting to run through the joined hands of another group barring the route in a road cutting. Historically they have involved the members of one part of the village in a struggle for a ball with the members of another part of the village which is the precursor of modern football. A recent copy of the *New York Times* quotes a beautiful example still played in Afghanistan (October 24, 1968, 49):

"The King of Afghanistan sat on a brocade-covered sofa and sipped teas as he watched some of the fiercest, most agile horsemen in Central Asia play a form of mounted football with the carcass of a beheaded calf.

"This gentle pastime is played here every year at this time in honor of the birthday of the king, Mohammed Zahir Shah, who has now turned 54.

"To score in the game — known as buzkashi — all a rider has to do is snatch the carcass from the ground, gallop with it a quarter of a mile down the field, then gallop back and throw it in a chalked circle near the point where he started.

"Grabbing the carcass can be a bit tricky, however, for it weighs 75 to 100 pounds. Also, at the moment the rider leans from his saddle to hoist this weight, several of his opponents' powerful horses are likely to come slamming into his in an attempt to knock the carcass loose.

"For a moment the men and animals shove and heave like a wave on the verge of breaking. Then with shouts and a cracking of whips, one of the horsemen breaks loose from the pack at a hard gallop, somehow throwing a leg over the heavy carcass to hold it to the side of his mount.

"At that instant buzkashi has more than a touch of epic beauty as the horsemen stretch out across the landscape in thunderous pursuit.

"Often, when the lead rider is caught, a tug-of-war results with the carcass stretched between two galloping horses, their riders leaning away at angles of 45 degrees or more to break the opponent's hold.

"That's how buzkashi gets its name. Kashi means pull and buz means goat, calves being only one of several possibilities for the carcass.

"The buzkashi matches sponsored here by the National Olympic Federation for His Majesty's pleasure are as rugged and dangerous a sport spectacle as can be seen anywhere — except on the far side of the mountain barrier called the Hindu Kush, near the Soviet border, where Turkmen and Uzbek horsemen play it without any reference to the rule book the Olympic Federation has attempted to write.

"Here there are 10 men on a side playing on a field with marked boundaries under the supervision of a referee who is supposed to call a foul if one of the players uses such traditional buzkashi tactics as whipping an opponent across the face or pulling him from his horse.

"In the north, there can be 100 men on a side or, so it is said, there can even be no sides at all — each man pitted against the rest. That sounds like certain death, but apparently it isn't for the best horsemen, called chapandaz, survive to play before the King on his birthday.

"One of today's stars, Hakim Pahlavon, has only half of one ear, a minor example of the kinds of injuries a chapandaz can sustain."

Those who are familiar with descriptions of the play of children in the lower socioeconomic strata of this society will recognize similarities. W. F. Whyte in his classic *Street Corner Society,* gives an account of the way in which the dominance of the lower class gang leader affects the scores of the other players, so that while better than him at bowling, they never manage to consistently outscore him. Maas describes the hierarchical character of play relationships amongst lower class pre-adolescents as compared with the egalitarian character of those amongst middle class boys (1951, 1954). But in general accounts of gang life and gang play in modern civilization have focused on these phenomena as if they were rather peculiar reactions to modern circumstances of deprivation, whereas ethnological accounts would suggest that such age-graded and hierarchical play groups are a much older and more general cultural form than the more egalitarian peer groups of modern society. Again if the picture I have presented here makes any sense, it follows that the play patterning thus traced is of a systemic character. Because deprived children cannot play imaginative games, and instead prefer hierarchical relationships involving power and aggression does not mean they are outside of culture. It would seem to mean rather that they are still persisting with cultural forms of far greater antiquity and generality than those that have come to have influence in the Western world.

ACHIEVEMENT GAME CULTURES

In my own earlier studies of historical changes in children's games over the past 100 years first in New Zealand and then later in the United States, I reached the following conclusions:

1. Children today play fewer status games. There is less mention of roles for Kings, Queens, Priests, Aunt Sallys, Brother Ebenezers, Julius Caesars, Dukes, etc. There are fewer Singing Games, Dialogue Games and Parlor Games. While there are remnant circle games, the older line and couple games of marriage have disappeared.

2. Children today show more verbal slickness and smart answers. The verbal elements in games has increased as indicated by the proliferation of joke cycles (Sutton-Smith, 1960).

3. There is less physical aggression in both games and playground than was formerly the case. Fewer penalty games, fewer games prone to cause accidents. Less fighting.

4. Girls show increasing preference for boys' games (Rosenberg and Sutton-Smith, 1960).

5. There is more verbal freedom of expression including verbal aggression than was formerly the case (see 2 above) (Sutton-Smith, Morgan Rosenberg, 1961).

6. There is a greater emphasis on organized games and sports.

7. There is a changing trend away from formal sports and games to informal pursuits (swimming, boating, fishing, skating, etc.) Even the fairly ritualized play-party marriage games have given way to more informal kissing games. The ritualized singing games have been replaced by the more open jump rope games (Sutton-Smith, 1959).

Until recently I had interpreted these various historical changes in games in terms of the increasing use of psychological (symbolic) discipline within the family, the increased emphasis on achievement for girls, and the relatively egalitarian as compared with hierarchial structure of the modern family. These points are not negated by my present analysis, but they do need to be considerably amplified. I might add that in a return visit to New Zealand in 1967, on which I administered the same game lists to several of the same schools that had been used in 1949, one of my chief findings was that the children's responses were much more heterogeneous than had previously been the case.

To understand these historical changes one has to return again to the Aries approach in *Centuries of Childhood*. He suggests, in effect, that childhood as we currently know it was created at the beginning of the modern era (in the Seventeenth Century or thereabout).* The development of the middle class family, the nuclear family, schools, and privacy in daily life were associated with the treatment of childhood as a distinctive period of life. Children became separated from the life going on around them. More recently in a book *The Changing Nature of Man*, J. H. Van den Berg (1964) has argued, in addition, that the child's segregation from the rest of society was also brought about by the scientific revolution in knowledge. The differentiation of knowledge he suggests meant that reality was no longer the same for all men. There were various canons of truth. Men could no longer make judgments in confidence and in terms of immediate perceptual information. The affairs and understanding of adults became increasingly invisible to children. As a result children were, in fact, increasingly innocent. If a child asked a question about green leaves, he could no longer be given an immediate answer in terms of the vernal spirit of Spring, but was given instead some mystifying information about chlorophyll and the conversion of carbon dioxide into carbohydrates. His innocence too was emphasized by his inability to read, his inability to follow adults into that private world of the mind's eye fostered by the development of printing (McCluhan) as well as the heresy of Martin Luther.

In these terms, of course, my playground changes recorded above simply meant that as time has passed, more and more children have acquired at earlier ages some of the symbolic masteries previously restricted to adults, and at some far distant time restricted even more completely to the priestly classes, or to those military leaders playing some form of chess in preparation for battle. So today's children play fewer status (or ascriptive) games, show less aggression, are more verbal, and girls are more interested in games of achievement.

But it would be wrong to pretend that we fully understand this transition to an achievement culture that has been going on these past several hundred years and is now upon us in mass form; although some of those who have studied cultural deprivation have acted as if the deprived had not only a resistance to acquiring middle class American culture, but also no culture of their own. These same scholars have shown a considerable inability to define the essence of that middle class culture itself.

Perhaps children acquire this culture, as Van den Berg implies, by not being given straight answers. Some remedial programs are based on this premise. One of the most successful of such programs has focused on having

---

*One of my students, The Reverend Benedict J. Groeschel of Children's Village, Dobbs Ferry, New York, argues contrarily that the concept of childhood was rediscovered, not invented.

the children discuss situations which did not exist in front of them at the moment. On the other hand, a Freudian might well argue that the real change came with the historical shift from the extended to nuclear families and with the great changes in infant socialization that came about at that time. From the 1550's to the 1750's there was a great shift towards more restrictive forms of infant socialization (oral, anal, sex, dependecy) (Ryerson, 1961). This might well imply that the total patterning of middle class reality became one that directed the child away from immediate impulse satisfaction, towards the fulfillment of distant abstractions ("good behavior") both in behavioral as well as linguistic terms.

If we turn from such possibilities to reports of the development of play and games in middle class Western children, there are some parallels, but the account is not entirely clear. If we follow Smilansky's account and enlarge upon it with Piaget's middle class observations, we get an outline of the development of play in Achievement Culture something along the following lines.

There is no systematic data on the sensory-motor play of infants in the two different game cultures we are here discussing. One's tendency is to grant that even if games and imaginative play are not universal, then at least motor play is everywhere the same. But this is probably not true. There are studies indicating (at least on the case level), that mothers vary a great deal in the extent to which they play with their infants. Some mothers play with their infants' fingers while feeding them, others do a great deal of tickling, lifting, laughing and peek-a-boo. We might expect that such activities would induce a readiness for playfulness; that the alternations, with humor, of motor position and social responses, might well be the precursor behaviors which are antecedent to a later readiness for flexibility on the role taking level. In a four month old baby, for example, laughter is readily evoked by suddenly placing the familiar person's head against the baby's stomach, rather than holding it in the customary position. Eible-Eibesfeldt has contended that the essence of animal play is such a combination of normal behavior sequences in a novel manner (1967). And Hutt (1966) has described the same phenomena amongst four year old children in terms of "transposition of function." One of the faults of Piaget's otherwise excellent account of infant play, is that too much attention is paid to the way in which the play episodes replicate the intellectual structures which they parallel, and not enough to the unique character of the novel combinations that are the essence of play. Though probably the greatest transformation at this age level, one that is discussed by Piaget, and the one to which Freud paid most attention is the transformation from passivity to activity. What we need to know is whether the child is helped towards such ludic flexibility by similar manifestations in the doting parent. My hypothesis would be that the relationship is positive.

By the age of two years we have the ascriptive game children in motor play closely imitative of that of their elders. There is the ludic transformation from passive to active. They now carry it out — instead of just witness-ing it. But this representative play follows in principle most of the sensory-motor play of the earlier motor period. It replicates, but does not transform. Or the transformation is affective rather than structural. Already by this time, as judged by Piaget's records, the middle class child is introducing into his play a greater variety of subject-object, object-object and self-other transformations. He uses a shell for a drinking cup, the same shell for a shovel and for a block. He imitates many people in his play, not just the power figure most immediate to him.

And by the third year the middle class child appears to have gone off into a new structural form in his solitary play — which if we read Smilansky correctly — is not found to any great extent in the ascriptive child's play. Namely, that he introduces various dialogues between characters who takes different roles in his play. There are dyadic and plural social relations por-trayed, and again there is flexibility as the members change over time. By four years imaginary characters enter the play activity, and in some cases even imaginary companions. A recent report from England indicated that middle class mothers felt that the presence of such companions was a good index of their children's developing imaginative powers, whereas working class mothers worried about the children's mental health when such charac-ters made their appearance (*New York Times,* November 3, 1968, 97-99).

Some figures from Smilansky are useful at this point, so that we don't dichotomize these two game cultures too severely. Observing three to five year old children both from achievement oriented middle class groups and from tradition oriented asiatic groups (ascriptive), she scored their play in terms of the following categories:
1. Imitative role play
2. Make believe with objects
3. Make believe with actions and situations
4. Persistence
5. Interaction
6. Verbal communication

It is of some interest that whereas only three per cent of the achievement group showed no play at all, 69 per cent of the traditional group showed no play. The differences in imitative role play were not great with approxi-mately 20 per cent of each group showing play of this sort. On the other hand when compared for sociodramatic play (which involves others, talk-ing, and make believe with situations, etc.) only 11 per cent of the traditional group and 78 per cent of the achievement group participated. The verbaliza-tion differences were equally striking. The achievement group used more words, a greater variety of words, longer sentences, longer statements.

I should perhaps mention that the intent of Smilansky's work was to induce sociodramatic play in traditional children by participating with them and by encouraging them in this play. Her ascriptive group made considerable movement into sociodramatic play as a result of her training procedures. If the relationships between play and cognition are fundamental, her finding has an important implication for Head Start programming (Sutton-Smith, 1967). But the readiness of the children to be triggered off by the example of adults, also suggests that ludic tendencies have something of an innate character, but must be released by appropriate external models.

By four years of age most children are playing alongside or with others. Despite good descriptive accounts of this play by various workers in the 1930's we do not have currently any systematic reports of the varieties and forms of this collective play. This is an imperative need because it seems that increasingly children's later play forms are an extension of this earlier informal play. Through literature we are acquainted with the fact that this has been the case with solitary and intelligent children for centuries. What is now occurring is that a larger segment of the population is more interested in its own solitary and imaginative social play for a longer chronological aged period than was previously the case. Fewer children are jumping the cultural gap from imaginative play, to ascriptive central person play, than used to be the case.

It is not that children today no longer have any experience of chase and capture and the like (though as I have mentioned many of the varieties of these games have gone. There is no more Sally is a Weeping or Mother Mother the Pot Boils Over).

But these more rigid structures seem less important to children whose relationships with parents are also more egalitarian. In traditional culture social life and games appear to have been largely synonymous in early childhood. The cry of "Tag" mobilized and structured social intercourse. The Achievement Culture children by contrast have their social life structured by the group shared fantasies of reading and of television. These children are capable of dialogue. They are not restricted to group action. Verbal humor plays a childlore role that was once taken by action.

The type of rule games with their considerable role complexity which have developed over the past hundred years are apparently the natural successor to this increasing flexibility. The team game of several hundred years ago or of Afghanistan today was that of the mob and the emergent powerful individuals. The game of today (particularly football) is that of a complex organization. While professionals usually settled on particular roles, it is true that the course of development in games throughout childhood requires considerable role flexibility, role exploration and the understanding of the roles of others. This sort of shifting about is a far cry from the relatively fixed statuses of ascriptive cultures.

There was one other finding in my earlier historical study, however, which seems to have even more far-reaching implications, and this was the move away from sports towards informal and individual sports (cycling, fishing, etc.). This was also the major change I found in my New Zealand sample over the past 20 years. Their levels of response were not different, but their heterogeneity was. There were more differences, more diversity.

It is already the case that fewer children are prepared to give themselves to modal activities like football and baseball. It perhaps follows that these team sports will continue to be sustained only as long as there is continued upward mobility of minority groups, but that in due course such modal pursuits of large population segments will give way to a relatively more differentiated picture of play and sports. It is not likely that team sports are doomed, but it is likely they will become the hobbies rather than the avocations of mankind.

Still I don't suppose we should protest if sports cease to be a form of national mania and become recreations.

CONCLUSION

I began by suggesting that at the beginning of our era game scholarship focused on the universality of forms of games and play. My approach and material today has indicated the untenability of that older approach. In addition, however, the data seems to imply that play and games are not as trivial as they were thought to be but are instead part and parcel of the cultural systems within which they function. In turn, the present account of two game cultures (while over-simplified), further modifies unilinear notions of development through play. There are instead a variety of cultural systems of psychological development through play and games.

REFERENCES

Aries, P. *Centuries of Childhood*. New York: Knopf, 1962.

Eibl-Eibesfeldt, I. Concepts of ethology and their significance in the study of human behavior. In Stevenson, H. W., Eckhard, H., and Rheingold, H. (Eds.) *Early Behavior*. New York: Wiley, 1967.

Goffman, E. *Interactional Ritual*. New York: Doubleday Anchor #596, 1967.

Gomme, A. B. *The Traditional Games of England, Ireland and Scotland*. London: Nutt, 1894.

Huizinga, J. *Homo Ludens*. London: Routledge, 1949.

Maas, H. S. "The role of members in clubs of lower class and middle class adolescents," *Child Development*, 1954, 25, 241-251.

Newall, W. W. *Games and Songs of American Children*. New York: Dover, 1963.

Piaget, J. *Play, Dreams and Imitation in Childhood*. London: Heinemann, 1951.

Roberts, J. M., and Sutton-Smith, B. "Cross cultural correlates of games of chance," *Behavior Science Notes*, 1966, 3, 131-144.

Rosenberg, B. G., and Sutton- Smith, B. "A revised conception of masculine-feminine differences in play activities," *Journal of Genetic Psychology*, 1960, 96, 165-170.

Ryerson, A. J. "Medical advice on child rearing 1550-1900," *Harvard Educational Review*, 1961, 31, 302-323.

Smilansky, S. *The Effects of Sociodramatic Play on Disadvantaged Preschool Children*. New York: Wiley, 1968.

Sutton-Smith, B. *The Games of New Zealand Children*. Berkeley: University of California, 1959.

Sutton-Smith, B. "The kissing games of adolescents in Ohio," *Midwestern Folklore*, 1959, 9, 189-211.

Sutton-Smith, B. "The cruel joke series," *Midwestern Folklore*, 1960, 10, 11-22.

Sutton-Smith, B., and Rosenberg, B. G. "Sixty years of historical change in the game preferences of American children," *Journal of American Folklore*, 1961, 74, 17-46.

Sutton-Smith, B., Rosenberg, B. G., and Morgan, E. "Historical changes in the freedom with which children express themselves on personality inventories," *Journal of Genetic Psychology,* 1961, 99, 309-315.

Sutton-Smith, B. "The role of play in cognitive development," *Young Children,* 1967, 6, 361-370.

Sutton-Smith, B. "Games, play and daydreams," *Quest,* 1968, 10, 47-58.

Sutton-Smith, B. "The folkgames of the children." In Tristram P. Coffin (Ed.) *Our Living Traditions.* New York: Basic Books, 1968, 179-191.

Strutt, J. *The Sports and Pastimes of the People of England.* London: Methuen, 1801.

Van den Berg, J. H. *The Changing Nature of Man.* New York: Delta, 1961.

Whyte, W. F. *Street Corner Society.* Chicago: University of Chicago Press, 1931.

I want to begin by saying that I'm tremendously impressed and excited by Professor Sutton-Smith's paper. I have really nothing in the way of criticism. Thus I'd like to build on the paper rather than destroy it. I'd like to suggest that as a sociologist I would begin with society and then work down to games rather than beginning with games and working up to society, which I think is the general direction that Sutton-Smith's paper takes.

Supposing I begin this way. I was present as a graduate student when David Riesman first presented his observations which led to *The Lonely Crowd,* a book that I think has had a profound influence on our society and on sociology. As he was presenting his three well-known types, tradition-directed, the inner-directed and the other-directed character, Ellsworth Ferris got up in the back of the room and in a quavering voice said, "Well, doesn't that remind you of W. I. Thomas' Philistine, Bohemian and creative types of personality?" and I suppose I have to ask Professor Sutton-Smith, doesn't the ascriptive culture and the achievement culture somewhat remind you of tradition-direction, indeed, he uses the term in the paper, and inner-direction, and then what about beyond that, beyond achievement, a point that I'll return to.

For at least a hundred years sociologists have been talking about transitions in society. We can begin with David Riesman's tradition-direction and inner-direction, but in terms essentially of changes in the division of labor in society or really the economic problems of the society. In such societies which are often called tradition directed, the economic problem is one in the sense of subsistence, or if you like, primary industry, in terms of the direct exploitation of natural resources, such as hunting and fishing, with relatively little manufacturing or tooling industries, and that in the inner-directed society we find the rise of manufacturing, and where the problem really becomes one of production of goods rather than the direct gathering of resources, the production of resources. Riesman, in this wonderful way he has of developing catch phrases, points out that with such changes there are also changes in socialization problems, that the problem of socialization and the tradition-directed society is one of succession; simply replacing the various units of the society, while the problem here is one of success as we will find out later, getting ahead. Now, of course, this involves a fantastic change in the division of labor and with the proliferation of occupations in society there are all kinds of consequences but for one thing in the tradition directed society or the ascriptive culture where the problem of socialization is one of succession there aren't very many occupations, although it is very difficult to know because such societies have no written histories, and very often I think people tend to treat such societies as static in character simply because they have no evidence to the contrary. If I had time I could provide some anecdotes which would cast doubt on the relative static character of such societies but assuming this particular sociological myth is correct, in such societies there aren't very many occupations and the problem, as I say, is one of succession — there is a high birth rate, a high death rate, the period of life expectancy is short, and the problem is to get little children to take the place of fathers and mothers, simply to maintain this relatively simple level of organization. As such, as Sutton-Smith has indicated, there really may not be much childhood, maybe there are no children in such societies, maybe there are only infants and adults, and consequently we don't see the proliferation of play and games in many of such societies, that we see in our own complicated society.

Now as the division of labor increases, in the first place the possibility of succession, of following precisely into the father's career, is reduced. There are several reasons for this. One, the occupation moves out of the domestic milieu into a factory and the child simply doesn't get a chance to see what the father is doing so that the possibility of his engaging in what Sutton-Smith calls imitative play with any kind of sophistication is reduced. Second, with this fantastic increase in the division of labor, occupations die and new occupations arise so that, for example, it is best not really to go in training to be a blacksmith these days, although, we do need some of them in some places. It's probably also a good idea not to spend too much time playing cowboy as a child because there is not a great demand for cowboys in the labor force. So occupations die and the problem then, in terms of socialization, if we can think of one consequence of socialization, is training children for occupational participation — I think this is a sort of archaic idea, which I'll come to in a moment — the problem is one of training children not to replace or succeed the parent in whatever occupation is involved, but training the child to select an occupation that he may have practically no familiarity with. Hence, I would suspect the greatly enhanced role of child's play and games in the so-called achievement society or what I prefer to call the industrial society. In short, all I'm saying is simply that with this proliferation of occupations the child simply cannot expect to replace his father in the labor market, let's say the male child, and of course now with women having entered in, I think by 1940, all occupations in our society, including that of garbage collector — they're really getting up there now — the daughter cannot expect merely to replace her mother in a particular occupation. Garbage collection probably will also be obsolete fairly soon. I know that in talking to Buckminster Fuller, who's a marvelously imaginative person, that they are developing large garbage disposals which can be placed in the garage and will chew up jars and cans and everything, as well as just cantaloupe rinds and banana skins and that sort of thing.

So the problem is to get the child to choose. This means the child must try out a variety of occupations in his play rather than just imitate the occupation of a parent, and here you get this proliferation. It is in this period that George Mead developed his notions of socialization. It's interesting that he makes a distinction between play and games. In play, the child presumably imaginatively acts out the role of others or of a particular other, as when he plays school he acts out the role of teacher, or he plays house and he acts out the role of the parent. By the way, it's very difficult to get a child to "play child" in playing house. He plays Indian, cowboy, policeman, and this sort of thing. In taking such roles, according to Mead, in the stage of play he literally gets outside himself and can develop from this other perspective, from this other role, a conception of himself as different from but related to the teacher, the parent, the Indian, the cowboy, the policeman, et cetera.

Now for Mead this isn't enough, because what develops from this stage of play is a highly atomized kind of agglomeration of different selves and Mead then says that the child must somewhere, probably around the age of seven or eight, enter into a different stage, namely the game. The thing that distinguishes play from games for George Mead is that in the game, and he takes baseball as an example, one must take all other roles simultaneously, one must generalize his conception of the other positions on the team and literally take the role of the team and govern his own conduct with reference to his generalized expectations of the entire team. And you can see why this is important. If you take the first baseman, for example, he couldn't say, "Now if I were the second baseman, where would I want the first baseman to be and if I were the shortstop where would I want the first baseman to be and the third baseman, and if this person were at bat and this were the pitcher, and that the catcher," and so on, by the time he had figured this all out the game would probably be over; although we have a player sort of like that on the Twins whose name is Harmon Killebrew, he can hit quite well but whether he can take the generalized role of the team is another question. So, with the stage of the game then the team becomes a synonym, for the community. We can look at communities as teams and the child by analogy then, as taking the role of the entire community and developing a conception of himself from the standpoint of the expectations of that community.

Now this was a time you see, when people lived in communities, when people sometimes died in the same communities they were born in, which doesn't happen too frequently these days, and sometimes they were even buried there; although some small towns are trying to keep people there by asking them the question, "Where are you going to be buried?" It's kind of a morbid way to keep people in the town, but I suppose it does have some influence on some morbid types — I suppose indicating something of the morbid nature of a small town. But, there were a number of communities that developed with the proliferation of occupations. The city at the time I think was characterized probably best by Lewis Mumford as a factory and a slum. The city isn't quite the same at this point. So the point is that play and games in this period of industry, where the primary problem was one of work and production, become a very important part of socialization. But life today isn't the way George Mead saw it. Mead himself was born and spent considerable part of his life in a small town before he went to Chicago. He did very little research, and developed his notions by speculating,

I would guess, about his own childhood. Now, things are of a quite different nature. It doesn't matter so much where one lives anymore, given our fantastic rate of transportation, but more important I think the central organizing economic problem of the society has changed. I think this is what Riesman is saying when he talks about other directions, where, in a sense, we have solved the problem of work in our society. This causes a tremendous amount of difficulty because we believe that work is good and indeed there is enough Protestantism in all of us, including the Catholics, to think that work is really the key to the gates of heaven. And yet the central problem of society has become one of distribution, or from the standpoint of the individual the problem is one of work for consumption and we are really poorly equipped for handling this problem in our society. You can see, by the way, in terms of sports, which in what I call the industrial society, were *played,* while in the consumer society, or the society where the problem is one of distribution, sports are *consumed* and watched. Obviously we are going a bit beyond Sutton-Smith's notion of an achievement society. The problem isn't one really of getting ahead and I think this accounts for some of the discontent of our students because we want them to get down to work and get ahead, but it's really one of getting along. This is C. Wright Mills' happy caricature of the situation.

Now, what are the consequences for socialization? It's very difficult to say; certainly much socialization takes place over the TV as Sutton-Smith indicates in his paper. Kids become what some of us consider to be precocious although there were very precocious young people, perhaps not children, around the 17th and 18th centuries as Aries indicates in his *Centuries of Childhood,* but myths tend to disappear in a society and I think myths are rather important, a thing I'll get to later.

I don't exactly know what's happening to the role of play and games in socialization. I feel that my children have been, in a sense, deprived because they have the TV rather than the radio, and as I think back in my own childhood, I still remember Jack Armstrong. I think I can sing the Hudson High Anthem right now, but what the radio did as opposed to the TV was to permit imagination. You see, one had to fill in the visual void with some conception of what Jack Armstrong must have looked like. Usually these conceptions, these imaginary conceptions, were way off base and perhaps some of you can recall finally having seen some figure on the radio in person and having been completely disappointed by the appearance of this person, like the Lone Ranger, for example. But certainly something is going on and I developed this notion that something is going on in terms of childhood play through observations of Halloween. It was about seven or eight years ago when my patience wore thin in terms of these little beggars coming around every Halloween night holding out their shopping bags — you see it's a consumption problem — and I even became a bit disturbed at myself for being conned into this whole scheme by having to buy the corn candy and so forth that I threw into their shopping bags. But then

I thought, well, after all, either you are a sociologist or you are not, and here is a nice sample of people coming to your door and you might as well interview them. So I interviewed them. They would ring on the door — by the way, interestingly, behind them you know, beyond the shadow shafts cast by my porch light, there were parents, often more parents than there were children, which I also thought was disgusting in terms of my own reminiscences of Halloween — and so I would answer the door and say, "What do you want?" Most of them couldn't say anything — and this made the parents very nervous by the way — and then I said, "Well, do you want — I mean is it trick or treat?" and they'd say "Yah," or something like that and I'd say, "Well, supposing I said 'trick,' what would you do?" Now that evening, out of about thirty children, one said "I don't know," and one said, "I'd go home and I'd get some sand and throw it on your porch." Notice that the means of production are at home now and not in the factory. Another said, "I'd go home and get a water pistol and squirt your windows," which needed squirting, by the way. So the tricks weren't very dire. The rest had absolutely no response, they had no conception of a trick. Tricks are really productions while treats are consumptions. Now when I think back on some of the tricks that I perpetrated in my childhood, my first childhood, they were fantastic productions. In the first place we had the means of production with us, we didn't have to go home to get them, and we made them. We had these little serrated spools that you put on a pencil and rattle the window, and pins that we put in doorbells, and soap — we had a whole kit with us. And moreover we had a hierarchy of values. We decided which people in the neighborhood were most worthy of our productions and which were not so worthy, and one fellow was very worthy of our productions and we detached his evetroughs — right now I don't even have the energy to clean mine out, let alone detach them. We detached his eavetroughs. He had at that time a set of porch stairs that could be moved away and we pulled away his porch steps, and then threw the eavetroughs on his porch, and he responded perfectly by running out and falling flat on his face as we giggled in the distance. Well, this was a fantastic production and we had no conception of a treat.

Now, as I say, there is no conception of tricks really, it's all treats. This last Halloween I was just amazed when I said "Now what do you want?" and one little urchin said "Candy" and grabbed. That was Halloween for that person.

Let me make one observation — that we have gone beyond Marx; for Marx, consumption in a sense was the cost of work. One consumed so that he could work. This was a very important part of Marx's notion, that the tendency would be to pay for work only in terms of the amount it took to provide clothing, food, shelter and reproduction of the labor force. But now work is the cost of consumption, and if you look at ads for occupations particularly in the engineering field you find that people are lured to work with companies not because of the conditions of employment, but because of the amenities that are provided by the company itself and by the location of the company. "Come to our company," and, by the way, factories are beginning to look more and more like ranch houses, while tool shops are found at home in the basement in terms of the do-it-yourself materials; but they say, "Come to our company so you can hunt and fish and play golf." Well, this must have some consequence for socialization in the role of play and games and I think that we need to go beyond the achievement and the notion of an achievement society and fit the contemporary play and games of children into this notion of a society of, as Rostov calls it, of high mass consumption.

I want to make some specific comments on Sutton-Smith's paper. On the first page he made a nice statement that child psychologists continued to write about the language of play as if there were no foreign languages. To get back to some of our earlier arguments I think that sociologists of sport tend to talk about the world as if there were no foreign languages. Thus, for example, we presume a Greek grammar in our attempts to cut up the world, and there is a difference I think between Greek knowledge and what might be called Jewish knowledge, or between cognitive knowledge and carnal knowledge, if you want to put it that way. I think we ought to begin thinking a bit more carnally about problems of sport. For example, when Gerry Kenyon says a proposition — he's distinguishing between a concept and a proposition — consists of a statement of a relationship between two or more concepts, I know Gerry Kenyon doesn't know anything about Turkish. That's why I welcomed Sutton-Smith's observation on this wonderful Afghan game of buzkashi. "Kashi" means pull, and "buz" means goat, and there it is all in one word, and in Turkish, an agglutinative language, it's possible to state propositions with only one word. So we tend to get trapped in this Greek view of the world and in spite of Chomsky's attempts to develop a nice notion of syntactic analysis where I think he really merely is saying that we can translate languages from one into the other, I would say that things lose something in the translation. In other words, what I'm really trying to get at here, I'm very serious about this, is that our grammars very much determine our conception of the world because grammars are rules which tell us how to put things together and, consequently, how to break them up.

I certainly like this observation that children were really rediscovered in 17th century France rather than discovered there as Aries suggests because certainly in periods of Rome and Greece there were children as social identities.

I'd like to comment briefly on the importance of myth for children and I think this is what Sutton-Smith is getting at when he says, "If a child asked a question about green leaves he could no longer be given an immediate answer in terms of the vernal spirit of spring, but was given instead some mystifying information about chlorophyll and the conversion of carbon dioxide into carbohydrates." Why it is I don't know, but I'm convinced that children need myths and I think adults need them too, by the way. We spent a good part of yesterday discussing the way in which we reconstruct our pasts, because it makes it much easier if we build a mythical past for ourselves to live in the present. Thus I'm not surprised in terms of John Loy's data that some sportsmen who lettered in track will report that they lettered in football. It's a very important myth to build and help them live in the present time. But children will often know that myths are in fact myths and almost insist that in spite of their knowledge that they be maintained. I think of my own son, who I'm sure knew there was no Santa Claus by the age of four and I knew that he knew there was no Santa Claus, and he knew that I knew that he knew there was no Santa Claus, but I insisted on playing Santa Claus. I refused to let Christmas morning creep into Christmas Eve the way it does in most houses these days, and I put the kids to bed on Christmas Eve and then I put the presents under the tree and laughed "ho-ho-ho, ho-ho-ho" and so on. And my son enjoyed that; and this was a very important part of his socialization even though he knew that it was his old man who was providing laughter and going through this seemingly nonsensical ritual, perpetuating a myth that nobody believed in.

There's a problem then in terms of Mead's notion of play. Mead uses a very general term "play." I have yet to be able to define "play," by the way. He uses a very general term "play" for what I think is better called "drama." By "drama" I simply mean the misrepresentation of the self and the consequent enactment of the role that is misrepresented. There are two types of drama. One is directly related to socialization. It might be called "anticipatory" drama, where the child plays the role of teacher, of parent, of grocer, and I speak of these kinds of childhood dramas as anticipatory in the sense that they prepare the child to assume roles which he can reasonably expect to enact or encounter in later life, in adult life. So this is a form of preparation for him. But, there is another part of drama which might be called "fantastic" drama, and this gets us into playing cowboys and Indians and pirates, this sort of enactment of roles, that is, the enactment of a role that cannot reasonably be expected to be enacted or encountered in later life. Perhaps Sutton-Smith can tell us, but I know of no study of the consequences of fantastic drama. There are two things that happen. One, through fantastic drama the myths of the society are perpetuated, and by the way, this is what Aries emphasizes in *Centuries of Childhood* when he calls children the most conservative in this sense of all the animals — but I don't think he really likes children very much. Another part of fantastic drama is the creative consequence, the fact that much of what is happening today was anticipated, for example, in the Buck Rogers' comic strip of thirty or forty years ago. I recall playing with a Buck Rogers rocket gun that went "zap." So this problem of myth I think is a very important one, and how to perpetuate it is important.

One last point. Sutton-Smith says that this representative play, this would be anticipatory drama, by the way, follows in principle most of the sensory motor play of the earlier motor period. It replicates but does not transform so that playing the role of grocer is a replication of the role of grocer. I'm not sure about this. Again Mead assumes a sort of open-awareness, that everybody knows everything about the role that he's playing, that when a child plays grocer he really, in fact, knows what grocers are supposed to do. I don't think this follows at all. But also, we all know that some of this drama is really a ruse and that we engage in this drama, as children, really to do something else. I think of playing doctor — and perhaps you've all had the experience as children of playing doctor or nurse — and you know darn well what was in your mind. It wasn't really preparing yourselves to encounter doctors or nurses in later life. This gave you a certain license to explore parts of the body that when you were children were mysterious and also very appealing. The only place that I know where this is mentioned is in Oscar Lewis' *Levita* where the discussion of playing doctor, for precisely this reason is presented in a study of Puerto Rican families in New York and that, to me, is interesting because we find that very kind of calculated play in a highly tradition-directed segment of our population. This suggests then that although these historical notions are interesting and help us organize our perspectives, we don't know very much about tradition-direction and the place of play and games in the tradition-directed society. We know most about play, in what Sutton-Smith calls the achievement society.

DISCUSSION

BRIAN SUTTON-SMITH: I think that last remark was very intriguing because you remember Caillois' *Mask Societies*. He doesn't give any explanation of where the masks come from but he does associate them with these tradition-directed societies and what you are suggesting, and of course, is missing in the Smilansky document and any other record that I know of, is the possibility that what appear as very direct and replicatory anticipatory activities might actually be a preparation for the mask societies if these roles were being used in that covering fashion. I don't know how we'd ever get to such data, but the existence of masks in tradition societies would seem to apply some preparation for it, some preparation for a sort of structured deception.

Let me go back. We have this dialectic going in this group: do you start with Parsons in an involvement theory, or do you work with sports, and now, again, should you be with games or should you be with society. It's a persisting theme in this conference as to the level of discourse on which our problems should be attacked and, of course, it's got quite a bit to do with dualism of the membership of the conference probably. If there's any persistent dialectic in this conference it's this and it's re-echoed again.

Cowboys . . . they are fantastic and they're so persistent, and I suppose what we usually assume is that they are not anticipatory. By the way, they are fading also. What I used to say about cowboys was that the virtue of these fantastic characters was that they, in a sense, did personify the sorts of qualities of manhood, the dispositions of manhood even if not the actual exemplifications which the kid could see, and of course he was always presented with these in the cultural media and so on. I asked last night, too, the question "What is the third society?" and said I felt we were *in* a third society. I like this system, I had forgotten about it. I like the notion of the consumer society. You remember last night I talked about the much greater ease of children today to converse and indulge in a dialogue about what they saw on TV and react with humor to commercials in parody. I find that they are much more capable of free dramatic enactment and caricature of what they see. So this is a part apparently of the behavior of the third society. It's consumer sophistication, perhaps. That's one of the things that impresses me.

With respect, again to your notion of the fantastic, there really hasn't been anything except that there are glimmers throughout the literature. You will find people will note it but ignore it. When you work with studies on gifted children you will often notice that there is more solitary play, more imaginative activity, and they're really referring to this fantastic behavior thing. Kagan and Moss in their *From Birth to Maturity**have a nice relationship between later intellectuality and the child's involvement in model worlds when young, the worlds which he creates himself. To me this is one of the most important findings in the book, but they don't do anything with it at all. I've always felt that a great deal of our adult character persistence, the imaginative worlds we inhabit as adults in a sense have precursors in these sorts of model involvements. So I think we can say we know that there are connections there, but nobody has really thought it worthwhile to study the character of the fantastic world and its shape and form and so on. Well, those are a few of the things that I enjoyed in what you said.

STONE: Could I make just one comment. In terms of this shift, whether it's true or not is another question, but what I want to get at here is we have to consider the historical transformations that are going on in society. I don't know whether these are the transformations. Somewhere Sutton-Smith has a statement that our games are becoming more informal, "There is a changing trend away from formal sports and games to informal pursuits — swimming, boating, fishing . . ." and I'll stop there, I won't say skating — but what's happening here, of course, is that in changes in sport there are mutual transformations of work and play and I would now add drama, having just completed a study of wrestlers. What swimming, boating and fishing are, are, of course, earlier work forms and one of the things that may be happening here in terms of this shift away from the centrality of work to the centrality of consumption is that we begin playing at work, playing at let's say what were once earlier work forms and we begin working

*New York: Wiley, 1962.

at play in terms of professional sports, and this is the kind of thing you talked about.

SUTTON-SMITH: A similar thing perhaps are the very fleeting and informal psychodramas which now occur constantly in little children's activity which do not take on a ritualized form. They don't need it. They seem to be able to do this and react to each other, in caricature, or laugh and make another reaction without it ever being called a game. This is again an indication of sort of a breakdown there.

STONE: Well, I don't know whether they don't need it or don't get it, that's one thing. Whether it's happening with the children or whether it's happening with the parents, they don't seem to be involved so much in rituals.

SUTTON-SMITH: Well, let me give you a reaction — I was talking to a professor of English a few weeks ago and he was recounting a game he played and it really struck a chord of recognition in me. He played this game: The kids next door would come in and they'd sit down and he'd say, "I wonder why all the houses down the street are green," and the kids, you know, the three year olds would look at him and the four year olds would, and by five years of age they would say, "Yes, and those ones over there are purple," and so on. In other words, they caught on and this struck a recognitory note in myself because I've always done this from the very beginning of playing with my children. I've always enjoyed playing jokes with my children, above anything else. Playing most games is a bore, but making something, making the world different than it seems and pretending and reacting to a word with its other meaning has always seemed to me the most exciting and enjoyable thing I did with my children. Now here I am only using myself as a case study. But when this other person said that that was what he did, I immediately recognized that this is what in effect I had been doing, ever since my children were young. I wonder if this in itself isn't sort of a preparatory introduction, a little bit like Smilansky. But what we in a sense are saying is that the world we live in now is a world of intellectual differentiation and the ability to see any particular thing in many different ways and to enjoy this change in perspective is a sort of play. This is our recognition of the way the world is, and is going, and this is the thing that we've been doing in a semiconscious way with our children. Perhaps that tells us something about the world of play. That is what I see in the kids themselves and the children they bring home. Of course, they are their peers and they come from similar sorts of professional homes and so on. They show this same sort of an enjoyment of varying perspectives.

GÜNTHER LÜSCHEN: I found the comments of Dr. Stone very interesting indeed, but I think, however, that you did not complete your comment that you should start off with society and not go into games.

STONE: And then go into games.

LÜSCHEN: Yes. With regard to your comments on the Halloween

situation, could it also be that it's just that this particular material, this type of game, has changed positions and that maybe achievement or productivity is now expressed somewhere else? For example I have just observed with my children, who are very early in this culture, a certain competition for productivity based on who collects the highest number of candies in the neighborhood, so it may well have a shift.

Yesterday I also had some similar problems when you, Dr. Sutton-Smith, made the remarks that the interest in football was fading among higher status groups and in a way implicitly seemed to infer from that that in general the interest in competition is fading.

SUTTON-SMITH: I think it depends on what sort of socio-economic groups you are talking about. These are speculations and I don't really know, but you have to raise the questions because it's like the stuff that kids play. Nobody is really looking at this formal material in any society. It's the same situation.

LÜSCHEN: Well, okay. I just wanted to say at this point that what you very often would conclude from that is that they have no interest anymore, but it may well be that certain other games now replace on that level the former interest in football, for instance.

SUTTON-SMITH: Yes, this is what I found. In the New Zealand study the kids were playing games still, but it was just that they were more widely dispersed.

LÜSCHEN: The general achievement orientation that we have found traditionally in work, seems also to be creeping quite strongly into leisure, and I would for instance, see the increase in interest in sport indicating very much this type of shift, so that now you have to achieve in leisure time and have to produce enough somewhere to secure your status.

STONE: I think your point is well taken that I, I think, wrongly emphasized the too close connection between achievement and work because certainly one can achieve in consumption or play or any other area of life.

REX BILLINGTON: I was interested in Dr. Stone's comment about the parents lurking in the background at Halloween and I began thinking it seems to me that there is an increase in adult participation in children's games or at least there is more emphasis on games that the whole family play. Do you see this as having any other sort of implications for children's play?

STONE: Yes, I think that there is something about Riesman's notion, also, about calling the consumer society the homogenized society. He talks about the homogenization of the sexes in the age grades. Charles Winick, for example, had an article fairly recently in the *Antioch Review* called "Dear Sir or Madam, As the Case May Be." It's quite possible, and this is speculation, that with this homogenization of the age grades where you have fifty year old boys and girls, that maybe the children will disappear again. It makes a little bit of sense in terms of Sutton-Smith's observations on the increasing rationalization for the childhood experience, and so on.

SUTTON-SMITH: Yes, I think we have a developing family game. Children and parents today share ambivalences about each other and psychological information puts them in the business of having many choice points. It's not only the parents, it's the kids. It's amazing how psychologically sophisticated many nine and ten year old kids are, having grown up in a home where they have psychological coinage going around all the time. Now I don't think anybody studies whether it's just words, but in fact I think there is no question that children show a great deal more insight. I know that my wife and I are sometimes surprised by being called "children" by our oldest daughter, and she's been doing this since she was nine or ten and she would call it what it was in terms of the conflicting feelings of my wife and myself about something. You know, you sit there and think "My God, I've a psychotherapist in the house!" The problem with this, if we are going to go back histronically, is as Aries points out, that there isn't any restriction on sexual information or anything else. The whole thing is open. Are some things going to be left out or is the beginning of the hippie movement an indication that even sex is not going to be left out in the long run? These are interesting possibilities in the family game.

Harry Webb

8. Professionalization of Attitudes Toward Play Among Adolescents

In the transition from communal-agrarian to urban-industrialized society, "achievement" criteria are presumed to replace "ascription" ones as a basis for the allocation of positions and the distribution of rewards. The urban-industrialized society, based as it is on technological knowledge and a consequent division of labor, presumably requires a distribution of roles, at least in the economic and political institutions, based on qualifications of training and ability, and not necessarily on family background. "To the swift goes the prize," goes the saying, indicating not only the constant connection between sport values and those of the economy, but the emphasis on individual differences in ability, training, and desire, and their consequences for influencing excellence presumably rewarded in a free competitive atmosphere. Involved in the notion, endemic to Western urban thinking, are the components of skill, equity, and victory.

Since those institutions most isomorphic in their structure and operation to society's dominant ones may bask in the glow of the latter's prestige, stand protected by their power, and be promulgated by their interest, it is no surprise that sport, given its considerable popularity, reflects in its operation this inviolate trinity, and thus provides to the rationalization and defense processes of the economy, which dominates Western society, a ready object example for illustrating its most highly touted values at work: fairness, skill, and victory. And by useful implication, it transfers both success of value implementation and even language of description to its own more complex operations. Thus, willy-nilly, and later partly by public-relations design, sport becomes a ready vehicle for making analogies favorable to the economy, and those in simple panegyrics which glowingly describe its activities.

Therefore, in part due to the increasing rationalization of the problem solving process and the consequent increase in the complexity and size of its productive units combined with an increasing concentration of wealth, these values, as they occur in the economy, become less readily recognizable in both the fact of their existence and the success of their implementation, and so reference to a simpler network increases in importance; particularly reference to one in which demonstration of superiority, awarded by victory, and based on skill in an atmosphere of equity, is clearcut and unequivocable. And largely for that reason the frequency of analogies to sport structure develops in the self-descriptions of both businessmen and business.

The success of the analogy is based on the fact that it is (like most cliches) partially true: to some extent, at least at the lower levels of business and industrial hierarchies, and particularly in those demanding extensive technological training, allocation to positions is based on skill, and rewards are to some lesser extent, based on success. And the same goes for sport. The crucial difference is in the *extent* of such allocation and reward processes existing in the two, and when this is considered, sport develops it largely as fact, but in business it appears primarily as *ideology;* thus the neat fit of the two, and their reflecting, or mirroring connection otherwise assumed in the sparse commentary on that relation.

Sport *is* a reflection, in that sense, as it provides in fact in one institution what is essentially ideology in another. But skill, fairness, and victory do not exist as a particularly harmonious tandem, especially when the third (read "success") increases in importance, as it must in a society emphasizing its primary standing above most other values. Since skill may produce it, and equity may actually inhibit it, it may reasonably be expected that the older a person gets in such a system, the greater the value he places on skill (in this sense it includes "training"), the less the value on equity.[1] Thus fairness can be viewed as a sometime limitation on winning, while skill is ordinarily not.

So that achievement criteria, characterizing the industrial society's at least ideological method of allocating positions and distributing rewards, in an emphasis on its desired end, success, may in the process undermine part of its basis, i.e., equity or fairness. It should be clear that competition has as a constituent part the equality, except in matters of skill and strategy, of any competitors. They are to begin the contest without advantage, except in those matters of skill and strategy, to ensure not only a clearcut victory, but a "deserved" one, based on genuine superiority in whatever quality is under test. Much the same thing goes on in the scientist's attempt to "control" otherwise "intervening" variables in demonstrating the effects of a

---

[1]See Kingsley Davis, "The Sociology of Parent-Youth Conflict," *American Sociological Review,* 5(August, 1940), p. 523. This is probably why the son calls the father "cynical," and the father calls the son "unrealistic." "Don't argue (with your superiors)," he tells the son (translated as "forget about principle," i.e., equity), "get the degree (or training or whatever else may be instrumental in the son's achievement of "success")."

selected one on another. "Fairness" guarantees the control and lack of effect on outcome of such "intervening variables."

The changes in the relations between the members of the trinity can be observed in the rationalization of play itself, as it grows progressively formalized over the play life of any given child. That is, the child's activities themselves become more formalized, more rationalized, as he makes the jump from jacks to linebacker. But concomitant with that structural change is a change in attitude, one progressing from an emphasis on "fairness" to one on "skill," as the admission policy to play activities changes from ascription to achievement criteria.

It may seem obvious to state it, but it should be clear that it is precisely this change which makes possible later effective participation in the economy. Thus sport and economic structures are related not only on the basis of shared values, largely fact in one and ideology in the other, but sport experience additionally makes an important contribution, to this point largely ignored, by providing a basis for attitudes and beliefs appropriate to later adult participation, in politics as well as in the economy.

This contribution not only culminates in justification of a distribution process existing in name only, one in which goods presumably go to the worker based on the importance of his functional contribution (his "skill")[2] but it diminishes the emphasis on "equity" (an equal starting point), and increases that given to "success." It may be the case that it is in part because of this early experience, and its extension to much larger and more complex institutional arrangements, that considerable opposition is marshalled, e.g., against attempts to reduce discrimination in such areas as jobs and housing, the expressed argument being "skill deserves rewards," the unexpressed reason being "equity may actually inhibit success." No child escapes this experience, although some are more subject to its strictures than others (for example males over females, and Catholics over Protestants). Thus play experience in play institutions prepares the young for later participation in an "achievement" economy and a "democratic" polity, but its contribution may be at odds with that ordinarily asserted, and asserted in terms of the components of "sportsmanship" whose major constituent, it should be emphasized, is "fairness."

In any case, the notion of "equity" surrounding "child's play" may be undermined by the desire for success, growing with the rationalization of the activities themselves, with increased emphasis on the element of skill at the expense of the element of fairness.

"Child's play" is child's play because it is simple, has relatively little

---

[2]Kingsley Davis and Wilbert E. Moore, "Some Principles of Stratification," *American Sociological Review*, 10(April, 1945), p. 242. The authors connect reward distribution and the skill-training combination as the way in which "more qualified individuals" are encouraged to take the "more responsible" positions in society. Without differential rewards, society would not motivate its "better people" (my quotes) to take the more important positions. Thus rewards presumably go to those with the highest skill, training, and apparently desire. Though it's not intended, this appears to be a "scientific" defense of the *status quo*, and as a result, this aspect and others precipitate a veritable barrage of often trenchant criticism.

organization, allows anyone to play, and offers few rewards based on measurable differences. It is in this sense that such play emphasizes ascription criteria: admission is determined by particularistic principles in involving notions of "likeability," "neighborhood residence," and so on, so that the question of skill is incidental, and often, at the earlier ages, virtually unrecognized. Not particularly consistent with those criteria, but present notwithstanding, is the notion of fairness which stands paramount in the child's approach to play. For this reason he needs few rules, often making them up as he proceeds, and no referees; he is capable, given his fairness, of enforcing them himself. Too, the very simplicity of his activities makes rules and enforcers superfluous. But with the emphasis on success, which he meets most formidably in his first formal experience, in the classroom with its institutionalized competitive framework, and there at about the fifth and sixth grades, skill begins to take precedence. Thus the transition from "child's play" to games, and then to sport, involves increasing complexity and rationalization of the activities and increasing professionalization of attitudes. By "professionalization" of course is meant the substitution of "skill" for "fairness" as the paramount factor in play activity, and the increasing importance of victory.

This rationalization process affecting the structure of activity and developing from childhood through adolescence and into early adulthood is obvious if not well remarked, but the process of professionalization of attitude, that is, the change in perception of play and approach to it, is not so obvious, and in my reading, only rarely remarked. And it is that process of professionalization of play attitude which constitutes the focus of this paper.

The items discussed so far clearly involve a change in those attitudes over age, but it is a change which may vary along certain other dimensions as well, particularly sex, family life style, religious preference, and race; although it is also clear that exposure to sports in the mass media may affect those attitudes too, especially as the mass media increase their impact on the socialization process. The first four of these factors are examined in the paper.

With these considerably extended thoughts in mind, an opportunity to test some of them came along when H.P.E.R. people at Michigan State University were invited to develop a new physical education program in the public school curriculum at Battle Creek, a middle-sized city in southwestern Michigan. To get as much information about the students enrolled in the system as possible, they asked me to sample the attitudes of those students toward the physical education program then in effect. The opportunity was there, and with the cooperation of both public and parochial school officials, we obtained a random sample of both systems ($n_1 = 920$, $n_2 = 354$), stratified by grades (3, 6, 8, 10, and 12), and administered a questionnaire developed for the study in the fall of 1967. The data presented here is derived from that Battle Creek survey.

Although a number of scales were developed for the study, only one is of interest here, the three item "play scale" which attempts a ranking of items "important" in play activity, and then a scale constructed from the permutations of ranks measuring degree of "professionalization." Two others were developed for the study, but are not discussed here, one designed to differentiate preferences for individual and team type activities, the other designed to distinguish "reasons" for participation, ranging from "companionship" to "prestige," thus indicating in another context, degree of professionalization.

Needless to say, those scales achieving the greatest simplicity in administration and both simplicity and specificity in construction, are probably more often than not the best in differentiating capacity, reliability, and (though the question is moot) validity. That is, the simpler and more differentiated the items, the greater the likelihood they will first be understood, and then second responded to accurately, both increasing the likelihood they will accurately measure whatever social quality the investigator has in mind. In addition, those scales identified with a specific social context are more likely to define attitudes actually in operation in that context. To the extent scales are generalized from such specified context, they may reasonably be expected to lose not only meaning, i.e., validity, but also their explanatory value.

Thus scales measuring, e.g., general "alienation," apart from a specified context, often have little meaning since, e.g., a person may be reasonably alienated from political institutions while effectively participating in family and educational ones, as in the case of some of our present undergraduates. And although persons may be firmly entrenched in the economic sector, such as H. L. Hunt and some John Birchers, they may feel considerable alienation from other major institutions, in this case the democratic political process. Thus when scales become so generalized that they attempt to differentiate attitude positions across very different social contexts, they may not only sacrifice meaning, and therefore usefulness, but may produce, as they sometimes do, conflicting and even contradictory results, thus sacrificing explanatory power as well.

Thus, in spite of their popularity, such over-generalized scales may have only limited utility, since attitudes appear to be a function of experience in given social networks, and ones not therefore generalizable over institutions sharply contrasted in values and organization.

The particular scale employed here does appear to have the virtues of simplicity and specificity, of measuring factors in a defined social situation, namely play activity. On the other hand, it should be clear that to the extent play intervenes in, or spills over into, other areas, the attitudes related to that context may transpose as well, and therefore the scale may have that much increased application. The scale is developed from the following questions, the first appearing on the questionnaire for grades three and six, the second for grades eight, ten, and twelve. As is clear, they are identical in content, but are differently designed to facilitate correct answering among two different age groups.

It should also be clear that they are intended to identify the members of the trinity, skill, equity, and victory, and provide a means for testing their relations with each other, and the effect on their ranking of the four independent variables, age, sex, religious preference, and father's occupation.

What do you think is MOST important in playing a game?

Place a "1" next to the one you think is MOST important.

Now place a "3" next to the one you think is LEAST important . . .

——— to play as well as you can

——— to beat the other player or team

——— to play the game fairly

What do you think is most important in playing a game?

Number the items below from 1 to 3, starting with the one you think is MOST important (1), and finishing with the one you think is LEAST important (3) . . .

——— to play it as well as you are able

——— to beat your opponent

——— to play it fairly

Although the items are only at a nominal, i.e., categorical level of measurement, their forced ranking on a "greater importance" basis provides an ordinal level of measurement subject to higher order statistical analysis. The permutations of the three items taken together are six and range from lesser to greater professionalization in terms of the differential ranking of "play," "beat," and "fair"; thus the scale derived achieves an ordinal measurement level as well.[3]

The permutations are presented in the following table:

TABLE 1. PERMUTATIONS OF ITEMS

Play Orientation			Professional Orientation		
1	2	3	4	5	6
Fair	Fair	Play	Play	Beat	Beat
Play	Beat	Fair	Beat	Fair	Play
Beat	Play	Beat	Fair	Play	Fair

---

[3]Ordinarily, for this level, examination of central tendencies would dictate the use of an appropriate non-parametric statistic such as Mann-Whitney U, but since its "power efficiency" relative to the t-test is about 96 per cent, preliminary runs contrasting both showed practically no difference in rejection of null hypotheses, and the t-test presented the possibility of figures graphically demonstrating differences based on calculated "means," the t-test was thus understandably employed. This seems to be an acceptable procedure, and in practice is the one most frequently employed.

The mean rank of the scale items by grade (age) is shown for males in Figure 1, and for females in Figure 2.[4] The contrast between male and female ranking by grade is demonstrated in Figure 3, an overlay of Figures 1 and 2. Kruskal-Wallis analysis of variance is significant at the .02 level or

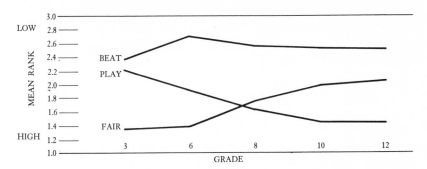

FIGURE 1

MEAN RANK OF SCALE ITEMS BY GRADE:
WHITE MALES ONLY

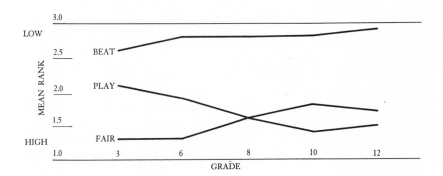

FIGURE 2

MEAN RANK OF SCALE ITEMS BY GRADE:
WHITE FEMALES ONLY

[4]Since black children are predominantly Protestant, and we are interested in the effects of religion, and are predominantly blue collar in occupational background, and we are interested in the effects of occupation, and since they differ significantly from whites on both these factors and others, they have been eliminated from the analysis, so that the effects of race will not influence the effects of religion and occupation.

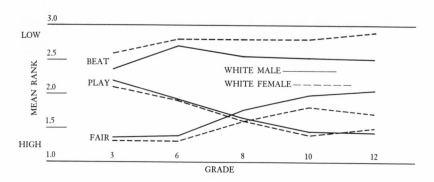

FIGURE 3

MEAN RANK OF SCALE ITEMS BY GRADE AND SEX

less for the ranking of each item by grade for both sexes. The greatest degree of difference occurs in the changing importance accorded both "play" and "fair" from grade three to grade twelve, thus supporting the assertion regarding the fact and the nature of that change discussed earlier in the paper. At the same time, although males accord significantly greater importance to "victory" following the drop in emphasis at grade six, females significantly rank it at lower levels as they mature. This would seem to be consistent with the different experience both groups acquire with respect to ascriptive and achievement criteria. For the males, expected job experience will dictate some submission to the latter, one of whose constituents is "success," thus the emphasis on it illustrates its importance in attitudes developed in play by age, at the same time it illustrates its utility in providing attitudes consistent with later adult activity. For the females on the other hand, such participation is neither as likely nor as expected, with a prime concern being choice of husband, and, notwithstanding the well-meant advice of parents, this is likely to occur on ascriptive bases rather carefully cultivated, and based on such items as looks, personality, height, body type, and so on.

Differences between the sexes at each grade level are most pronounced for that "beat" or success factor. Except for the sixth grade, these differences are significant at the .01 level or less. Although differences are systematic, that is, females consistently rank fair at higher levels than males, the variation in the line describing change is nearly identical, with both sexes ranking it lower by age. But only·in the tenth and twelfth grades is the difference statistically significant. The emphasis given skill by females is surprising to say the least. At every point on the line except the last, the twelfth grade, females consistently rank play higher than males, although at no point is the difference statistically significant. In any case, both sexes, tend, as they grow older, to give diminishing importance to fairness and increasing stature to skill, the first losing its primacy in the eighth grade to the second, the second attaining that eminence clearly at the expense of the component "fairness."

For both groups, a major jump occurs between the sixth and eighth grades, and it is during this period that they make the transition from the relative community atmosphere of the grade school to the society atmosphere of the junior high, where because of larger numbers, anonymity increases, and contact with individual teachers tends to fall off, as they change from a single classroom situation to one in which there are different rooms for each subject. With the decrease in contact, there is usually greater reliance placed on universalistic criteria in evaluating the standing of students; and this seems to be indicated by the increase in the ranking given the skill component. Skill is of course a major element in the universalistic approach, and the students' experience with its increased emphasis in the more formalized school situation, is probably related to the change in attitude in regard to play. In addition, play forms themselves have become more formalized, and admission to socially approved forms is increasingly based on those universalistic elements, and thus operates as an additional factor in the improved standing given to skill.

Figure 4 illustrates the gradual rise of both groups on the professionalization scale, with males rapidly increasing the distance between the sexes after the sixth grade, those differences statistically significant at the .01 level or less. Table 2 provides the same information, but for males only, and

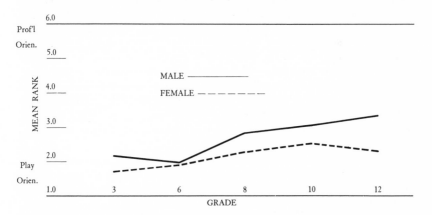

FIGURE 4

PLAY SCALE MEAN SCORE BY GRADE AND SEX

demonstrates more clearly the very considerable change in attitude toward play as age increases.

TABLE 2

PROFESSIONALIZATION OF ATTITUDE BY GRADE IN
PROPORTIONS: MALES

Scale Position	Grade				
	3 (83)	6 (94)	8 (76)	10 (131)	12 (88)
1-2 (low)	78.2	72.4	31.6	28.2	19.3
3-4	12.1	20.2	52.6	48.1	58.0
5-6 (high)	9.7	7.4	15.8	23.7	22.7
	100.0	100.0	100.0	100.0	100.0

Chi square $= 112.48$, $p < .001$

Thus it appears clear from the data that the hypotheses regarding the gradual professionalization of attitudes operating within play, the diminishing importance of fairness as a factor in the play situation, and the concomitant increase in importance of the skill factor, as age increases, receive rather substantial support.

Clearly, age and sex are important factors then in the differential ranking accorded the play components under discussion. But religious and occupational background differences appear to be important as well. The two are to some extent interrelated, but the nature of this possibly compounding aspect can be ignored for the time being while we consider the influence of religious preference, on its own grounds, as its affects differential ranking of the scale items.[5]

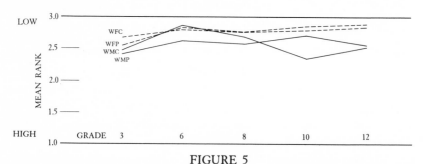

FIGURE 5

BEAT MEAN RANK BY GRADE, RELIGION AND SEX

[5]Public and parochial school Catholics have been combined for this analysis. Although differences between them occur, with parochial school Catholics somewhat more professional in attitudes than public school ones, their trend lines on the ranking dimensions are very similar and differ not so much with each other, as they both differ in the same direction from Protestants. Thus nothing is affected in the contrast with Protestants by the combination. The differences mentioned, with respect to variation by degree of "authority" are examined in another, but unpublished, paper.

Figure 5 not only demonstrates the previous distinction in ranking between the sexes on the "beat opponent" or "success" item, but it demonstrates the difference among males, occurring along religious lines, in its ranking. Up to the eighth grade Protestant males rank it higher, but after that, with some modification, Catholic males rank it somewhat higher. For the males, only the differences at the sixth and tenth grade are significant, but what has occurred between those ages is a reversal of emphasis. Figure 6 illustrates the differential ranking on the skill factor with Catholic males and females tending over age to rank it somewhat higher than their Protestant counterparts. The result is, that by the twelfth grade, both Catholic groups rank it significantly ·higher than either Protestant group. As before, the increasing importance accorded skill, tends to develop at the expense of fairness. Figure 7 indicates this transposition, with differences in ranking occuring between the sexes, but in both cases, within the sexes, Catholics rank it lower than Protestants. These differences develop as trends after the sixth grade are statistically significant by the tenth grade.

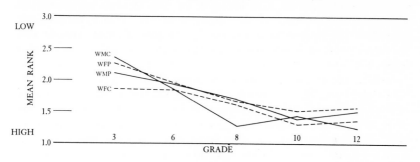

FIGURE 6

PLAY MEAN RANK BY GRADE, RELIGION AND SEX

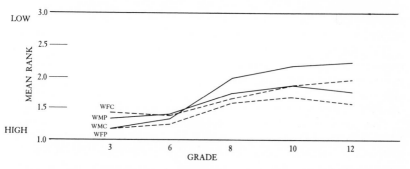

FIGURE 7

FAIR MEAN RANK BY GRADE, RELIGION AND SEX

What seems to be happening is the pounding of another nail in the coffin of the "melting pot" notion dear to the American heart; which can be maintained without fear of contradiction, in that heart of hearts, with the contradictory notion, as it is conveniently employed, of the "pluralist" system; both by intellectuals as well as their self-described "down-to-earth" critics. Cleavages do exist in our society along religious, as well as class and ethnic lines, and our refusal to admit them is in part responsible for much of the dissatisfaction in our political and economic systems today. Whether any given "minority" actually experiences discrimination or not is incidental, compared to its conscious perception of a distinct identity, and one which it is prepared to promulgate and defend. For example, part of the Negro's increasingly well-publicized difficulty is that, unlike the religious aspect, he cannot promulgate his difference, and he is hard put, given his lack of financial resource and political power, to defend it. On the other hand, class and religious groups can do both.

At the earlier ages, excepting differences along color lines, these variations are not nearly so pronounced, since they depend on socialization in a given context, and this is a function of age. Too, these differences depend on participation in rather formally developed social networks, and the consequent exposure to variations in dogma and belief, both again a function of age. So it's not until they are older, that these developing variations affect things like the play disposition.

To the extent the group views itself as the subject of discrimination (and whether it is or not is beside the point, since such assertions have obvious value in promoting lasting commitment and current solidarity), it can be expected to emphasize the value of success, and its attainment, as concrete proof of its worthiness and even superiority. And as has been demonstrated, as emphasis on success increases, there is a corresponding emphasis on the importance accorded the skill factor. Only those groups convinced of their superiority and worthiness can afford the relative luxury of an emphasis on equity and fairness, since in a way, they view themselves as already possessors of "success." There is considerable support of this assertion in addition to the quite convincing data presented here; thus, for example it substantiates once again the frequent finding in political science and sociology of the over-representation of professional (and thus prestigious and to lesser extent well-paid) groups among those characterized by "liberal" values, and their membership in such organizations as the American Civil Liberties Union.

Thus the differential emphasis on both skill and fairness, and to a lesser extent, on success (between males), may be a result of the developing consciousness of "minority" status based on religious difference. This is strongly suggested by the fact that such differentiation develops only after the sixth grade, and then at about the time formal participation in religious activities seriously begins, and awareness of religious difference begins to grow. Figure 8 trenchantly illustrates this difference in variations in the professionalization

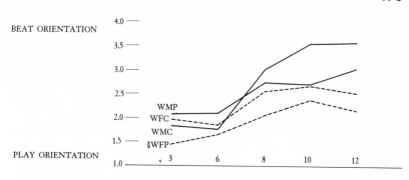

FIGURE 8

PLAY SCALE MEAN RANK BY GRADE, RELIGION AND SEX

of play attitude developing after the sixth grade. It is clear that the effect by sex is not the same, with females increasing by degree but less so than the males. In both cases the mean rank of Catholics is higher than their Protestant cohorts. But what is most marked is the steep and continued rise of the Catholic males' curve which climbs precipitously in the period between the sixth and eighth grades, continuing to the tenth and leveling off by the twelfth. The Protestant male increase is marked as well, but not nearly to the extent of that of the Catholic male. Although the trend is clear, statistically significant differences between Protestant and Catholic male occur only in the tenth and twelfth grades. But the differences are clear, and are probably associated with the growing awareness of minority group status, and a consequent concern with success as a mitigating factor to that status, resulting in a rapidly diminished concern with fairness or equity and more pronounced emphasis on skill. To that extent it can be argued that the Catholic male is more rapidly and more completely socialized to achievement criteria and to participation in the industrial economy. This of course is an attitude developing in the play situation, but with obvious consequences for other kinds of participation. It is in this sense that play experience does provide an arena for first learning, and then experiencing, value and behavior patterns appropriate to participation in other institutional sectors, most particularly of course, the economy.

Introduction of the occupational background factor does tend to delete statistical significance for differences based on religious variation among white males, grades eight to twelve, but the tendencies described in the foregoing section remain consistent. This is because occupational background does appear to have systematic, though not statistically significant, effect on item ranking. Though there is no statistical significance to the variation between this group of Catholics and Protestants on occupational background, as demonstrated in Table 3, it is clear that among this group Catholics are over-represented at the upper occupational levels.

TABLE 3

OCCUPATIONAL BACKGROUND BY RELIGION, WHITE MALES,
GRADES EIGHTH THROUGH TWELVE

Religion	Occupational Background			
	Blue Collar	White Collar	Professional	
Protestant (131)	48.9	27.5	23.6	100.0
Catholic (122)	36.0	30.4	33.6	100.0

Chi square = 4.79, n.s.

If occupational background is controlled, as in Tables 4, 5, and 6, statistical significance, at least as determined by chi square, is deleted, although as above, the differences remain, and are systematic in direction:

TABLE 4

PROFESSIONALIZATION OF PLAY ATTITUDE BY
"BLUE COLLAR" OCCUPATIONAL BACKGROUND,
WHITE MALES, GRADES EIGHT THROUGH TWELVE

Religion	Scale Position			
	1-2 (low)	3-4	5-6 (high)	
Protestant (61)	36.1	50.9	13.0	100.0
Catholic (38)	21.1	52.7	26.2	100.0

Chi square = 4.00, n.s.

TABLE 5

PROFESSIONALIZATION OF PLAY ATTITUDE BY
"WHITE COLLAR" OCCUPATIONAL BACKGROUND,
WHITE MALES, GRADES EIGHT THROUGH TWELVE

Religion	Scale Position			
	1-2 (low)	3-4	5-6 (high)	
Protestant (31)	35.4	45.2	19.4	100.0
Catholic (31)	16.1	63.8	16.1	100.0

Chi square = 3.74, n.s.

TABLE 6*

PROFESSIONALIZATION OF PLAY ATTITUDE BY
"PROFESSIONAL" OCCUPATIONAL BACKGROUND,
WHITE MALES, GRADES EIGHT THROUGH TWELVE

Religion	Scale Position			
	1-2 (low)	3-4	5-6 (high)	
Protestant (27)	22.2	63.0	14.8	100.0
Catholic (37)	2.7	62.1	35.2	100.0

*Chi square is not computed for this table since more than 25 per cent of the categories have expected frequencies less than five.

TABLE 7

PROFESSIONALIZATION OF PLAY ATTITUDES BY
OCCUPATIONAL BACKGROUND, WHITE PROTESTANT MALES,
GRADES EIGHT THROUGH TWELVE

Occupation	Scale Position			
	1-2 (low)	3-4	5-6 (high)	
Blue Collar (61)	36.1	50.9	13.0	100.0
White Collar (31)	35.4	45.2	19.4	100.0
Professional (27)	22.2	63.0	14.8	100.0

Chi square = 2.64, n.s.

Thus, although statistical significance is deleted, the differences are clear and remain in the predicted direction. That occupation also appears to affect standing in degree of professionalization is indicated by Tables 7 and 8, where this time religious background is controlled. Again, though the differences are not satistically significant, they are consistent in direction for both Catholic and Protestant males.

TABLE 8

PROFESSIONALIZATION OF PLAY ATTITUDES BY
OCCUPATIONAL BACKGROUND, WHITE CATHOLIC MALES,
GRADES EIGHT THROUGH TWELVE

Occupation		Scale Position		
	1-2 (low)	3-4	5-6 (high)	
Blue Collar (38)	21.1	52.7	26.2	100.0
White Collar (31)	16.1	63.8	16.1	100.0
Professional (37)	2.7	62.1	35.2	100.0

Chi square = 8.05, n.s.

Occupational background thus appears to make a difference in the de-velopment of attitudes toward play, especially those consistent with later economic success. That is, the higher the occupational standing, the greater the emphasis on skill (position rank 3 and 4), and for Catholic males, the greater the emphasis on success (position rank 5 and 6). And although the difference it makes is consistent for both religious orientations, it ap-pears to be much more emphatic in its effect on the professionalization of attitude in the Catholic male. The direction of difference may appear at odds with an argument made earlier, namely that "liberal" attitudes and emphasis on "fairness" are probably stronger among those groups confident of their standing, which could reasonably be argued to include those in the upper occupational strata, independent of religious preference. But the over-riding influence of religion, even where occupation is controlled would seem reasonably to negate this, at least for the Catholic males, given the apparent strength of "minority" identification.

But among Protestants, the difference remains; and there appears to be a differential emphasis on fairness in favor of those at the bottom of the occupational hierarchy. This is of course with respect to play orientation; but it may also indicate a feeling that, even on the field, equity is not as widespread as it should be, and without it, successful participation in this area or its economic counterpart is not probable, and probably is not pos-sible. If true, this would help explain the greater emphasis on skill among Protestants at the upper ranks: since their starting point is advantaged, they can sponsor greater interest in the basis of success, given equity, namely skill.

And finally, it could be argued that since this is a play orientation, and success on an athletic field is clear proof of personal ability, aside from other factors, a greater need exists among those from the upper strata to demonstrate individual superiority independent of advantages provided them by background. In this case, the boy from the lower occupational levels is said to have succeeded "in spite of his background," e.g., he has " 'overcome' it." Thus a modicum of success would provide distinction for the lower class boy, while somewhat greater success would be necessary for the upper class boy as evidence that he had overcome the advantage, rather than disadvantage, of background. In this sense, it constitutes a peculiar case of "differential expectation." (That is, rather than "self," it is "other," who "expects.") Thus in an unusual way the background may be something to be overcome, and given the emphasis on skill developed in that advantaged background, it should not be surprising that it appears to influence the upper class adolescent's approach to participation in play.

* * * * *

In attempting to analyze the direction and degree of influence of items isolated only with considerable difficulty and operating in contexts of very great complexity, it is difficult to reasonably assert much effect for any given factor. But it does seem to be clear that although experience in the school setting promotes attitudes appropriate to a society maintaining universalistic criteria in its major institutions, experience in the play sphere influences their development as well. In turn background factors such as religious orientation and father's occupation become increasingly important in the development of those attitudes as the student grows older. And as play activities themselves become more rationalized with an increase in age, standards appropriate to the rationalization process develop, and an emphasis on success through skill replaces the equity factor which is pronounced at earlier stages where those standards do not operate in the same degree.

The personality produced at the end of the process thus appears to be a result of experiences in both major areas, school and play, together with the gradually increasing importance of class and religious background, but to this point, with very few exceptions (among them Mead, Cooley and Piaget) the importance of play experience in that process has been virtually ignored. Clearly, if nothing else, this investigation demonstrates that participation in the play world is substantially influential in producing that final result, the urban-industrial man. Although it is true that play attitudes, as demonstrated, are extensively influenced by other factors, it is the final isomorphism of the play arena to the economic structure, and the fact of participation in it, at a time when participation in other areas is virtually nonexistent, that makes that participation the significant factor it now appears to be. Thus to continue the sophomoric and even moronic insistence on play's contribution to the development of such "sweetheart" characteristics as steadfastness, honor, generosity, courage, tolerance, and the rest of the Horatio Alger contingent, is to ignore its structural and value similarities to the economic structure dominating our institutional network, and the substantial contribution that participation in the play arena thus makes to committed and effective participation in that wider system.

REACTION TO WEBB PAPER — Günther Lüschen

When I read Professor Webb's paper, I was very much reminded of my first attempt to read Max Weber. I had an awfully hard time with him. I had a pretty hard time with the present paper also, because of the flavor that Mr. Webb likes to put into his language, his highly idiomatic style. My dictionary didn't show all his terms. On the other hand, this, of course, makes the paper quite enjoyable, as it did for me after I caught a grasp of the meaning of certain phrases. There is another parallel to Max Weber; Professor Webb takes stands on issues. A difference, however, is in Professor Webb putting implicitly into his paper his worries about social situations. Again I believe this makes the paper more interesting than it would be without it.

His problem in general is professionalization as it occurs in play. As he defines it, he sees this as the emergence of skill over other orientations like the orientation towards play and the orientation towards fairness. In a way, it seems to me that he suggests that the integration hypothesis, which is implicit in the concept of professionalization, is not supported by his data. It is a crucial question whether, for instance, the other orientations move out or whether they don't stay in and whether or not the system of play, as I would call it here, which goes with professionalization, may not allow fairness to remain in the game although there is a stronger emphasis now on skill. I would also like to add that the development over age as I see it, seems not to be linear. An analysis of this situation is difficult, and I think a child psychologist would like to add here certain things out of his experience. The notion of fairness in children's games which Professor Webb thinks to be quite prominent, may not necessarily be that strong in the early stage of the development of children's games, for instance at the age of five. Of course, as far as that early stage is concerned, we don't know very much. We know that children start pretty early comparing one another's products for instance, and in a way competing with one another, but on a very low level. The open question is what comes first.

Is it first the group orientation, the orientation toward sociability, or is the competitive aspect first? Out of some studies students of mine have done in kindergartens it seems as if the competitive aspect is there very early and that the controlling sociability aspect emerges later. In a way that also seems to be quite obvious in the study that Piaget has done where actual insight into group structure, the meaning of norms, and the reciprocity of norms, comes at the age of eleven and twelve. So there I would perhaps expect the highest emphasis on fairness and if I'm not mistaken there seems to be a slight tendency in Professor Webb's data supporting this.

Professor Webb points to the difficulties in using scales, and insofar as he would use them in a very general context, here again I would have some reservations in view of the different situational context of these data. He uses the same test over age and it may well be that the same wording may have a completely different meaning to an eighteen year old compared with a twelve year old.

I would also remark that perhaps the professionalization of skill, the phrase that Professor Webb puts in here, may have a rather broad connotation still. It may, in a way, refer to working in the realm of the rules of responding to the group. It may also have a certain connotation for certain levels of personal or individual skill.

The problem of the difference Professor Webb found as far as Catholics are concerned, although not significant when controlled for occupation, may well show something, and therefore, I would like to ask about the Catholic community in Battle Creek. Are these, for instance, which could be possible, highly urbanized Catholics, or Catholics who have come into this country rather recently? The Protestants may have been citizens for quite some time already, whereas the Catholics may be, in a way, less integrated, and as such less affected by social control, and thus more able to get away with a more beat attitude. Or, is it that the Protestants in the sample have lived over a time in rural areas, whereas the Catholics lived from the beginning in urban areas? So this might be quite an interesting case of perhaps the more urbanized American Catholic — that the results run contrary to our expectations here then, and in that way, may be explained. You may also know that in recent years some investigations have revealed that Catholics in urban areas exceeded Protestants in occupational status, quite surprisingly so.

Well, I shall close off my remarks at this point. The problem is, of course, once you discuss research projects you either buy the data or you make a certain critique of its validity or the methods employed. As far as the statistics are concerned, I have no reservations. Problems of why you should have used non-parametric statistics seem indeed, as far as our recent experiences in sociology go, not that relevant. This is by and large a more theoretical question. In general I think we should be quite thankful for Professor Webb's most stimulating and interesting paper.

DISCUSSION

LEON SMITH: Professor Webb, your paper is mainly based on attitude, that's my first premise — a brilliant deduction. We have had problems in getting reliability with the younger group, especially grade three in past studies, and I wondered if you did a test-retest on reliability with the lower group of persons.

WEBB: We did all five groups, three through twelve and the reliability is very, very high.

SMITH: Have you any figures?

WEBB: Yes. The point of the thing is, the simpler the scale the easier it is to answer and probably the greater the reliability. In other words, if he understands and it is a relatively simple concept and for a specified time test, he's going to answer in the same way on another occasion, and he did. It varied, of course, from the twelfth graders that we used down to the third graders, that is true, but it was always at or above a .90 level; .96

was the highest and I think that was for eighth or tenth graders. There is an additional point which should be discussed, too. This does not refer to how they behaved. It's an attitude, it's their approach which we are interested in, attitudes which are appropriate to the situation. It is not an attempt to identify behavior. To that extent the scale gains in value too, because many scales are concerned not so much with attitudes in fact as they are with the prediction of activities. We are not concerned with that, we are concerned with an aspect of the socialization process in which a kind of perceptual format is developed, and in that sense then, the attitudes. It's a good point.

GUY REIFF: I had a couple of questions on design. First, in the selection of this sample did you sample children or classrooms?

WEBB: We sampled the classrooms. We discussed the possibility of having them collect in the auditorium those kids selected on a random sample basis, but it seemed much more difficult that way than to do it by classrooms. At the same time we were careful to make sure there were no overlaps. In other words, there was no kid in the same class twice or more.

REIFF: In other words, each youngster was represented once in each single class?

WEBB: Right. The way it turned out every kid had the same probability of being chosen in a given grade sector as any other kid.

REIFF: Which gets at the probability sample. You took the classrooms and then all the kids in the classroom. So, the question I wanted to get at was, in the calculations of the variability of responses what type or what method did you use? Did you use the classic difference from the mean analysis like in the calculation of the variability for the t-test, and so forth, and also in the calculation of the variability in the Mann-Whitney U test, which is a very powerful non-parametric test, do you recall how that variability was calculated?

WEBB: No, I can say this though, and Lüschen brings that problem up too, that the only t-test differences mentioned that are mentioned in the paper are differences at that level or less on the Mann-Whitney U as well. So far as variability between the factors taken together is concerned, they were run on Kruskal-Wallis analysis of variance.

REIFF: The point I wanted to make is that in the calculation of the variance in the clustered sample, you don't use, as you probably know, the standard techniques because of the fact that each kid does not have an equal, an independent chance, but his probability of selection is the same across the board. So therefore if you calculate the variability in a classic manner you will overestimate the actual variance, sometimes in a ratio of 3 or 4 to 1, which we call a design effect, over what would it be calculated if the variance were taken from a simple random sample. So, therefore, if we looked at the significance here it would have no effect, that the design effect would have no effect on the differences that you have that are significant because you will have a larger variance in the numerator and so forth.

But it might where you have no significance. It's a sticky thing to handle and there actually is no true method in calculating the variability from a clustered sample, but it is something to keep in mind and especially when we look at variability responses of younger age groups.

WESLEY WHITE: Concerning class and responses to fair play, one could put a reasonable rationale for the lower classes being more concerned with fair play than the upper classes — one could put a reasonable rationale for them being more concerned with success in the upper classes, as you did. I would go for the hypothesis concerning the lower classes being more concerned with fair play because this is one note of explanation they give for them being less in effort. But this has consequences for the question which was posed because I think it could be split into two dimensions. The lower classes would go for one dimension and the upper classes would go for the other dimension in this way. When asked the question, "Do you think the game should be played fairly?" I think the lower classes would say, "Yes." Other people should play the game fairly, as it were, *they* should play the game fairly but when the upper classes are asked, "Should the game be played fairly?," they would tend to respond, "Yes, *we* should play the game fairly rather than they." So the lower classes when you ask them this question may say yes, they should play the game fairly, *people* should play the game fairly, and the upper classes may say that we should play the game fairly.

WEBB: That would apply if the notion of "ought" as indicated by "should" were included and it was deliberately not. They are not asked who should play or how should I play, but what is most important in play — rank the following items. I think that that might control the "should" or "ought" concern, although it is possible, as a great many things are possible, that it could intervene, as well.

WHITE: I think the lower classes would tend to respond for people at large and particularly other people, whereas the upper classes may refer to themselves, *we* should play fairly and there could be a difference here, of course.

JOHN ALBISON: I was wondering if you looked at the data with respect to those who play and those who don't and their difference in ranking.

WEBB: No. We are in the process of doing that now. We have some information on kids who have been involved in activities outside school, kids who have been involved in intramurals for boys and girls, and kids who have been interested in or have been involved in interscholastic athletics. We are in the process of running that now. The other thing is in answer to another question: "What would you rather do with respect to your favorite activity, play it or watch it?" Given any situation, would you rather play or watch? These two groups were then contrasted which would, in some sense, get at that information as well. The kids who watch tend to rank, surprisingly, the fairness thing much lower. They are watching for other kinds really. A kind of vicarious success experience is involved in spectating, I suppose. I think that this is what Gregory was saying yesterday. But we are in the process of making those runs, so I wouldn't want to speculate on them.

SEYMOUR KLEINMAN: I was just going to ask whether you are satisfied with the use of this kind of forced choice in making kids make a decision about what is most important in these concepts because when a kid is forced to make a choice that fairness is more important or skill is more important, we really don't know in a way whether he really thinks it's a lot more important or on the same level of importance and so on. In the light of a forced choice, are you satisfied with that as a fairly accurate way of doing it?

WEBB: Thankfully, satisfaction is not one of those qualities which is without degree. I am *relatively* satisfied. The problem is, as you can guess, and we ran into this problem before, approaching something from an ideal kind of situation and approaching something from a trivial, a largely trivial situation. The problem is generating hypotheses that are interesting and are important, have some meaning in them, and then finding a way of testing these. The great difficulty attached to any social research, of course, is the extent to which as the paper mentions, the extent to which these kinds of items actually measure what's going on, and that involves as well, as you point out, the notion of degree. I am satisfied, relatively satisfied, with the forced choice thing because I'm not so much concerned about whether play is 14 per cent important at this point, as I am in contrast to these other things. What is happening in the relationship between the three, and there is really no way you can get at that, at least in terms of my own experience, unless you force their ranking, and you then proceed to an examination of how they vary in that ranking across age.

KLEINMAN: Just one more thing. There appears to be, at least to me, an element in games or sport, related to the way we participate in them or view them that might be interesting to try and get at — and that is when we are talking about games there appears to be some sort of a stoicism about it. You know, you play the game and accept the breaks of the game, you win, you lose, on the way the ball bounces sometimes, not necessarily depending on skill, not necessarily depending on playing fairly or on that third category you mentioned, but just this stoicism about being in a game situation and acceptance of the result regardless of what was necessarily involved, and this may be also carried over into the general society as you tried to point out in these categories. You know, you kind of get ahead or you are successful in our world, a lot depends upon the "breaks of the game," regardless.

WEBB: It's interesting you use that phrase, the "breaks of the game," which is applied to economic experience. Very good. No, that is an interesting point. But it's again with respect to that analogy which constantly goes on, the analogies that are made in terms of sport operations with respect to their application into much more complex economic activities. What is the other interesting thing, and the one that you are actually getting at, is the way in which people reduce tension. In a very complex society we look for simple solutions, simple outcomes, you want something black or white. it's finished or it isn't finished, damn it, it's done or it isn't done, and let's not have all this in Viet Nam. The sport activity to the extent that it is rationalized, is the same thing. The greater the degree of rationalization the greater the probability of acceptance of that direct outcome. In other words, there is a victor. And because of the need for simple solutions — don't forget that we are relatively simple men operating in enormously complex situations and that creates a great many problems for us — these values have a way of maintaining themselves over long periods of time even when the structure itself has changed and it's that thing that creates a great deal of conflict. In terms of this discussion, Gregory had mentioned before the change from a production to a consumption economy, and that would predicate then the development of a new set of attitudes, but those attitudes will not develop to the same extent, they'll be held over for a very long period of time. So that we in many senses are very simple men. Our nervous system, for example, is organized on a closed and open circuit basis just like our computers. It operates then on a bivalent or two-valued logic. It's no accident that we develop the computers we do, we develop the Aristotelian truth-false kind of logic. It's an outcome in part of the construction of our nervous system itself. Those things do not change; at the same time our social systems change very, very rapidly. So that we come to them with almost dictated kinds of approaches, and when we can get, as the paper points out, very clear and simple decisions in an area which makes a difference, and of course sport does, that kind of thing serves not only to reduce tension but to show us that relatively simple solutions to complex situations are possible when, in fact, of course, they are not. That is an interesting problem and of course when it comes back to the socialization experience, well, the kid loses but the adult loses as well, and he simply accepts it then as not necessarily a matter of fate but the winner has been decided, something like that. That relates to the comment in back too. You remember that book about meritocracy, Michael Young's "Meritocracy," where a position in a system is genuinely attached to the degree of his skill, to the degree of his merit, and this intergenerational exchange of funds and the control and power process that develop from their control is not possible. The people at the very top wind up buying the bright sons and daughters of those at the very bottom. Those at the very bottom see themselves as not able to achieve and their lack of ability to achieve is demonstrated by their position. I wander around a good deal in blue collar bars and as I sit there, you know, you start talking with the guys and they say "Well, you know, my folks had to have me go to work and I just didn't have a chance, but I could have made it. I really could have done it if I had had an opportunity." In a meritocracy that's not possible. At the same time, of course, that he's making this kind of justification, in other words, he could have done something else but for circumstance, the guy at the top wanders through the streets and may from time to time say to himself "There but for the grace of God go I." In other words "My being where I am is a result of a great many factors not necessarily related to my ability or my skill or my merit." There is some tendency to modify this kind of thing and it serves a very important social process. In other words, it does not bring these two together in a tremendous clash, as eventually happens for example in the meritocracy, in that book a dystopian novel like *1984*.

DONALD CASADY: One of the problems that I'm sure you considered, and it's I think quite complex, when you're assessing attitudes you often get what their professed attitude is and perhaps even some indication of what they think the desired answer is, not what they are truly thinking. Did you give any thought to try to check behavior at any stage? Did it coincide with how they approached it?

WEBB: We haven't so far. Its' a good point. To what extent are these attitudes related to activity? Do those kids placing emphasis on skill, for example, wind up in varsity sports? That is something that I will do. Although the data were collected in the fall of 1967, every single piece of work including the coding of the cards, not the punching which I did not do, but the programming for computer runs, the translation of material and everything else, its organization, I've had to do myself. There were virtually no funds to operate with in this kind of research. I suppose to the greater extent that such work appears in the literature there will be a corresponding increase in availability of funds, but that means that there are things that you want to do that take time. That's another one that I've got in mind. Thank you.

BRIAN SUTTON-SMITH: I've done some of these studies where you actually compare the kids and their preferences on a scale where playing games is what he actually does and it is a very tricky world. We did it over two summers and we changed the scale on one of the occasions so we had more mature items in and that produced results that were completely different. This gets me back now to what sort of projective test this really is, whether or not the people who have the highest professional attitudes are the ones that really have the least professional behavior. Now I think some of your data suggestions fit fine with your hypotheses. You know, the age trends nicely. The female and the Catholic data suggest that maybe there is another thing in the world, there is an interaction in influences going. Michael Maccoby at Harvard many years ago did a study in which he gave kids marbels and he said "Now, when you are playing marbles with your father and you have each got ten marbles, how many are you prepared to lose to your father or how many are you prepared to win off him, and when you are playing with your best friend how many marbles will you lose and how many will you win?" Now, the five year old kids playing with their father say they want to lose a lot; playing with their best friend, they want to win a lot. At the age of eleven years they want to win the lot from their father, but win five and lose five to their best friend. In other words equality comes later, fairness is a more sophisticated attitude.

WEBB: We could assume that from the data. At the same time, of course, we cannot criticize the way in which it was developed, which is an important effect too.

SUTTON-SMITH: There is something at variance here in terms of your description of the younger boys as concerned with fairness. This doesn't really fit what we know, the Piaget stuff you have alluded to. I think it is true they play in a very sloppy way but if asked about rules they are very definite, deifically rendered and so forth. My feeling is with respect to both the Catholic and the female response in your data, that these are like the boys wanting to win when they were five years of age, that they are actually less mature responses in terms of one's attitude to play. They are the sort of responses of people before they really are in the system of play-ing, where they want equality and matching of the opponent and that you. do have genuine play data. I don't know how it reflects the larger achieve-ment system but it's reflecting discrepancies in maturity. They are marvelous data, by the way, and it's just fantastic the way this paper carries on the conversation of the early part of this morning.

BRYAN PETRIE: My question is directed to you, Doctor Lüschen. In your last statement I was wondering whether you intended to imply that parametric statistics may be used with equal thoroughness with survey and attitude data. You seemed to imply that non-parametric versus parametric was perhaps not quite the distinction we should make in our research. I feel that we have to be very careful with our use of statistics particularly when information can not be assured.

GÜNTHER LÜSCHEN: My one basic point is that most times as far as I know there is not that much difference occurring whether you use parametric or non-parametric. On the other hand what my basic conviction with the whole game is that we have so lousy data that the highly sophisti-cated statistics very often will not show that much. It is actually that we need an awful lot of theoretical insight in what is needed to make the problems really meaningful.

PETRIE: The point I wish to go on with, actually the only particular parametric test which is being shown to any extent to be robust enough to use with survey data is the t-test, and that we are using continually in our research analysis of variance techniques which have highly sophisticated as-sumptions. I don't feel at this stage in the development of our particu-lar sub-discipline that we can afford to be sloppy with our parametric de-signs and perhaps we should go back to non-parametrics until we are more sophisticated in our techniques of approaching data.

LÜSCHEN: My point is that very often we have to deal with very weak data. For example, Doctor Webb's data are not — I think you would agree — superior, hard-core data. These are attitudinal data first of all. What is the validity of the attiudes that you are really measuring here? The reliability may be very good but you may lose on validity by using very simple questions. But, this is nothing special to Doctor Webb's research here, it is a general question in sociology. Also, for instance, we make here certain inferences on change over time where we actually should use the same people and observe them over time. That's another problem. If we just dealt with a thing as it is, very often we would just stay there and do nothing.

GREGORY STONE: I just want to carry on the dialogue a bit further. It seems to me that your conception of professionalization — again, presuppose the industrial society rather than the society of high mass consumption — as you mentioned yesterday in terms of the changing labels of occupations — this is part of the professionalization of labor, and changing labels as professionalization means getting status for the occupation, or at least believing one is getting status for the occupation — then you can change from undertaker to funeral director to mortuary scientist. This has to be tied up with the school system, because the schools, particularly the universities, more and more bestow status upon occupational groups. So my question is this: You mentioned an item about the prestige one gets from playing — I wish you would mention enjoyment; some kids might like to play for fun. . . .

WEBB: We try to get at this — the fun thing — in another scale — a "selfsatisfaction" scale.

STONE: . . . do you think there would be any difference in this respect? In some early work Bill Foreman did, it was found that there was a much greater emphasis among those of lower socio-economic levels on class symbolism, and at the middle and higher levels, on status symbolism. Do you think this sorts of thing would show up in your groups?

WEBB: That is a very interesting question. It would be hard to get at with our data. We might be able to, but I'm not sure at this point. Certainties should never be expressed!

Charles H. Page

9. Symposium Summary, with Reflections Upon the Sociology of Sport As a Research Field

Needless to say, I feel a number of things but among them I feel guilty about having this wind-up exercise as a responsibility, guilty primarily of course because I'm afraid I've monopolized a good deal of the discussion during some of the meetings. At the same time, however, I have a feeling of relief, not from what Gerry has said so kindly, but rather because several of us are absent or not here as yet, including my good friend and very severe critic, Gregory Stone; I hope that he doesn't show until I've finished my comments. I do see, however, sitting in the rear of the room, another friend who is also a severe critic and this fills me with trepidation. I'm referring to Jay Demerath of the faculty of Wisconsin.

I'd like to make several introductory comments, and one of course sanctioned by my age. My own interest in sport goes back to the 1920's and '30's, the early '30's, when I was active in some sports as a participant and later as a coach of three or four different teams. Since about 1950 I have been working from time to time on a general study of sport and society — a book, if it ever becomes that, which deals with most sports; but certainly not all of them, not the sport of kings about which I know nothing, nor sporting houses which have been referred to during our deliberations here and about which I know little. I concentrate on three sports for reasons I think that may become evident in a few moments — professional baseball, professional boxing, and tennis, both amateur and professional tennis (which I guess are the same today, at least at the top levels).

It's been pointed out several times during the conference — at the outset and often since — that until fairly recently this subject has been neglected by social scientists. It is still viewed, according to Mr. Sutton-Smith and others who have spoken, by many scholars in a variety of disciplines, as a trivial subject, in spite of the obvious (I think obvious) large and conspicuous role of sport in social and cultural life. And one of the situations that triggered my own efforts to put something on paper almost twenty years ago about the situation was the fact that during the years following World War II there was a spate of books about American society, American culture, American character, for the most part, but not entirely, written by notable anthropologists or anthropologists who subsequently became notable because they wrote such books. I'm thinking of people like Margaret Mead and Geoffrey Gorer. I was reading these books at the time because I was teaching an undergraduate course on American society. I was struck then by the almost complete absence of any mention of sport in American life. There are some casual references in passing, but it seemed to me that, and I have in mind anthropologists particularly here, these people were writing books of a kind that one might write about certain primitive societies with no reference to magic or, to exaggerate the comparison, no reference to kinship systems. I'm not implying that sport has a comparable structural role in American life, but this seemed to me a kind of blindness, sheer blindness, on the part of otherwise very brilliant and perceptive people. Of course I couldn't have been blind to sport by virtue of the fact that I had been a sometimes participant in this world.

Now since those years, as you know, there have been some efforts to correct this situation, and I'm not speaking now of the kinds of papers that we have heard and discussed. I will refer to those as I go along, but I'm thinking of a book such as that written by the two physical education people, by Cozens and Stumpf, *Sports in American Life,* which I think was the first book on sport reviewed in *The American Sociological Review;* or again, in Britain, McIntosh's *Sport and Society* — it came out in the early 1960's and is a general and largely a historical study; and again, as we have been reminded during the last two days, there is a growing number of research projects in the United States and France and Britain and Scandinavia and Eastern Europe, and elsewhere concerned with sport and sport activities. And now, of course, the partial reputability and the partial intellectualization of this subject are signalized by a number of things: by the forthcoming publication of at least two readers in the field, one edited by Gerry Kenyon and John Loy and the other by Eric Dunning in England; by the formation of a committee of distinguished men — I don't know if the committee has any women, if not they should have immediately — a committee that is a double agency of UNESCO and the International Sociological Association; by such meetings as this one, the recent one in Boston, and the meeting in Dallas; and so on.

So far as sociologists are concerned, of course, sport became, inevitably, a subject for investigation because some sociologists, quite a few, in fact, as Irving Goffman says, follow the action, whatever it is. Sociology is a notoriously fickle field and I think correctly so. This is one of my biases. Some of us are up to our ears today studying youth. Why? Because youth is active today, doing interesting things. We study black power today for obvious reasons. We study the culture of poverty (we seem to have forgotten the fact for several years that we have a "culture of poverty" in the United States and now we've rediscovered it). We study crimes without victims, we study hustlers and other so-called deviants — and I think this is all to the good. And finally a handful of sociologists, ever growing in size, are discovering, so to speak, that sport is a large and significant area of action, of human activity.

I might say in this connection as an aside that I think that the exploitation of this area of action, of sport, by sociologists on the one hand (as well as by representatives of other scholarly disciplines) and on the other the exploitation of sociologists and members of other disciplines by people in physical education and who are directly involved in sport, this kind of reciprocal exploitative pattern that we now see going on and are illustrating by being together at a conference such as this is all to the good. This is a *social* pattern — I'm not referring to the motivations of people here, which I know nothing about. When I use the word "exploitative," I mean nothing invidious. Whatever the reasons for this development and whatever the motivations of specific individuals — why you, for example, Mr. Kenyon, are involved up to your neck in this field, or why an old coot like myself is bothering with it — it may have some positive intellectual and scholarly dividends. One of the things I will try to suggest as I talk is that the papers we have heard at this meeting promise such positive results.

Now certainly it has become evident, if it hadn't been already evident before we assembled on Monday, that there are many different ways to study sport, sociologically. And I suspect that the various ways that have been discussed and about which we have argued some, are each quite legitimate in terms of intellectual criteria. (Note that I don't use the word "science" because I'm not qualified to do so, but I do sometimes refer to scholarship or intellectuality). We have heard considerable discussion of alternative theoretical and methodological perspectives or orientations with respect to the field of sport. Let me remind you of two or three of these and add two or three.

Until this morning, I thought that I'd start off by pointing out that a Marxist or a neo-Marxist approach to the study of sport had not been illustrated in this conference. This is an orientation or perspective that has played and continues to play, as you all know, a very important role in the social sciences. But that would not be correct because we have heard Harry Webb's paper this morning, and his paper is an illustration (however lost we might have gotten in those twenty-seven or so tables) as Harry made abundantly clear, of this orientation. The paper is written not merely in the spirit of a Marxist or a neo-Marxist approach, but indeed the theoretical propositions that he brought to his paper and from which he peeled off hypotheses stemmed directly from this perspective. He didn't suggest, as someone might who took Karl Marx literally, that one of the important functions of sport in contemporary society — maybe this came out in the discussion of his paper which I could not hear — might be that of the opium of the masses — in the same way that Marx depicted the major social function of religion. This is an interesting idea, and sports writers frequently write about it. Sociologists never do, at least so far as I know. Well, this is one type of perspective.

Another that we heard a good deal about is the structural-functional approach, and one way to use that approach is to develop an exhaustive or what seems to be an exhaustive paradigm of the kind that Günther Lüschen presented for us on Monday. Or it might be a more modest effort of the kind that Gerry Kenyon made to order our concepts, that is, to develop the "strategic variables" to study in this area, or variables that at least have the potentiality of being strategic. Although I did not hear his paper last night, Mr. Sutton-Smith's discussion of the two cultures of play includes (among many other fine things) some effort to make use of a theoretical conceptual scheme in distinguishing between the two cultures of play, one which he calls ascriptive and one achieving.

A third and closely related perspective to this field, which has also been illustrated in the last few days, is brought out in what Robert Merton calls "middle range" theory (or "short range" theory, in the case of studies that focus on very specific relationships between a very small number of variables). We have had some very nice illustrations of this kind of effort this week — Walter Schafer's paper on "Delinquency and Sport Involvement"; the paper by John Loy on "Athletic Participation and Mobility"; and I must add Harry Webb's study of the same subject which he brought into the discussion when he commented on John's paper. So this is another perspective and one I think that the majority of sociologists in this country would find most agreeable: you can get your teeth into this sort of study, you know what you're looking for. You're looking for a relationship, say, between so-called delinquent behavior and athletic performance or athletic involvement. You may find a double relationship (as I suspect there is in this case — it came out in the study), which is both a positive relationship due in part to the delinquency of sport itself, a concept I suggested, and a negative relationship for reasons that were discussed at length.

Still another approach is one that (and here I'm going to misuse a term, one of the reasons I hate to see Jay Demerath sitting back there) I'll simply call "cultural." Here I'm referring to efforts to get at what might be called the intrinsic nature or "quality" of this world of human behavior and evaluation — of sport. An extreme illustration of this approach is that of the "ethnomethodologists," Harold Garfinkle and a seemingly growing number of young sociologists who advocate this version of a phenomenological approach today. Phenomenology is more widespread than ethnomethodology itself, so that pretty soon we are going to have some papers, I think, on what sport "really is" in everyday life. In order to find out what sport "really is" these people will discover that they are going to have to learn about it, they're going to have to go in the field and feel it and sense it and probably participate in it. This is a point I've tried to suggest from time to time during the discussions.

And there are other illustrations of this orientation. We heard Gregory Stone describe himself, and I believe correctly, as an exponent of symbolic interactionism as a theoretical perspective. (I'm not talking about theories, remember, but *perspectives*). Some of Gregory's work, not only the research he reported here but earlier work on the meaning of sport and particularly as a part of communication patterns and the whole symbolic aspect of sport, clearly illustrates this orientation.

As I suggested before, all of these orientations, and no doubt others, I think, have a legitimacy and probably will help us if we continue to exploit this field. And they may help us to write learned tomes about sport.

Well, now I'm going to forego any kind of sophisticated theoretical and methodological approach in saying some things about a few of what I think are (and I believe that most of us would agree) the major research areas in this field. In a quite eclectic and simplistic way, I plan to use a set of substantive categories to depict such areas. At least most of them are substantive categories about sport, not analytical categories, not highly abstract theoretical categories. I'd like to say a few things about culture — the culture *of* sport and sport *and* culture; about sport and the community; about sport and social stratification; and about sport and organization. As you know, these are longstanding areas of sociological interest and the comments I'll have to make about these areas will be for the most part "old hat."

Now sport and *culture*. I'm using the term "culture" here pretty much as my mentor, Robert MacIver, developed it in his writings, and to some extent as both Talcott Parsons and Robert Merton have used the term. "Culture," then, refers to value systems, to values, to thought styles, to patterns that have end or terminal interest for human beings — and I've invoked this notion in the course of the discussions from time to time. I've suggested, for example, that sport, like sex, is fun, the most obvious thing about it, and yet we say the least about it.

Of course sport involves all sorts of other types of interest, instrumental interest. Sport is both a social and cultural institution in modern society. I'm certain that there is a very important instrumental aspect to it, but let me say some things first about the cultural aspect. Probably there are two, overlapping to be sure, principal research areas here. First, there is quite a bit of work, (to be sure, it's fugitive) on the interaction of sport and the larger culture, both in American society and other societies. There are historical studies, for example, that deal with this relationship. Some of you may know about the first serious book that I'm aware of that was written by a historian on sport, which came out in 1928, written by the American historian John Krout. And I'm sure many of you know recent volumes on specific sports, such as Seymour's study of the history of base-ball, books on professional baseball, or even Thomas Mendenhall's little known book (Mendenhall now being the president of a small girls' school in the East known as Smith College) on the history of the Yale crew. This is a fascinating book — for example, probably very few of you know that in the early years of the Yale crew many of the crew members were re-cruited in the Pennsylvania mining areas, their names were changed and they didn't attend class, but they rowed for Yale. If you think of crew as somehow an upper status sport, historical information such as this is fascinating.

One looks at investigations of this sort and sees a good deal, usually put forward in a very unsystematic way, of concern with the relationship between sport in general or a specific sport and the larger culture. Some-times there is a good deal of attention given, for example, to the way in which specific sports are shaped or moulded by certain cultural circum-stances or even generated by certain cultural circumstances surrounding their development. The history of baseball is fascinating to read about for precisely this reason. It does, to be sure, according to Seymour, have some shadowy English origins, but it's essentially an American sport historically and otherwise, and it was certainly shaped in our kind of society. A great deal has been written about this, mostly by sports writers. Or again, with respect to American football, the whole switch from the rugby type of thing to this idiotic game that we play in the United States, certainly the impact of the cultural surrounding is very important. Or cases of sports that are transplanted from one society, one culture to another and take on a different shape. Note, for example, what happened to tennis in the Ameri-can environment after it moved from the British scene to this country and joined the private and expensive country clubs of the Eastern seaboard. Within two or three decades after it arrived here it became something differ-ent, it became a disreputable activity in the eyes of many people because it became a good game. Big tennis developed because of some American and Australian players, such as the great "Red Comet" from Australia.

BRIAN SUTTON-SMITH: McLaughlin.

PAGE: McLaughlin, thanks, who came over and the big game de-veloped and it's quite something else today. What happened to golf? You know, it really didn't take that caddy from Boston, Francis Ouimet, who beat the two British professionals, to make golf a different kind of game.

With respect to cultural influence, read that fine little book (I'm curious to know if any of you have ever seen it) by Neville Cardus on English cricket, which came out in the middle '40's; this tiny book (you can read it in about forty-five minutes) is a magnificent essay on not only the cul-ture of cricket, but on cricket within the British culture. This is marvelous stuff, and now, of course, people like Eric Dunning are pursuing studies of this order. — These are historical in the roughest sense, perhaps anthropological, types of studies. They are not too many in number, but they've been going on for a long time.

How about the converse process, the impact of sport on the larger culture, the less obvious thing? This question has received only skimpy and largely speculative attention. We see general statements from time to time — for example, a good many years ago Aldous Huxley wrote that sport is the dominant characteristic of our time; he didn't explain why in any detail, but this was his formulation. We read in Huizinga's *Homo Ludens* very insightful comments, as in the more recent observations by some of the French sociologists, such as Dumazedier and other people who came out of the Georges Friedmann shop in French sociology. What about American sociologists? We have heard a number of references during the week to essays on sport — the kind of sociology that I like to read. Discursive, undisciplined, impressionistic, unscientific work by people like Reuel Denney and David Riesman and others in this country who have had some very insightful things to say about the impact of the sport on the larger culture. But there's not much of this, and this is fascinating.

It's a fascinating sociological question as to why this is the case. For the influence of sport, I would say in my impressionistic way, on the larger culture rivals the influence of Negro culture on the larger culture; it rivals even — I hate to say this, but none of my students is here at the moment — the impact of so-called youth culture on the larger culture. This is illustrated in many ways: in the informal evaluative patterns used by Americans to evaluate one another; in our political rhetoric — we've heard for several presidential elections now running back into the 1930's the rhetoric of sport becoming the rhetoric of politics (it's not something that our President-elect invented); in our child raising patterns; increasingly, by the lexicon of our folk heroes, and we remake our folk heroes. Of course, Father George did not throw that silver dollar across the Potomac, but we have had him doing it for a long time — it's important that he do it in our way of thinking. Calvin Coolidge was not a great athlete, but we made him an outdoor man in the public image. FDR was not a great swimmer, but we made him one after he became President; and so on. There are any number of ways to illustrate the cultural significance of sport, for our general life style is increasingly a sporting style. I'll venture the general hypothesis here, if I may misuse the term "hypothesis" for a moment, that the playing field and the gymnasium provide a salient measure of the worthwhile, at least in modern American life. And I believe that this question deserves much more attention than it's gotten by intellectuals, whether they are sociologists or physical educators or whatever.

Now how about the culture *of* sport itself and the culture of specific sports? Sport is a way of life involving both sacred and secular traditions, as you all know. It involves ever-changing lores and customs, different styles of rhetoric, and, as I suggested earlier, both terminal and instrumental values.

All of this is vividly depicted in a huge body of literature, namely that written by sports writers, or by many sports writers. And, of course, some of the sports writers are among my favorite list of sociologists. They wouldn't use this term about themselves normally, but certainly their writing is an important source for sociologists. Similarly, a few of our novelists and other fiction writers fall into this category — all of us talk about Ring Lardner and, more recently, about Red Smith. Some people even refer to Hemingway's stories in which sport is a theme (although treated rather poorly, in my view). And there are a few wonderful books such as *The Sweet Science* by Leibling (if you haven't read it, do so — it's a joy esthetically, and it tells a great deal about the history of professional boxing). This reportage and this literature are, I think, required reading for the sociologists who are now investigating the culture of sports, trying to find out something about their phenomenological nature. They are required reading unless our studies are to be as anthropologically limited as much of the sociological writings on popular culture in general was ten or fifteen years ago, most of which was pretty shoddy stuff partly because sociologists didn't know much about popular culture itself.

All of this has something to do with Gerry Kenyon's paper. At one point I suggested that the paper was a wonderful effort in helping to tidy up our concepts with respect to the study of the sport field. But I think that even in the process of tidying up our concepts a good place to look, way beyond the sociological literature, is the descriptive and interpretive literature written by the people who know the scene.

Let me turn to my second category, sport in the *community*. I won't say too much here. In his recent book on leisure Dumazedier holds that institutionalized leisure has become — he takes an extreme position — an essential component of modern industrial society; and sport, as he has tried to show, and others have tried to show, is a very large and a growing part of this component of modern industrial society. And I think that this is brought out in a good many studies of community life in both the small local community and in the larger mass scale community, the mass cities of present day.

In small towns, in towns, in small cities and probably to a less extent in residential suburbs, and in both European countries and in this country, certain sports, as you know, provide community-wide events of great importance — high school basketball and little league baseball teams in American towns, and in European towns the local football (soccer) teams. Much of the collective life of the community is centered around such activities.

The more individualized sports, such as bowling and golf and hunting and fishing — notice that I include these as sports — are an important part, of course, of leisure patterns at almost all class levels now in the United States (except at the ragged bottom margin, the poverty stricken, a substantial percentage of American people). These activities rival and are often associated with the other kinds of grass roots activities, such as social drinking and sexual sport, as anyone knows who has done any casual field observation in small towns in American society.

Now within the larger "mass society," the persistence of these local town activities and of local community life, or community life on a localized basis, I think it may be suggested, is partly dependent on community-wide sports events and also the guarantee of opportunity for individualized sport activities. This dependency, I think, is much greater today than say when Robert and Helen Lynd wrote their Middletown books in the '20's and '30's, which give a good picture of leisure and sport in Muncie, Indiana at that time. And if we are to believe what Dumazedier and his students are reporting in French society about Annecy, for example, a community he has studied intensively, this dependency is very much the case. This relationship is also suggested by Kenyon's paper in which at one point he dealt, I think so nicely, with sport involvement as important for the maintenance of a variety of institutions. This formulation stems from a functional orientation, at least at that point in his paper; I think that this is a very suggestive hypothesis and I would guess a correct formulation, particularly at the level of local community life.

What about the larger communities, the great cities? Here, of course, we have a situation of spectacles, of mass spectatorship, whether in stadiums or in private homes, and of course the big centers of professional sport. As I tried to suggest once during the discussion, as spectatorship and professionalism grow in our society, and figures bear this out, so does participation grow. Though I don't know of any causal relationship that has been established between those two trends, I think that the interpretation is fairly simple to make. In any event, we see a great demand, an increasing demand, for facilities for *both* spectators and participants.

Now there are several important aspects of this situation. Let me mention just a couple. In the urban ghettos, whether black or white, professional athletes, as you know and some studies have made clear, like other entertainers and some criminals, are apt to be heroes and become models for youth. This has been a feature of youth culture in such areas for many decades and all kinds of studies bring this out — studies that are not focused on sport but bring out this aspect of sport.

Again in recent years, as investigations in Britain and France and Germany and this country show, a rapidly growing number of working-class people and families, very much like middle-class people, participate in flight from the city sports. More and more they get out of the big cities in order to recreate and to have fun, so more and more in the working-class segment of the population we have skiing, both in snow and on water (particularly water for working-class people) and golf and fishing, and so on. This trend, I think, reflects a pressing leisure need in industrial and urban society, as Dumazedier states.

Well, these are trite observations but I think they suggest that the mass scale community provides enormous opportunities for sociological research on a variety of different problems.

How about sport and *social stratification?* This of course is the socio-logist's most favorite area nowadays, and we've heard a good deal about this subject during the last two days. The class dimension and the ethnic di-mension of sport are probably of greater interest to sociologists than other problems, both in Europe and in this country. Here I'd like to distinguish three sub-areas, inter-related of course.

First, there is the class structuring of sports, which I referred to earlier when talking about the histories of specific sports. Seymour on baseball, Leibling on boxing (which is really not history in a technical sense) and Allison Danzig on the history of tennis in the United States tell us a good deal about the class factor in the development of these sports.

Many sports originate and persist for some time as class linked recrea-tion, as you know. So with baseball, which in this country began as a leisure time activity for middle-class businessmen in New York, and became some-thing else quite rapidly. Boxing, which began historically, I believe, as a British but essentially working-class phenomenon (always followed by an aristocratic fringe of people, as the historians point out), has become some-thing else. American tennis, as I suggested earlier, began as an upper-class importation from England long associated with exclusive clubs, is something quite different today. Sometimes the histories show interesting anomalies. I mentioned one of them, the working-class hired hands rowing for Ivy League crews in the 19th century. Or consider the Texas cowboys in the 1920's and '30's who became ten-goal ranking polo players.

Although the class linkage of most sports has greatly declined, of course, in the United States or even disappeared in the case of many sports (and I'll return to this in a minute), some traits of their class origins often per-sist as traits of the cultures of the sport. For example, the relative decorum of tennis audiences and indeed tennis players, so when a bad boy "mis-behaves" on the tennis courts the sport writers write about him today; this has something to do with the class origins. The old school tie tradition of football, particularly as it developed in the Eastern schools, persists in some measure. The conspicuous violence-seeking among the audiences or many members of the audience of boxing and especially professional wrestling exhibitions has something to do with the history of the sport, I think. And I think that checking such impressionistic observations would give a prom-ising research opportunity to students with a historical and anthropological bent.

A second aspect of the stratification picture has to do with what's often referred to as the "democratization" of sports, the transition of sport in general and numerous specific sports from class status, or class-linked sports, to community-wide or mass status sports. This transition is frequently pointed out and has been documented quite extensively in Europe and in this country, and again the cases of baseball, tennis and boxing are suggestive. The history of each of these sports illustrates the shift from a class basis origin to a "mass" situation. Even in tennis, as in golf and in swimming, and in spite of the persistence of discrimination and of limited opportunities for athletes of working class origin, black athletes, Mexican athletes, and others, the historical pattern is to be seen. These one-time prestigeful or upper status sports are becoming, in some measure, "democratized."

As sport becomes more *mass* — as it becomes the "peoples'" activity as in Communist countries, or as it becomes "everybody's" in the United States — the athlete himself tends to become de-classed. Or, as we put it in the American context, he becomes a representative of that modal group, the so-called "middle class," at least in public image if not in fact — and I think that there is some evidence that suggests that this happens in fact. In the public image (at least) the athlete becomes a representative of middle-class virtues and middle-class vices, he becomes a good family man and all the rest, as you know. So with professional football and baseball players, and even some boxers. They become solid businessmen. Conversely tennis players and golf players no longer have high social status the way they used to: they too are part of this mass situation. On the one hand, the disreputability of the tough guy — the boxer who was supposed to bury his fists in salt water three hours a day (of course he never did that, he would have no hands left), the Babe Ruths in baseball, the bad boy, the drunken bum, the cussing man, and so on — this image is changing in favor of that of the solid citizen, the middle class man. And on the other hand, the country club snob type — the tennis player in immaculate white garb — is disappearing too into a kind of mass or middle-class "democratic" situation. This process, I would suggest, is directly related to a number of things: to the rise of mass leisure, to the "middle" classification of a big segment of the working class (its *embourgeoisement*), to the growing organization or bureaucratization of sport (which I want to move to very shortly) and to the mobility picture and sport which has been discussed at some length here.

In sport, as in the arts and some of the professions, performance (or universalistic criteria) counts, as was stressed this morning in Harry Webb's paper; every aspiring athlete knows this. Some research, not a great deal — this is one of the big reasons for the importance of the recent work by John Loy and Harry Webb — on mobility and baseball and boxing was pointed out by Loy yesterday; together with some work on professional sport as presumably an opportunity avenue for members of socially handicapped and discriminated groups and on changing patterns of recruitment into sports. You are all aware, for example, of the very large number of Irish Americans and quite a few Jews in professional baseball in the early part of this century and the end of the 19th century; many of the Jews in professional baseball played under Irish names for obvious public reasons. The same ethnic or minority groups were well represented in professional boxing, but are not today — there are easier ways to "get ahead." Everyone is aware of the long standing position of Negroes in boxing; and they are joined by Puerto Ricans and other Latin Americans. The relatively recent opening up of professional baseball and football and basketball to members of certain minority groups is widely evident. And so on.

Now what are some of the implications of all of this? First of all, the success stories of these spectacular rises to riches and fame on the part of a few people, however few in fact, like the success stories of movie stars, singers, and other entertainment heroes, receive enormous publicity and these people receive great attention, as I said before, as folk heroes. One of the functions of this, whatever the objective facts concerning mobility may be, and this was a question that was discussed here at some length, is helping to maintain the psychology of opportunity, the American method, the American dream, whatever you want to call it. Support of this myth takes place where it is especially important (in our myth system) for it to be maintained — among segments of the lower classes.

A different aspect of mobility is the fact that school sports serve more and more as a pre-professional training and sifting agency for professional athletes, both amateur and professional. As sport becomes more and more a part of social mobility patterns the relationship between school and opportunity in this area (as in others) becomes increasingly significant. As all of you who ever coached teams at the college level know, the relationship is quite explicit — as it is at the high school level in some schools (such as those "football schools" in Ohio). When the kid who at fifteen or sixteen has tremendous promise coaches are apt to think in career terms: "you go to Michigan State, we have connections with such-and-such pro team." In this way, coaches become career specialists.

Now this is an important situation, and these trends raise more intriguing questions about careers. What happens to the majority of ex-professional athletes? Is downward skidding typical? Unusual? This question was raised during the discussions, and is directly related to the question of identity crisis, as someone brought out in connection with both Walter Schafer's and John Loy's papers. The discussion of those papers also raised the question, "What happens to the athlete *after* his successful career, particularly for those athletes who don't make it?" Is this a real "identity crisis" (to use what has become a cliche' for many Americans)? I have met, in the last twenty-five years or so, at least six or eight ex-great athletes from the Ivy League schools, Princeton, Harvard, and particularly Yale (I don't know why) who didn't make it, in their terms. They came from upper middle-class families, were great football stars, didn't become distinguished attorneys, physicians, businessmen, bankers and faced terrific crises in their lives (this is often portrayed in fiction) about the age of 35 or 40 — they can no longer cash in, psychologically speaking, on the hero role they once had. In other words I'm suggesting that this sort of thing happens not only to kids coming out of working-class families, but is a much more widely spread pattern.

How do different sports compare with respect to career opportunity? There were some suggestions in the papers about this theme as to tennis players and especially fencers, in comparison with those in the combative types of sports. Is it true that there are real patterns developing? They seem to be if one is to believe the newspapers and the television reports: professional athlete to sports announcer (each one of us can name nine guys, ex-professional athletes, who are now announcing sports on TV or radio or both). Is this a pattern? Athlete to insurance salesman — this seems to be very popular, especially among football players (I don't know why). Do these represent modalities of any kind with reference to any groups, or are these the unusual cases? Are these replacing older patterns? There was an older pattern, presumably — professional athlete to saloon keeper, to bartender, or in some lucky cases to restauranteur (one case is Jack Dempsey; I suppose there are others). These are interesting questions and I think they are grist for the sociological mill.

Let me turn then finally to sport and *organizations.* There is very little work beyond impressionistic essays (including a piece of my own on "Sport and Bureaucracy") as well as some insightful articles (again) by those great sociologists, Red Smith and some other sports writers. That is, there is little work on the bureaucratization, the formal organization, of sport, in spite of the evident fact that man's greatest social invention, as Max Weber called bureaucracy, as Harry Webb suggested in connection with play and sport, pervades both amateur and professional sport activity.

Some organizational roles have been studied. There is a nice little piece in the *American Journal of Sociology* on the baseball manager, for example. But the focus is not upon the organizational problem. The problem is the function of the manager: it raises the question of whether or not he has any role with regard to team success.

Farm systems and little leagues have both been described in detail as to their organizational features. The regulatory systems of certain sports, such as professional baseball, football, and basketball, have been described in great detail. But most of this writing of course has been done by members of the sport fraternity itself, and as students of formal organization only a few sociologists are now beginning to go into this area. They will go in. It's a nice area to exploit, as I suggested before.

In this connection, a fascinating program, which has only been alluded to in passing this week, is the way in which sport or at least quite a bit of sport, even at the most professionalized level as in professional baseball, football and basketball, *combines,* in the play activity of sport, highly rational organization on and off the field or the court with great opportunity for unique individual performance. Here is a situation in which Weber's two great problems of order and freedom (which he sometimes discussed in terms of "bureaucracy" and "charisma") are involved. Order and spontaneity somehow get together even in the most professionalized forms of sport — it is by no means true that all the athlete does is carry out the orders. Certainly that is not true, I know, in professional baseball, and I suspect it is not the case in professional football. I think that this combination has something to do with Mr. Lüschen's continuum — a very useful continuum — that he presented his paper when he drew the distinction between casual play groups, the least organized types of groups, and, to use his expression, teams of top competitors, the most organized types of groups. I would suggest that spontaneity is found at both ends of the scale and that there is not necessarily a positive correlation between these free little fellows who develop spontaneous play groups and spontaneity itself.

In the other arts, to use "arts" in a general sense, whether the performing arts or the graphic arts, discipline and creativity go hand in hand: in order to be creative you have to be highly disciplined. Doesn't this relationship hold for what I'll call for the moment the artistic field or cultural field of sport, where a high degree of discipline seems to go along with creativity? If you talk with someone like the pitcher Gibson of St. Louis, his observations about play on the diamond bring out this relationship, as do those of Bill Russell about the Boston Celtics with respect to basketball. To be sure, athletes have to be disciplined strongly, but if they don't also have that creative or spontaneous spark, they leave, say, the Cardinals or the Celtics. Well, these are impressions but they deserve research, I think.

Here are four large problem areas, then, calling for attention. There are many others, of course. I believe that all or most fields of investigation in sport intersect at some points, including what I have called the cultural, communal, class, and organizational features of sport.

I would say simply in conclusion that by far the most interesting for me, and perhaps even the most enlightening, aspect of our three days together has not been what has been presented in formal papers (because we can always read these and study them carefully), but what has been said in response to the papers. The major contribution has been made by the participants — by those of you who *have* participated. This is why I hope conferences of this sort which get together members of the disreputable proffessoriat, on the one hand, and the reputable physical education people, on the other, will continue.

DISCUSSION

GERALD KENYON: Thank you, Mr. Page, for your remarkable array of insights into sport. I'm not sure that there is much more that needs to be said or even can be said at this point but I would like to give an opportunity to any of our speakers and any of the persons here to comment or reflect on Mr. Page's remarks or some other subject that is in any way related to sport.

LEON SMITH: I'd like Professor Page to make one of his famous impressionistic comments on the massive transplant of the foreign-oriented game of soccer to the United States.

PAGE: Well, this sure will be impressionistic, because it's a sport (although I've played it some and coached it for five years at a small private school in New York City once a long time ago) I really don't know much about and have never followed with any great interest. I do think, and maybe this is really a strong bias on my part, that soccer is probably the most fascinating field sport to both play and watch that we have. And I think that it requires, for American people, some socialization, some adult socialization as well as early socialization. It's fascinating to me that for many years, and this may still hold true (my source for this is hard data, *The World Almanac*) there were more soccer players in the United States in organized teams — starting with 4th, 5th, and 6th grade teams — than there were playing any other single organized team sport in this country. Yet professional soccer, as I understand, is having a hell of a time financially and with respect to getting a big mass audience, but it is played a great deal. As all of you people know, in many schools where no football is played at all, soccer is played extensively. As I say, I don't know anything about this sport. I'm just talking off the cuff and adding impressions but maybe you could explain this situation.

GÜNTHER LÜSCHEN: I've some comments, because I have played soccer. I think this game is not adjusted to the American culture, so when the soccer league started I made inquiries on how it was perceived. One thing, one criterion, is that soccer is perhaps one of the sports where the most amount of chance is involved. So, for instance, it is possible to have outcomes which are not very just. The better team may lose just out of accident, for example when somebody slaps the ball from the middle line in some crazy movement, and somehow moves it into the goal, so that the one who deserves the reward is not really rewarded.

When I asked people, they were very impressed with the high skill of some of the soccer players, but on the other hand they complained strongly about the dramatic aspects that the soccer players introduced, or the way they would moan with just a minor accident that they had had on the playing field. That, of course, is part of soccer and that was what the Europeans and the South Americans were used to. In order, for instance, to get a penalty for the opponent you will just pretend to be seriously hurt, or something like that.

Of course, in Europe the experiment has been followed with great interest, but my prediction was from the beginning that it would be a failure, which does not mean that for instance as a participant sport there cannot be a high interest, but as a spectator sport for the time being I wouldn't expect that there would be that much.

CHARLES PAGE: I was interested to hear this. As you were talking I tried to think of some things about soccer. One of the appeals, that is for spectators, at least, of some sports in this country, is the combatitive aspect. I think many people think of football as a truly combative sport and soccer as not by virtue of the fact that players wear light uniforms, and so on. Another feature of popularity in this country is high scoring, you know;

hence the phenomenon of basketball, the whole shift in the rules, and so on, in speeding up the game. Now interestingly enough we can think of at least one professional sport that is greatly popular in this country, hockey, which has only one of these features, namely, it's very combative from the spectator's point of view, but has very low scoring as soccer does. Maybe these are aspects of the whole situation too. I think you're right that soccer is foreign to our culture. Perhaps it doesn't meet the rugged frontier, open country tradition that still pervades the mythology that Americans have about themselves. You know, hell, that we are a nation of dainty pants people for the most part, and these rugged guys if they ever existed in American societies certainly are not around now — except when they get signed up for the big time professional football teams; and the ones I've interviewed, they're not particularly tough guys except when they're out on the field. But we do seem to have this kind of myth. We love combat. How do you explain the popularity of professional wrestling exhibitions? (Notice how correct I am, incidentally, in my terminology). But these exhibitions, well, certainly one of the appeals — I don't know why these old ladies with their knitting needles scream and holler and so on any more than most of us do — one of the appeals is that it looks like something that is truly primeval, it's "real combat." These God-awful exhibitions (I can't stand them, they revolt me) have some sort of a true appeal, where soccer is a game of great skill, teamwork, and so on. Again our tennis crowds have never been big (it happens to be *my* favorite game to watch, it used to be my favorite game to play though I was never any good) — even the greatest matches are not heavily attended.

JOHN POOLEY: I have one or two points to add to this about soccer. You mentioned the low scoring. I think another factor closely resembling this is the number of tied games. In American sports clearly the American public wishes to have a result and many of the games that are played are tied. I've heard many observations made about this.

PAGE: Yes, that's right. Someone has to win.

POOLEY: The other point I think that needs to be emphasized much more is the foreign game element. Every other sport, that I can think of, I believe, possibly with the exception of hockey — I'm not sure of its derivation — has been so changed that it has become truly an American sport, where soccer hitherto is still a foreign sport, with foreign rules.

PAGE: It's an international sport, I mean it's non-American. Its' a non-American international sport.

POOLEY: Yes, and as it's played in this country it's so far not been modified as Doctor Lüschen pointed out to the American culture. The other point connected with that is many of the players still are foreign players. It's not a question of names, but they are from foreign countries having been imported, so clearly I would think there needs to be a grass roots development here. One other point that I found in a rather modest study that I did in Milwaukee, looking at the active soccer clubs there, the ten ethnic soccer clubs, I found that virtually the clubs were closed shops, closed shops, that is, to the American population, that because of the constitutions of the clubs either implied or otherwise —

PAGE: Were these nationally based?

POOLEY: Yes, they were based very much on ethnic groups and one found that although they may have said and paid lip service to the idea of entertaining people from the core society that in fact, very few, if any, ever became connected with these clubs. There were many reasons for this. One certainly was the language factor; that they still continued to speak their own language and, therefore, in so doing excluded others who may have been interested, having played in high school.

JOHN LOY: I've always felt just as with the sport of baseball there's really less there than meets the eye, and I carry on a debate all the time with my wife. My wife and her girl friends love the sport of soccer, and I point out well, perhaps as Riesman suggests in his piece that the appeal of the sport is quite high in the less well developed parts of the world and it has appeal to those who cannot deal with abstract concepts. So, I keep telling my wife it's because of her love for the less developed parts of the world and the fact that she and her girl friends are not well developed with respect to abstract concepts that the game has no appeal to her. This may account for the decline of baseball, too. It doesn't fit in with our modern world.

PAGE: It probably also accounts for a certain amount of tension in your marriage.

LOY: Although we get a kick out of both games.

KENYON: Any other comments to this point?

DENISE PALMER: I have heard said at a meeting of someone promoting soccer in the elementary schools in this country, that we had to develop at the grass roots good soccer players because this is the only sport in America at the present time that is an international sport, and yet, America hasn't made an opening.

PAGE: This is a very nice point. I've referred to this some place, not in writing but in a so-called speech or talk of this sort, as the Bolshevik syndrome which is so important in the United States. We outdo the Russians in all sorts of ways. Soviet Russia has developed quite deliberately a fabulously organized and highly bureaucratized and well financed and symbolically supported sports program, including, and in a remarkably short period of time, as we are all aware, fabulous performers, athletes in almost all the major sports and all the minor sports. Well, there is this business, you know: we cannot let those guys outdo us. We've got to have three, four times more nuclear weaponry than they have. We also have to develop some gymnasts that can compete with the Russians, and the Czechs and Japanese. We also have to, perhaps, develop some soccer at some point.

WESLEY WHITE: I agree with you when you say the Americans outdo the Russians in many ways. I don't think the Russians for instance could afford to have towels tucked down behind their pants when they are playing football, or a kind of game like that. I'd like to refer to Doctor Lüschen's comments and John Pooley's. When you say that there is more, or they perceive soccer as containing more chance as it were, or the team which doesn't deserve to win can really win, although they perceive it this way and I'm sure they do, I don't think it is true. I would say that the Americans can tolerate less uncertainty perhaps than some other people. This has been mentioned by numerous authors. I think this is reflected also in the American society at large, that they cannot tolerate uncertainty as much as some other nations, but because society is moving in the direction where they will have to tolerate more uncertainty, I think the Americans are doing that, having to tolerate more uncertainty now. I think the Viet Nam situation, as it has developed, has pointed to this. It may be that if the Americans tolerate more uncertainty in their lives, then soccer will have a better chance later on of coming into the culture.

PAGE: This is a marvelous suggestion. I would hate to call it a hypothesis. I don't know the general theory from which you peal it, but there is some implicit, general conception here. It's a marvelous suggestion, I think.

WHITE: If uncertainty does exist in the American football system then they can smash it down, but you cannot do this in soccer.

PAGE: If this were a group of all sociologists, I'd say "Stop that idea," you know, because we too often don't want ideas in sociology. This is an idea, it's a real fruitful kind of idea. When I was editor of the *American Sociological Review* for ten years of my life, which took up chronologically only three years, I had an associate editor who kept writing in notes after he would evaluate manuscripts and say "We can't publish this piece, it's a 'think' piece." This is, I think, a very perceptive observation.

GREGORY STONE: I just have one idea from Professor Page's talk and I just want to throw it out so it gets in the record somewhere. I hadn't thought of it before, but I'm just wondering historically, because I think we have to get a historical dimension to our studies, whether particular sports in a sense originate somehow among the masses, and I won't call them the lower classes, but from your discussion of boxing I began rethinking my whole vague knowledge of the history of boxing, if the sport somehow germinates in the masses and among the masses and is caught up then by the classes who then have to have rules because they don't really know what is going on — it's almost like Riesman and Denney's football thing — they impose the rules and in this sense create sport and then, of course, with the subsequent democratization, increase in spectatorship, and the problems of course of the box office and the take for sport, then the sport rules get realtered. I'm concerned about this because I'd like to know where rules come from and I don't think they come from Muzafer Sherif's study.

PAGE: Yes, this is another idea, and very interesting.

STONE: I am just thinking of where the Marquis of Queensbury rules came from.

PAGE: I can tell you — I've written about that and years ago (it's in this dusty manuscript that you belabor me about). But as you developed this notion — from mass to class, to use the shorthand terms, and then the rediffusion into an activity of popular reputability, or in the American scene that would be "middle class," it occurred to me that there is a real parallel between your description of what happened with respect to some sports historically and what happens to a great deal of fashion in general. During the 1930's, for example, when what we used to call "work clothes" (work shirts — you're too young to remember this — and other items of apparel that historically had been associated with manual work and manual workers) took on a kind of popularity among, first, a handful of middle-class kids, many of whom were "Young Communist Leaguers" or fellow travelers, but not entirely that group. Very soon in fairly characteristic fashion these clothes got into the swankiest shops of New York and other cities so that you could buy a wonderful work shirt for 22 dollars, about the same shirt that you would buy down at the Army & Navy Store for 98 cents; it looked the same.

STONE: I'm talking about the rules.

PAGE: Well, then there became a kind of formalization of this dress, this mode of attire, and this might be a kind of parallel with the rules as you refer to them, a kind of a formalization of this dress as the mode became popular so that every other person on the beaches of Cape Cod, for example, in the East, by 1944 was wearing a certain mode of dress which had its origins, in this instance, among manual workers. And so I think one could take fashion after fashion and follow a similar pattern. Today I have a graduate student working on the innovating role of youth and, of course, the most obvious illustration — there are many others — is popular music and the next and just as obvious is dress. So we have middle aged people walking around now, thousands of them, including distinguished college professors (such as Gregory) with their beads, and so on. In New York City (not in Minneapolis yet, I gather, perhaps not in Madison, Wisconsin, although I wouldn't know) you walk into a Madison Avenue Restaurant to have your martini before a meeting with the publisher and you see three guys sitting there with beautiful, expensive mod clothing, a mod turtle neck and a beautiful set of beads or medallion, and you discover that this one is an assistant bank president, this fellow is in charge of the insurance salesmen for one of the big firms, and somebody else is the vice president of a publishing house. Well now look at the speed with which this now happens — the time factor here is almost unbelievable: the time factor historically speaking, you know, is so shrunken today. We can do things overnight. How long did it take the beard to become a conventional, middle-class mode of dress? At most a year.

LÜSCHEN: I have one short comment on the problem of masses as being fertile for cultural traits like sports.

STONE: Can I say I deliberately used the term "masses."

LÜSCHEN: Right, I do it too. I have had one article in my life which has been rejected and in that the basic phrase was "also, masses can be fertile in the development of culture." Of course, I sent that to a very conservative newspaper, however, on request. Now I want to make just one point here. There is one good example historically where you could see that indeed the masses have been the fertile ground for development of a game, and that has been in France, the game of *longue paume,* the long ball game, which is the ancestor of tennis. This long ball game was taken up also by the upper classes and then after a while the upper classes wanted, of course, to exclude the others and put a fence around their playing field. They used the fence also as part of the play, and since it was raining they finally put a roof on it and what came out of it is the French ball house which you know has had quite a high distribution all over Europe. The other game, the long ball game, has still survived in the countryside and as far as my estimate is concerned it was perhaps the most popular game all over Europe, although seldom in physical education histories will you hear it mentioned. However, I may just mention that the last relic of that — no I think there is more than one — is in the Netherlands, a sport which is named as *kaatsen* which goes back to catball. I think one of the relics is also in New York, in the children's game of *one o' cat.* That seems to belong there. Well, these are all offsprings of that game. This game has, as far as I know, lasted to the beginning of the 19th century in Germany; with the oncoming of urbanization and industrialization it has died out, for reasons I still would have to go into. I have been able to trace it down after the beginning of the century in the most remote Catholic area in Germany, an area which was completely secluded from communication. There it was still. Well, this is just an example that indeed here the offspring was in the lower class.

STONE: May I just make a comment. In terms of our discussions of socialization, what it sounds like if this is true, is that the classes capture the creativity of the masses.

PAGE: You see it happens the other way around, historically, too. That is, the masses capture the creativity of the restricted classes.

LÜSCHEN: Correct, yes, yes. But, this is no one-way street. This is, as I would see it, a consistent interchange.

STONE: Yes, but we have been talking as though there is this impoverished life in the lower class and I wouldn't call the masses the lower class. I'm deliberately protecting myself by using that term, but it really sounds as though the classes capture the creativity of the masses.

KENYON: Stop! I've been naive about one aspect of this program, and that's this last session. I thought after two and a half days that we would have run out of ideas. I suppose I should have known better, knowing the people I had invited. Nevertheless, I don't think I was naive in the selection of those people. I would like, therefore, to express my gratitude publicly to all of you for coming and spending this much time away from your other commitments.

A question has been raised with me by a member of the group as to where do you suppose the field of sport sociology will be in five or ten years' time. I would have liked to have had Mr. Page react to that question, but as an alternative, and as an empiricist of sorts, I suggest that we wait for five years, see what happens, and perhaps bring all of these people together again at that time. Thank you all very much for coming. We stand adjourned.

BACKGROUND OF CIC SYMPOSIUM SERIES*

KING L. McCRISTAL

University of Illinois

The Western Conference Physical Education Directors Organization is an informal group which has met annually since 1930. This symposium is the child of that group and was sanctioned last December at the annual meetings in Chicago.

The symposium which starts today is the culmination of a plan started more than six years ago at an informal session between myself and the late Arthur Daniels, Dean of the School of Health, Physical Education and Recreation at Indiana University. We had previously discussed the need for identifying and building the body of knowledge in physical education, and two years after our initial conversation, met in the Summer of 1964 to lay out plans for the Big Ten Directors annual meeting which was to be held the following December at the University of Illinois.

During the Summer of 1965, the Big Ten Body of Knowledge Steering Committee met with Dr. Stanley Salwak, Director of the Committee on Institutional Cooperation (University of Chicago and Big Ten Universities) to inquire about planning money to assist with the development of this project. Later the C.I.C. provided a seed grant of $1,500 to the Big Ten deans and directors for this purpose. Subsequent meetings of the Steering Committee established the format associated with disciplines closely related to the field of Physical Education. It was decided that the following six areas were those on which the Body of Knowledge Project should concentrate: (1) Exercise Physiology, (2) Biomechanics, (3) Motor Learning and Sports Psychology, (4) Sociology of Sport, (5) History and Philosophy of Sport, and (6) Administrative Theory. These have comprised the areas of concentration for the agenda of our annual meetings for the past two years.

Various efforts have been made to finance the proposed series of symposiums. I spent several days in Washington last year running down leads in the U. S. Office of Education and the National Science Foundation, to no avail. I have also been in contact with 15 foundations based in Illinois with similar results. As chairman of the Body of Knowledge Steering Committee, I finally obtained permission from Dr. Salwak's office to use our remaining seed grant money to finance the symposium which starts today. I also prevailed upon Big Ten physical education directors to contribute to the cause and am happy to report that we received 100 per cent cooperation.

---

*These introductory remarks were made at the opening session of the Symposium on the Sociology of Sport at the University of Wisconsin Monday, November 18, 1968.

We are particularly grateful to the Athletic Institute of Chicago, whose Board of Directors has agreed to underwrite the publication of this symposium's proceedings. The request was initiated through the Institute's President, the late Laurence Mullins, and I was notified of the Institute Board's approval by Dr. Frank B. Jones, who succeeded Mr. Mullins.

Dr. Gerald Kenyon, a member of our Steering Committee, has handled all of the details of these meetings and has done this, I might add, in the short space of a very few months. The decision to go ahead with the symposium at this time was made when Dr. Kenyon and I were riding back to our hotel on a bus at the AAHPER meetings last March in St. Louis. His boss, Dr. Leonard Larson, had earlier committed him to chair the meetings which he was prepared to do if I could come up with the money to pay expenses. The fact that we are here today precludes my having to tell you what happened in the interim.

Obviously, we have high hopes for these meetings. It is our plan that this shall comprise the first in a series of symposiums which have been laid out by the Steering Committee. In closing let me say that we are greatly indebted to Dr. Larson and to the University of Wisconsin for hosting these meetings and to Dr. Gerald Kenyon, the symposium chairman. I know that the meetings are going to be all we hoped for. Thank you.

SYMPOSIUM ON THE SOCIOLOGY OF SPORT

UNIVERSITY OF WISCONSIN

November 18, 29, 20, 1968

SPEAKERS

GERALD S. KENYON
University of Wisconsin

JOHN W. LOY, JR.
U.C.L.A.

GÜNTHER LÜSCHEN
University of Illinois

CHARLES H. PAGE
University of Massachusetts

WALTER E. SCHAFER
University of Oregon

GREGORY P. STONE
University of Minnesota

BRIAN SUTTON-SMITH
Columbia University

HARRY WEBB
Michigan State University

PARTICIPANTS

JOHN ALBISON
University of Michigan

JOHN ALEXANDER
University of Minnesota

NANCY BALDWIN
Ohio State University

REX D. BILLINGTON
University of Iowa

JAMES R. BROWN
Indiana University

BURTON C. BRUNNER
University of Iowa

JAMES F. CARMODY
University of Iowa

DONALD CASADY
University of Iowa

FRANCES Z. CUMBEE
University of Wisconsin

DICK DeSCHRIVER
University of Minnesota

MICHAEL C. FINCH
University of Wisconsin

WALTER GREGG
Northwestern University

TOM GROGG
University of Wisconsin

DONALD R. HELLISON
Ohio State University

EVALYN K. HOWE
Indiana University

MAXWELL L. HOWELL
University of Alberta

ANDREW S. JACKSON
Indiana University

COLIN C. KELLY
University of Wisconsin

ERIK K. M. KJELDSEN
University of Massachusetts

SEYMOUR KLEINMAN
Ohio State University

BILL KOZAR
University of Iowa

DAN LANDERS
University of Illinois

DAVID K. LESLIE
University of Iowa

BEN LOWE
University of Wisconsin

RAINER MARTENS
University of Illinois

KING J. McCRISTAL
University of Illinois

BARRY D. McPHERSON
University of Wisconsin

JOANNA MIDTLYNG
Indiana University

LAURIE K. NEWTON
University of Iowa

DENISE PALMER
Southwest Minnesota State College

D. VERDELLE PARKER
Purdue University

BRIAN M. PETRIE
Michigan State University

JOHN C. POOLEY
University of Wisconsin

GUY GENE REIFF
University of Michigan

GLYN C. ROBERTS
University of Illinois

DEAN RYAN
Universities of Calif. and Wis.

JUDI SMITH
University of Wisconsin

LEON E. SMITH
University of Iowa

MICHAEL P. SONNENBERG
University of Wisconsin

LEE R. VANDER VELDEN
University of Wisconsin

GILAD WEINGARTEN
University of Minnesota

CYRIL M. WHITE
University of Illinois

WESLEY WHITE
University of Wisconsin

GARY WODDEN
Northwestern University

MARY L. YOUNG
University of Minnesota